D1250856

Jazz from
the Beginning

Michigan American Music Series

Richard Crawford, Editor

Jazz from the Beginning
By Garvin Bushell as Told to Mark Tucker

JAZZ
FROM THE BEGINNING

By Garvin Bushell
as Told to Mark Tucker

Introduction by
Lawrence Gushee

Ann Arbor

The University of Michigan Press

780.92
13
c.1

Copyright © by the University of Michigan 1988

All rights reserved

Published in the United States of America by

The University of Michigan Press

Manufactured in the United States of America

1991 1990 1989 1988 4 3 2 1

Library of Congress Cataloging-in-Publication Data

Bushell, Garvin, 1902–
   Jazz from the beginning / by Garvin Bushell as told to Mark Tucker;
introduction by Lawrence Gushee.
     p.   cm.—(Michigan American music series)
   "A Garvin Bushell discography": p.
   Includes index.
   ISBN 0-472-10098-X (alk. paper)
   1. Bushell, Garvin, 1902–   . 2. Jazz musicians—Biography.
I. Tucker, Mark, 1954–   . II. Title. III. Series.
ML419.B89A3 1988
788'.6'0924—dc19
  [B] .   88-16922
                                                   CIP
                                                   MN

NEW YORK SOCIETY LIBRARY
53 EAST 79 STREET
NEW YORK, NEW YORK 10021

To the memory of Sam Wooding

FOREWORD

My introduction to Garvin Bushell came through Nat Hentoff's three-part article, "Garvin Bushell and New York Jazz in the 1920s," that appeared in an anthology of writings from *Jazz Review*.[1] Like others who have read that piece—an edited transcript of Hentoff's interview with Bushell—I was struck by the keen observations, the strong opinions, and the finely detailed recollections of a distant musical era. I also responded to Bushell's gift for storytelling, as when he recounted being pursued by Tiny Tally, the ultra-amorous brothel owner in Louisville, or when he sketched a portrait of Charlie Creath, the legendary trumpeter from St. Louis:

> Creath had a Joe Smith-like tone, but with much feeling and drive. He had beautiful sound and soul, and the blues were his forte. . . I've heard Tommy Ladnier say: "When Charlie used to hit certain notes, the whores would just fall out and throw up their legs." He made his biggest impression on women—not so much his looks as his playing. The way he played the blues mellowed you; people threw their glasses in the air. He'd hit a seventh chord and sustain it and people fell out. He later committed suicide; a woman was involved in some way.[2]

In a few sentences, Bushell could distill the essence of an obscure yet important regional musician and suggest the environment that could produce—and destroy—such a player.

Some years later, while working on my doctoral dissertation about Duke Ellington, I was looking for musicians to interview who had been active in New York in the 1920s. Dan Morgenstern, director of the Institute of Jazz Studies at Rutgers University–Newark, suggested I get in touch with Garvin Bushell in Las Vegas (where he has lived since 1976), and the writer and critic Stanley Dance helped me make the initial contact.

In early April of 1985, my wife Carol Oja and I went out to Nevada to meet Garvin and Louise Bushell. That first visit was strange and wonderful, a bit like stepping through the wardrobe in C. S. Lewis's Narnia chronicles. One moment we were in a pleasant suburban neighborhood on the east side of Las Vegas, surrounded by dry desert and barren mountains; but as soon as we entered Garvin's studio and he began talking, we were transported far away through the active agent of his memory—we saw the smoky interiors of Harlem nightclubs, visited European capitals in the company of Sam Wooding and the *Chocolate Kiddies* troupe, and perceived the dark landscapes of the Jim Crow South through the eyes of a touring black musician who still carried the pain and anger of that degrading experience deep within. A few hours later we emerged, blinking in the bright sunlight, and knew we had been in the presence of an extraordinary man.

The following year we returned to Las Vegas, this time for a longer stay. On 5 July 1986, I began what would turn out to be a series of thirty-one interviews with Garvin, taking time to cover as many aspects of his life story as he chose to recollect. We worked five or six days a week, starting in the morning and knocking off around noon. The interviews stretched into August, ending on the sixteenth of that month. When we finished, we had collected over sixty hours of conversation on tape.[3] During most of this period, Garvin was not in the best of health; yet he refused to let fatigue check the course of our progress.

While the initiative to compile Garvin's memoirs came from me, some years earlier he had conceived the idea of an autobiographical project. Among his papers, I found detailed outlines of his life story (undated, but probably from the 1950s) that may have been intended as guides for his memory while writing. There was also the fragment of a short story (apparently never finished) about a black child, Clifford Allen, who grew up in Centerville, Ohio, and eventually became a lawyer in New York.

More important for the present volume were two other written sources. The first was a six-page typescript account of Bushell's earliest musical memories; it appears, virtually untouched, as the Prologue that follows. The second was a 240-page journal kept by Bushell in the fall of 1964 during a three-month tour of Africa. Chapter 16 combines extracts from this journal with verbal accounts of the trip.

For the most part, however, my interviews with Garvin during the summer of 1986 make up the primary sources for this volume. In editing what Garvin said during our conversations, I have had a free hand in organizing and shaping the text to remove minor inconsistencies. While Garvin has reviewed the entire text and offered corrections and suggestions, I take full responsibility for its final form.

In chapters 2–4, I have incorporated sections of the article "Garvin Bushell and New York Jazz in the 1920s," with the kind permission of Nat Hentoff, Martin Williams (his coeditor at the *Jazz Review*), and Garvin himself. I have drawn upon two additional sources only sparingly (a phrase here, a sentence there): Monk Montgomery's interview of Bushell in August 1977 for the Jazz Oral History Project;[4] and Patrick Gaffey's profile of Bushell in *Arts Alive: The Southern Nevada Magazine of the Arts*.[5]

Chapter 6 has appeared previously, in slightly altered form, in *Storyville* 131 (1 September 1987) and 132 (1 December 1987).

I am grateful to Ted Panken, whose expert transcribing skills helped commit, with astonishing accuracy, many hours of taped interviews to paper. Thanks also to Laine Whitcomb and Martine Basagni, who assisted both Ted and me in the process of transcribing.

I owe a debt of gratitude to Dan Morgenstern of the Institute of Jazz Studies, who was extremely generous in offering practical help. I would also like to acknowledge the following for their support: the National Endowment for the Humanities, which helped me carry out the interviews through a Travel to Collections Grant in 1986; the Association for Recorded Sound Collections, which provided a research grant in 1986 to assist in the compilation of Garvin Bushell's discography; Walter E. Sears, former director of the University of Michigan Press, who believed in the project.

Carol Gabriel, curator at the Clark County Historical Society in Springfield, Ohio, read chapter 1, checked it against the historical record, and corroborated many details of Garvin's account. John Chilton combed the entire manuscript for accuracy and supplied additional biographical information on musicians. Garvin Bushell contributed the photographs from his personal collection.

For encouraging words and various kinds of assistance, thanks to Stanley Dance, Patrick Gaffey, Lawrence Gushee, Barry Kernfeld, Carol Oja, Phil Schaap, Alyn Shipton, Roland J. Wiley, Martin Williams, Laurie Wright, and Dean Thomas Wright of the University of Nevada–Las Vegas.

Finally, thanks to Louise Bushell for her warm hospitality, and to Garvin Bushell for speaking his mind and keeping the faith.

Mark Tucker

NOTES

1. The article was first published in *Jazz Review*, January 1959, 11–13; February 1959, 9–10, 41; April 1959, 16–17, 40; and was reprinted as

"Jazz in the Twenties: Garvin Bushell," in *Jazz Panorama*, ed. Martin Williams (New York: Crowell-Collier, 1962), 71–90.

2. "Jazz in the Twenties," 86.
3. The tapes and transcripts of these interviews are now housed at the Institute of Jazz Studies, together with over 150 reproductions of photographs from Bushell's personal collection.
4. The transcript of this interview is at the Institute of Jazz Studies, Rutgers University–Newark.
5. Patrick Gaffey, "Garvin Bushell: Jazz Roots from the Beginning," *Arts Alive* (Las Vegas, Nevada) 3, no. 3 (1983): 18–20, 33–34; "A Life in Jazz," Pt. 2, 3, no. 4 (1983): 20–22, 31; Pt. 3, 3, no. 5 (1983): 26–27; Pt. 4, 3, no. 6 (1983): 28–29.

INTRODUCTION

On a trip to New York a couple of months ago I walked past the corner of 49th Street and Seventh Avenue expecting to indulge in a bit of nostalgia by looking up at the windows of what I knew a generation ago as Garvin Bushell's studio—actually the studio of trumpet teacher John Costello in which Garvin had a small room, lit rather inadequately as I recall by one exceedingly grimy window. There he had sat, surrounded by a forest of woodwinds, dispensing technical and musical wisdom. Well, one shouldn't expect any Manhattan building to last the ages, but it was a shock to see that there was no building there at all. Like the unbelievably dense and cholesterol-laden cheesecake that one could eat after a lesson, at the Turf a block away, it was history.

All the more incredible that, as I write these lines, the man whose memories have been collected here is still practicing his art under the arid Nevada skies. And equally incredible that these memories span some seventy years, reaching back to a time before "jazz" had become the fashionable label for the vociferous New Orleans ragtime that spread through the country like wildfire between 1916 and 1919.

A moment's thought tells us that no other jazz biography embraces such a broad expanse of time. That the man who was inspired by Ted Lewis's playing on the Earl Fuller 1917 Victor recording of "Little Liza Jane" also loved Eric Dolphy's playing lends credence to the essential unity of jazz as a kind of music (or an attitude to music) despite incompatibilities of technique and style between 1917 and 1960. But it's not just a matter of timespan. Very few have had Garvin's breadth of experience. To me as a clarinetist, it's barely credible that the same man learned both from Ted Lewis and from Henri Selmer. At the conclusion of his life story he writes: "But all I wanted was to be a great jazz clarinet-player, a fine first alto player, and a first-chair bassoonist." Each of these roles involves a different strength: creativity, leadership, discipline; and it's probably impossible to keep all three balls in the air at once. This has made for a varied life, but one in which it's been difficult to transcend the faint praise of the label "musician's musician."

It's a truism that the jazz life was generally unhealthy—until musicians began to embrace clean living in the mid-1960s—and that too many performers have fallen victim too early to drugs, alcohol, impoverishment, or general debility. Apart from that, the premium placed on youthful energy and the merciless pace of stylistic change have often made back numbers out of performers still in their thirties. Garvin has been spectacularly successful at the art of survival; no doubt he would attribute this to wisdom and discipline rather than either luck or personal virtue. I hope he won't mind too much if I take a somewhat different view.

After decades of combing jazz biographies and autobiographies for penetrating observations concerning jazz style, for insights regarding the process of improvisation, for details of technique and instruments, I've come to the conclusion that they're extremely rare. But their rarity has nothing to do with the amount of formal training or education that a jazz musician happens to have had, since their classically trained brethren are equally inarticulate in recounting the part of their lives that's artistically significant. Perhaps it's the professional deformity of historians and analysts to assume that art belongs to the sphere of reflection—where in reality it belongs to that of action. It's a rare performer (or for that matter composer) who makes fully reasoned choices; and those who make much of their pet theories seem, more often than not, to think that fervency of belief is what makes a theory correct.

Garvin Bushell strikes one as unpretentious, thoughtful, and devoid of fanaticism. The guiding principle in his life appears to be that discipline taught by experience is the surest guide. He sees his own progress through professional life as the taming of a cocky, untutored hell-raiser through hard work and a love for many different kinds of music. And despite the fact that he impressed on all of his students the need for technical control of their instruments, jazz is to Garvin still a matter of authentic feeling. For example, the recording he singles out as containing some of his best playing is one that he made with Luckey Roberts in 1958 (Period RL1929). But why does he think so? Here are his words:

> I was as sharp on this date as I ever was. I was using a Selmer Albert system clarinet; I loved the sound of that horn. In this period I had a good, happy feeling about jazz. I didn't have any responsibilities, so I felt better.

Sometimes we can gain as much insight into a musician's character and artistic personality by knowing what else impassions them besides music. In Garvin's case, it seems to be fast, sporty motor cars: well-engineered and well-crafted machines that offer risky exhilaration to the knowledgeable and adventurous driver—not so different, really from a fine clarinet solo.

I have no sense in reading Garvin's memoirs that he's in any way disappointed, although the fact is that he makes none of the published listings of great or near-great jazz clarinetists. Perhaps some tinge of disappointment lies behind his sardonic comment on Benny Goodman's saxophone playing. And perhaps that's why there's so little about the playing of other clarinetists. When he does speak, though, his deepest love goes to players who embodied emotion, particularly Sidney Bechet and Eric Dolphy, and outside jazz, the Gypsy musicians whose music he learned in Budapest in 1925.

The pervasive neutrality and coolness of Garvin's narrative in no way diminishes the impact of the thread that perhaps inevitably runs through his professional career from beginning to end—that is, the automatic restriction of opportunity for Afro-Americans, even in a comparatively tolerant or liberal entertainment industry. Although Garvin does not use his autobiography as a soapbox, it would seem that once past his oat-sowing days he has consciously strived to demonstrate in his professional life that black musicians deserve respect to the extent that they earn it. Perhaps that has something to do with the important role discipline, versatility, and competence have played in his life.

Garvin's views of others are in the main charitable—perhaps the better word is balanced—although he convinces us once again that jazz musicians possibly have a longer memory for unpaid debts than for musical details. He finds the more original of his fellow musicians impenetrable as human beings: Ben Webster, Hilton Jefferson, Benny Morton, Dicky Wells, but does not indulge in amateur psychoanalysis. (To be sure, on some matters he has the discretion of someone born over eighty years ago, someone who was amazed—and no doubt delighted—to discover that ladies' ankles were attached to legs underneath the long skirts of his youth.)

But while generally charitable towards individuals, he seems often rather harsh towards jazz. His view is for me summed up by his understanding of Rex Stewart who, like others, was a great creator because jazz was his main object and not technique (rapid execution, good intonation, etc.). "Rex had a great ear, and could almost play whatever he heard. He could move fast and had the range. He just lipped and fingered his horn wrong." In contrast, today's youngsters, well-trained technically and able to read, don't depend on creativity. "The educational process is making fantastic imitators out of young players."

Well, here is a paradox Garvin doesn't resolve. This is hardly to his discredit, but makes us in the final analysis wonder whether the tension between music viewed as technical mastery (or a view of technique based on consistent intonation and fluent execution), and music viewed as inspiration is the spring that has kept Garvin an active performer for seventy years. I recall vividly one occasion on which he brought the two things together in a few minutes of supreme performance. It was the appearance of the Fletcher Henderson "reunion" band at the Great South Bay jazz festival of 1957, an occasion which inevitably would put one on one's mettle—although some musicians there declined the challenge. Garvin came to the front wearing a plaid sports jacket that seemed ten years out of style and played a solo that was not only totally assured but also beautifully formed. So, take it from an eye and ear witness, these are the memoirs not only of a survivor and a proficient sideman, but of an artist.

Lawrence Gushee

CONTENTS

PROLOGUE

It was Christmas morning of 1917 when I heard my first jazz band—the blare and noise of trombone, cornet, clarinet, piano, and drums, all playing ad lib, and none too sweetly. The occasion was the debut of a modern Victrola and the discarding of our old cylinder machine.

Back in those days, the phonograph was a sign of some degree of luxury with the slightly less than middle classes, and there was no better time to show off your rating than Sunday afternoon. This was done by setting the machine near a front window or open door in the summer and turning it on full blast. As passers-by looked in they would see this large, morning-glory-shaped horn, painted with all the colors of its floral prototype, protruding through a window or door. The larger the horn, the more convinced the neighbors were that the "Joneses" were quite successful. So you will understand my appreciation for this new contraption. A handsome bit of cabinetmaking it was, and possessed a very fine tone.

With the Victrola we were given six records free with the compliments of Wurlitzer & Co. Included in the lot was a copy of "Little Liza Jane," by Earl Fuller and His Jazz Band, featuring an unknown named Ted Lewis.[1] I played this record over and over. Noticing the lift the clarinet gave to the last chorus, I decided to forget all about Bach, Beethoven, and the others I had been studying on piano for the past four years. The seed of jazz had definitely been sown. I heard in that record great possibilities for me as a clarinetist. Although I didn't even own a clarinet, my knowledge of ragtime assured me I would not have any trouble with jazz. Since there was very little difference between the two, I knew I could master it.

As I recall, we also had copies of "Maple Leaf Rag," "Way Down Yonder in the Corn Field," "The Whistler and His Dog," and "Give My Regards to Broadway." Although poorly reproduced, these records contained the foundation of the jazz that was to come, particularly "Maple Leaf Rag." I make the statement with no fear of contradiction. Ragtime, as it was called then, had the technical essence that was later required in jazz. While ragtime was always played in a moderate or fast "two" tempo, jazz merely slowed it down to a fast or medium "four." Most all the old rags had a melodic pattern. Therefore I began to study rags on piano and omit the melodic pattern, just improvising on the harmonic pattern, and I began to hear results. But I still had to have a clarinet. Of course people were continually saying, "That sort of music won't be accepted. It's too noisy. You can't understand what they're playing." But that didn't change my intentions to play that "noisy music."

Since I was still in school, my earning power was of very little value, only enough for Sunday afternoon sodas and park amusements. Therefore I was open for ideas as to how I could purchase a clarinet.

First, I tried selling magazines and was doing fine, saving two dollars a week. After two weeks, the holiday issue came, so thinking I could make a big haul, I ordered four times my usual amount. I spent the entire four dollars on stock. Now for the payoff. I had been using my wagon with my favorite dog harnessed to it to make deliveries. Just one block from the publishing company Duke spied a cat, and down the street went my four dollars plus profit.

Well, the first thing that came to my mind was the clarinet I had hoped to buy, so I joined the chase. It was obvious after running one block that Duke had called upon all of his resources to catch his prey; but old Tom, seemingly conscious of just that, turned on a little extra steam of his own. With the result of their extra efforts I was hopelessly outclassed. Old Tom, as I was late to learn, was the real genius of the chase. In turning west into a side street, which led to a bridge crossing a narrow canal, he slowed down, allowing Duke to gain on him, thus increasing the dog's anxiety. As they approached the bridge with Duke nipping at Tom's tail, Tom made an abrupt turn at the bridge entrance instead of crossing. Duke made the same turn forgetting he was still harnessed to a wagon, carrying what I had hoped would be enough profit to make a down payment on my first clarinet. The front wheels of the wagon made the turn, but the back wheels refused and skidded towards the open canal, dumping every copy into the stream. Well, Tom went his way, but Duke and the wagon had become entangled with the bridge. Disgusted, I freed him from the harness, and, as usual, he jumped into the wagon to be hauled home.

After a few weeks, my Aunt Ella, with whom I lived, noticed my dwindling interest in the piano. With a troubled expression on her face, she began asking questions. After giving several poor excuses, which she didn't accept, I told her of my decision. She seemed shocked. Then staring into my eyes, she said, "Why would you want to be just on ol' horn player, when you could become a great concert pianist?" Tears began flowing down her face. Her mind probably went to two of my uncles who were members of circus bands, and the miserable conditions that existed for them. I'm sure she was saddened at the possibility of my becoming part of that life. She put her arm around me and led me to the front porch, and beckoned me to sit on a chair. Then she proceeded to go through the entire history of horn blowers, as she called them. Needless to say, it was not a pretty picture. In those days, a circus musician was classified in society as a person not accepted in most communities. People felt that members of the circus, particularly musicians and roustabouts, were a low element of people.

But I had a different vision of playing the clarinet. I had a picture of people accepting jazz as part of American music.

NOTE

1. The record was probably Victor 18394, recorded 10 September 1917. On the other side was Arthur Pryor's "A Coon Band Contest."

1

SPRINGFIELD

I was born in Springfield, Ohio, on September 25, 1902. Springfield is a development of the community that was created when they ran out of money building the continental road, Route 40. Some of the biggest factories grew up there: Springfield-Kelly Roller, Springfield-Kelly Truck, International Harvester, Lagonda Counter Plate, and others. It was a rather small town, but to us it was a metropolis.[1]

Springfield was also a prejudiced town. They lynched a Negro in 1904 and the mob came right by our house. We were upstairs, looking through the crack of the window, with all the lights out, naturally. I'll always remember the howl of that mob as they dragged the body, and the torchlights coming right through Fair Street. It seems as though this Negro didn't pay his rent, a white woman went to throw him out, and he smacked her. They dragged him down Clark Street, over onto Fair Street. I'll never forget that.[2]

My parents lived near Fair Street, which was black all the way through, from Center Street right on over to Yellow Springs. Dave Wilborn, of McKinney's Cotton Pickers, lived there on Fair Street; he had a big house, and his father was a rich undertaker.[3]

There were black businesses down on lower Center Street for about two blocks. But the main black business district was Washington Street, where the trains came through. Later it switched over to Fountain Avenue and onto Limestone Street. Of course, blacks could go in white-owned stores and businesses, but you couldn't sit down in a restaurant, bar, or soda fountain, and you couldn't go downstairs in a theater. We could sit in the back of two theaters in Springfield, the Pastime and the Dreamland. At the Fairbanks we had to go up in the gallery—that's the third tier, above the balcony. In the Columbia Theater we'd have to go around the alley and up the stairs.

Most people don't know what it's like to have gone through that. I revel in the fact that I've lived long enough to see change. In those days I thought so little of myself; my family and I, we weren't anything! Because for so long we'd been browbeaten and made to believe that our value in life was nothing other than servitude. They didn't let Negroes know that our ancestors had contributed something.

Still, Springfield wasn't as bad as a place like Mississippi. The schools were mixed, and there was no segregation in transportation. You lived where you wanted to live, if you could pay the rent. Negroes lived all over Springfield.

The poorest and most vicious Negroes lived in Needmore, on the other side of Yellow Springs Street. Their houses were made of dry goods boxes and tin, and they had dirt floors. Their stables were bigger than their houses. There was a stink factory out there, where they'd take horses that were ready to die and boil them up to make soap. People would buy them and try to fatten them up to get them to work. Todd Rhodes, also of McKinney's Cotton Pickers, came from Needmore.

When I was about six my parents went out on the road to teach school, and I went to live with Gram—that's what I called her, she was really my great-aunt, Ella Scott. My father, Joseph Davenport Bushell, was a preacher and a chorister. He had a whole book of spirituals he had written. He became president of the Brennan-Normal Industrial School in Austin, Texas. My mother, Effie Payne Bushell, taught school in Galveston, She could sing well, too. Later she told me she'd been offered a job by Williams and Walker to go out with a show before I was born, but had turned it down.[4]

Gram lived near the end of State Street, on the outskirts of town. Her husband Charlie Scott was part Indian and part Negro. He was born in a wigwam down on Buck Creek, south of Springfield. He couldn't read or write, but he worked as a steam engineer at the Springfield Machine Tool Company, which was right across the street from their house. He used to go to Columbus every year to get his license.

Charlie had been raised up around Germans and could speak a little German. But he hardly said anything. I don't think I heard him say five words in my life.

They still had Indians near Springfield and down in southern Ohio. I used to hear them sing when we'd go out to have our hogs butchered.

Every fall we'd have two hogs butchered, and the Indians would cut them up and salt them, then we'd bring the salt pork back to Springfield. Many Negroes in that section of Ohio were part Indian—Dave Wilborn was, so was Harold Gossett, Ray Price, and Bill McKinney. My mother's mother was part Indian and Negro. My father's mother was Irish, his father Negro with a little Indian. My great-grandfather was part German and Negro.

Unfortunately, I never learned too much about my ancestors. Some of them, I think, came from Virginia, others from sections of Ohio near Springfield and Xenia. I always regretted not knowing more about my background, my people. It wasn't important to my family, and they never took the time to tell me.

On Gram's block there was one other black family, the rest were white. All my playmates were white except when I would go over to my Aunt Eva's on Winter Street, which was a black street where Don Frye lived. That's when I got a chance to play with black kids. I wasn't allowed to play with the kids who lived in Needmore, because they were too dirty and were considered the lowest type of black people. My other friends were white—Irish and German. I'd sleep over at the house of Clarence Peck, an Irish boy, and we'd play with our model-builders and electric motors until it was time to go to bed. Or I'd go play with steam engines and trains with Harry Bradley, whose father was a machinist in the factory where my uncle was engineer.

I remember Gram whipping me once after I'd hopped on a freight train. She had just gotten off the streetcar and was coming up State Street, and she saw this red coat flare back. I was riding a box car across State Street. She screamed at me and I jumped off. She took me in the back yard, doubled up a clothesline, and whipped me all over the place. Now, my grandmother was a big woman. I never had the desire to hop a freight train again. Many kids in Springfield had one leg from hopping trains.

Another time, I got in a scrape with the owner of the factory where Uncle Charlie worked. I had access to the shop, and could sit and watch the engineers and machinists. I used to go through the trash bin and get automobile and engineering magazines. This time I saw a square box there, and figured I could make a good wagon from it.

As I was coming out the alley with the box to go home, the owner, Mr. Montanus,[5] said, "Put that box down!"

"I thought it was trash."

"You thought nothing!" And he turned around and kicked me in my behind.

I went home crying to Gram, saying, "Montanus kicked me. I thought the box was trash, and he kicked me and said I was stealing." Gram put a butcher knife under her apron and went over there. She took me with the other hand and walked right in the front office, screaming, "Montanus!"

"Mrs. Scott, what is it?"

"You kicked my boy! Why?"

"Oh, I didn't know it was your boy."

"Why'd you kick him?"

"Well, he was stealing . . ."

"He didn't know better. You know he's been here all his life. He don't steal." And she pulled out the knife. "If you ever lay your hands on him"—remember, this was a man who was a multimillionaire—"I'll chop your head off!"

"I'm sorry Mrs. Scott, I'm sorry."

I remember thinking, "Suppose he fires Uncle Charlie for that?" But instead he asked Charlie to give me his apologies. They didn't know I was the grandchild or nephew—they thought I was their boy. From then on they never bothered me. Mr. Montanus would say, "Hello, son, how are ya?" I wouldn't even speak to him.

My parents usually stayed out on the road for long stretches of time. My mother might visit for a couple days at a time, but she and my father never came back and located in Springfield. I always used to cry when my mother left. But I never discussed anything with her. That's why I was so very late in gaining any knowledge, and getting ordinary horse sense. And that's why Sam Wooding became so important to me later on. He had patience with me, and explained how I was doing things wrong. He became a big factor in my life.

GROWING UP

I had different jobs when I was young. After I had my paper route, I worked hoeing weeds in the vegetable and flower farms. I also worked in the foundry where Charlie was the engineer. I ran a core machine, and made one dollar a day, six dollars a week. This was in the summers.

My buddies and I would go across the railroad track into Peron's woods. We'd play in the cornfields and the cloverfields, then go out to Three Roots swimming hole, about two miles south of town.

Aviation was big in Springfield. Lincoln Beachey, I think, flew the first plane I ever saw. And one of my uncles knew Orville Wright. When the Wright brothers had a new plane—Fairfield [now Fairborn] was just a few miles away—they'd come up to Springfield and land on the racetrack. In 1911, I believe, they brought a twin-seater up, and I even went up with Orville.

The dirigibles used to take off from Fairfield. That's where I saw the first crash. This guy walked to the front of the gondola to nose the bag down, and a gust of wind hit the gondola and cut the bag. I saw a puff of smoke, and he fell. But the bag turned into a parachute—that's the only thing that saved his life.

During World War I, when aviation was in its infancy, they used to land in cornfields because those Liberty motors used to conk out on them anywhere.

I got exposed to automobiles at an early age in Springfield. At the fairgrounds they'd have races on the half-mile track. Racers like Louis DesBreaux, Louis Chevrolet, one of the Magellans, Ralph De Palma, and Jack Johnson, the fighter, all came there to race. Lincoln Beachey also drove cars, besides demonstrating his airplane. Barney Oldfield would fly an airplane 'round the track and Jack Johnson would race him in a car. I used to carry water for the merry-go-round and work in the pits, just to be around those cars and drivers. We made pushmobiles shaped after the cars we had seen. We raced with scooters. Then later, we'd go out on the track and race our bicycles. So the racing bug was well established with me before I left Springfield. Everybody was speed conscious there.

On Sundays I went sometimes with Gram and Uncle Charlie to evening service. As a rule, Uncle Charlie was a watchman at the factory on Sundays. But if he was off, he'd go out under the big tree on the railroad track and play cards all afternoon. Then later he'd go with us and ride the streetcar to church. If church got out later than eleven o'clock, when the streetcar stopped running, we'd walk clear across town back to State Street.

We were walking down Yellow Springs Street one night when we saw this low ball of fire with a long tail in the western sky. It was Halley's comet. We got back and sat out in the front yard. People were praying and singing spirituals, because the comet was big then, and close. People thought there was a possibility it might strike the earth. Some people jumped out of windows and committed suicide.

One time I went down to Nashville, Tennessee, where my mother and father were teaching. I was supposed to go down and stay for good, but I ended up staying only two weeks. My mother had quite a temper. She used to whip my bottom every day. So my father sent a telegram to Gram: "Come back and get the baby. His mother's not treating him right." This must have been around 1909 or 1910. The tune that was big at the time was "Steamboat Bill": "Steamboat Bill / Come down the levee / Trying to break the record of the Robert E. Lee." Later I played that in the circus.

MUSICAL BEGINNINGS

I started on piano when I was six or seven years old. My first teacher was Victor Johnson, grandfather—or great-granduncle—of Rafer Johnson, the decathlon star. He was an Antioch graduate, and used to drive up from Yellow Springs in his Ford. He was a big man with one of those Paul Robeson voices and a contagious smile. When he smiled his whole face smiled. He charged twenty-five cents a lesson. When he went up to fifty cents, Gram said, "Oh no, that's too much. Can't afford that."

Gram had a job as supervisor in a tobacco-stripping factory. That's where they take the stems out of the tobacco leaves, repack it, and send it to the cigar manufacturers. She said, "Well, I'll see what I can do about getting you a clarinet." She bought it on time, for something like $37.50. Paid $5 down, and the rest was $3 a week. I had no instructions how to play, and started out using the wrong hand. My uncle who was a musician wasn't around then.

Some of my buddies had organized a debating club, part of the Frederick Douglass Debating Society. We used to debate other clubs in Springfield. We'd meet at MacPherson's ice cream parlor, or at Dave Wilborn's or Don Frye's house. Lloyd Scott was the genius behind all this. He was a smart turkey. We had topics relating to Crispus Attucks and Toussaint L'Ouverture. Some of the kids had been to black schools where they taught about these things. There were some pretty intelligent kids who put us on the right track.

Our club put on a dance at the Odd Fellows' Hall on Fountain Avenue, and some of us were hired to play for it. There was Don Frye, Cecil and Lloyd Scott, Luther Watson, Dave Wilborn, and myself. We'd been practicing on Sundays trying to get something together. Later, after I left, a couple of other guys joined and that became the nucleus of McKinney's Cotton Pickers.

So we played our first dance, and they paid us a dollar and a half. Well, the music was so rotten, that at the next meeting the club voted to take back the dollar and a half! That wasn't encouraging, but I still wanted to play.

When we rehearsed, we'd play tunes like "I'll Say She Does"—this was very popular around 1916 or '17—also "Very Good Eddie" and "Jazz Dance." We'd get the latest tunes from Woolworth's. They had a demonstrator there, and we'd pick out songs, have him play them, and choose them that way.

We didn't call the music jazz when I was growing up, except for the final tag of a number. After the cadence was closed there'd be a one-bar break, and the second bar was the tag—5-6-5-1 (sol-la-sol-do)—that was called the jazz.

Ragtime piano was the major influence in that section of the country. Everybody tried to emulate Scott Joplin. The change began to come around 1912 to 1915, when the four-string banjo and saxophone came in. About the first tenor saxophonist anyone in that area heard was Milt Senior, who played with Willis and Wormack, and eventually joined McKinney's.

Negroes in Springfield were very aware of popular music as part of their life. They couldn't go to the theater, unless they went up to the gallery, and they didn't get to see a movie unless it was something at the Pastime. But there were dances all the time at the Odd Fellows' Hall and Memorial Hall, and they went to those. A lot of kids kept up with the music. It was considered an achievement to be a musician. I didn't want to be a preacher or undertaker, so I wanted to be a musician. My uncle was an engineer at the factory, but that was a freak thing, because he showed unusual talent with engines.

For some reason, central Ohio produced a lot of jazz musicians. McKinney's Cotton Pickers came out of Springfield. Ted Lewis was from Circleville. Willis and Wormack were in Dayton, so was John Brown, of Brown's Syncopators. Vic Dickenson came out of Xenia. Of course, Columbus had better musicians than Springfield—Sammy Stewart, the pianist, led bands there. But trombonist Quentin "Butter" Jackson came out of Springfield, as did Claude Jones, who taught him, and Earle Warren of the Basie band.

I went to Dibert Avenue School from first to fourth grade, to Franklin School on Fair Street for fifth through seventh, and then back to Dibert Avenue for eighth. I was taught solfège from the beginning in grade school, and to this day I can look at a note and know the pitch before I play it.

Time passed. I started at Springfield High School. Then I remember being taken out of school and being sent to live with my parents in Pittsburgh. We lived on Shetland Avenue, in an Italian neighborhood, and my father opened up a grocery story there. I attended Peabody High School.

I had my first experience with girls in Pittsburgh. In those days women wore their dresses down to the heels. Little dumb kid that I was, I thought women were solid all the way through; I didn't know they had legs, just thought their feet were connected to their dresses. People think I'm exaggerating. But when I first saw a woman's legs for the first time, I said, "Oh, she's got legs!"

Anyway, this girl and I went back into one of the ravines that run between the hills in Pittsburgh. I had on a fuzzy chinchilla overcoat, and I laid it down on the ground for her. Dark all around. Later, when we came up the steps on Larmer Avenue and walked over to Franklin to get a streetcar, I saw in the light that my coat was full of burrs. People laughed at me when I got on the streetcar. When I got home, I stayed up all night 'til seven o'clock picking off those burrs. That was my first experience.

But something happened in Pittsburgh—I'm not sure what—and they shipped me back to Springfield, where I had to work in the tobacco factory.

Gram decided I wasn't doing too much. My clarinet had broken in Pittsburgh, and we didn't know anything about repairmen. So she brought me out of the tobacco factory and sent me to Wilberforce. They had a high school division there, which is what I enrolled in.

SUMMER WITH THE CIRCUS

In 1916, during my first summer vacation from Wilberforce, my Uncle Charlie—one of my father's brothers who played clarinet—came to town and wanted me to go on the road with the Sells-Floto circus. I did about a month and a half with him in the sideshow band. I couldn't play very much, but Uncle Charlie showed me a few things, and a guy at Wilberforce had given me some pointers.

My salary with the circus was eighteen dollars a week, room and board. We rode in a dirty, stinking Pullman car. Nobody took a bath—the performers weren't particular about how they looked or smelled. Everybody in the band carried a gun and a knife. They were all mature men who'd been in the circus business a long time. I was the only youngster. Most of the time I was scared to death and stayed right under my uncle's coattail. But it gave me insights on people I didn't know. Traveling with show people, I learned a lot of things I shouldn't have learned in those days. It gave me an early start on experience.

When we arrived in a town we'd ride on a wagon for the parade and play "Beale Street Blues" or "The Memphis Blues" or "The Entertainer" in fast tempo, or else some old military marches. Other bands played them two to the bar, we'd play them four to the bar. We'd be next to last in the parade; the calliope always came at the end. We played "Rubber-necked Moon," out of the *Smart Set* show, "How Do You Do, Miss Mandy?," and "Snag It," which Joe Oliver used to play.

This was a three-ring circus, but our band only performed in the side-show. That's the little tent off the big top. In the sideshow there'd be the two-headed man, the bearded lady, the fat man, the frog boy, the fire eater, and the sword swallower. They also had Zip, the Monkey Man. He was an old Negro who had a head that went up to a point and looked just like a monkey. Each attraction had its own platform. After you made the circle round, the last attraction was the black band—it was minstrel entertainment, more or less. We had two or three girl dancers, a male dancer, and a blackface comedian.

The band consisted of several clarinets, baritone horn, alto horn, two trombones, two trumpets, tuba, and snare and bass drums. Most of the men came from Florida, Georgia, Tennessee, and Louisiana; I don't know how my uncle got in there. I think H. Qualli Clark, later an arranger for Black Swan in New York, was in charge of the band. The emcee would announce, "Straight from New Orleans, the Cotton Town Minstrels," and the chorus girls would come out and do gags, dance, and sing. We had about twenty or twenty-five minutes for our act.

We'd go on four times a day. The parade was usually around ten in the morning, then we'd do an afternoon show at two that lasted 'til about 4:30. In the evening we'd play in the sideshow before and after the big top performance.

I played with the circus in Florida and part of the South, also Indiana, Illinois, down into Kentucky, and back up into Ohio. Our audiences were mixed, but in the big top there was a segregated section for blacks. I remember asking Uncle Charlie, "Why is it the colored people have to sit way down at that end?"

He said, "Well, it's the same thing in Springfield. You know what you have to do there."

"Yes."

There were some great black clarinet players with circuses in those days. Percy Glascoe from Baltimore was one, and Fred Kewley from Detroit was another. Outside of players in the Jenkins' Orphanage Band, Kewley was the best black clarinet player in the country. In Tampa I heard the Pensacola Kid. Uncle Charlie brought me to a night spot and said, "I'm going to take you down and let you hear a clarinet player." Those guys had a style of clarinet playing that's been forgotten. Ernest Elliott had it, Jimmy O'Bryant had it, and Johnny Dodds had it.

Incidentally, I learned about the origin of the word jazz in the circus. It was just becoming popular then. I'm quite sure it originated in Louisiana. The perfume industry was very big in New Orleans in those days, since the French had brought it over with them. They used jasmine—oil of jasmine—in all different odors to pep it up. It gave more force to the scent. So they would say, "let's jass it up a bit," when something was a little dead. When you started improvising, then, they said "jazz it up," meaning give your own concept of the melody, give it more force, or presence. So if you improvised on the original melody of the composer, they said you were jazzing it up. It caught on in the red light district, when a woman would approach a man and say, "Is jazz on your mind tonight, young fellow?"

BACK TO SCHOOL

After that summer with the circus, I made it through another year or so at Wilberforce. I was concentrating on my clarinet and having a ball. But I wasn't too serious about my studies. In part that was the result of having parents who left their child at an early age, and didn't stick with him to formulate ideas and desires.

At Wilberforce we had a jazz band with Claude Jones, Pinky Starks, and Edgar Hayes on piano. Claude and I became like brothers. He was half-Indian, from Oklahoma. A lot of kids like that from Oklahoma were at Wilberforce. When I met Claude, he used to whoop and do his Indian dance out in the street. But he could play some trombone.

Our jazz band played for some proms, but they complained about my clarinet, saying it wasn't loud enough. I needed a new instrument. So a boy there said to me, "Well, Garvin, if you want to go over to Dayton and work, you could quit school, make some money, and get a new clarinet."

I said, "That's it."

So I left school and went over and stayed with him at his parents' house. I got a job at the National Cash Register Company. Every morning at five o'clock I walked to work along the bank of the Miami River. I stayed two weeks, and made enough to buy a clarinet and a pair of cordovan shoes.

Then I went back to Wilberforce. As soon as I got out of the cab, I saw a big man standing on the front steps of O'Neill Hall. It was my father: he'd come for me. The school had sent him a telegram saying they didn't know where I was. He didn't say anything to me except, "Go upstairs and pack your trunk."

The next morning I was on the train to New York.

NOTES

1. In 1900 the population of Springfield numbered 33,920 whites and 4,253 blacks.
2. On 7 March 1904 a mob lynched Richard Dixon, who was accused of killing Charles B. Collis, a white policeman. According to Benjamin F. Prince, in *A Standard History of Springfield and Clark County, Ohio* (Chicago and New York: American Historical Society, 1922), Dixon was having problems with a woman and appealed to Collis for help, then allegedly shot the policeman. That evening a mob stormed the jail where Dixon was being held, took the prisoner outside and shot him, then dragged him to Main Street and Fountain Avenue, where his body was hung from a telegraph pole.
3. For more on Wilborn and other members of McKinney's Cotton Pickers mentioned by Bushell, see John Chilton, *McKinney's Music* (London: Bloomsbury Book Shop, 1978).
4. The well-known black vaudeville team of Bert Williams and George Walker was active from 1892 to 1908.
5. P. E. Montanus founded the Springfield Machine Tool Company in 1891. In a history of Springfield published in 1908, he was listed as president and treasurer of the firm, and Paul A. and Edward S. Montanus were vice-presidents.

2

Early Years
in New York

Teddy Roosevelt was my father's idol. My father even
looked like a black Teddy Roosevelt, with his horn-rimmed glasses, thick
moustache, and Prince Albert coats.

When I arrived in Harlem with my family late in 1919, my father had
leased a house at 207 West 136th Street, between Seventh and Eighth
avenues. At the time he was a pastor at Walker Memorial Church, on
132nd Street, between Park Avenue and Lexington. Our house was a
typical brown-front: three stories, three rooms on each floor, with a dining room and kitchen on the ground floor, down a few feet below street
level.

We had three tenants on the top floor. One of them was the aunt of
Fletcher Henderson. When Fletcher came to New York from Atlanta, I
went down with his aunt to meet him at Penn Station. At the time his
name was James, and we called him Jimmy. When people first started
talking about Fletcher Henderson, I didn't know who they meant.[1]

My father wanted me to go to school, but I backed out of it. I kept giving
him excuses for not going, and every day went out looking for jobs.

My first job was as a porter at Weber and Heilbroner's, next to the U.S.
Stock Exchange on Broad Street—right around the corner from Wall
Street. I got the job through Leon Gross, who lived in our house, and who
was a truck driver at Weber and Heilbroner's. I happened to be there
when they tried to blow up J. P. Morgan at the Treasury Building. I had
seen the horse parked in front of the Treasury Building when I went to
work. (Back then there were more horses and wagons on the street than

automobiles). The explosion took place about 1:30. If it had happened during lunch it would have killed thousands of people.

But I didn't want to be a porter, so I left after not too long. Next I worked as assistant stock clerk at Loft's candy store on 42nd Street. I ate so much candy they fired me.

In the summer of 1920, while my parents were out in California at a convention, I applied for a job on the docks unloading banana boats. I wasn't very strong then, but I picked up two big stalks and wobbled off the gangplank. I went back to get another one and a big spider jumped out. I put that stalk down and walked right on off the job.

I also worked as a busboy at the Union League Club on Fifth Avenue, near 39th Street. Didn't stay there long, either. But I was still trying to duck going back to school. I finally wound up with an elevator job at 116th Street and St. Nicholas Avenue. All that neighborhood was still white, so they had Negro elevator operators. I didn't keep that job. I didn't keep any job much more than a week.

My first musical contact was with a fellow by the name of Clarence Potter. In his vaudeville act he wore kilts and did songs by Harry Lauder. His complexion was dark, but he had sharp features and looked something like a black Scotsman.

We organized a five-piece band and rehearsed on 136th Street. Then we did an audition, and they accepted us on the Independent time.[2] Our first date was at the Loew's Lyric Theater in Hoboken, New Jersey, on a Sunday concert. But the act was so bad, we were fired after one performance. After the first show the manager came up and gave us two dollars and a half for transportation back to New York. That was my first experience on stage with a New York group.

As word got around that a new clarinet player was in town, I began to get gigs. I met Leon Gardner, a saxophone player who lived on our block of 136th Street. We got a couple of jobs out in Larchmont; I remember the tune that was popular then was "Love Nest." I also got a few gigs out at Coney Island with a trombonist we called Race Horse.

These were just pickup bands. But there was also a rehearsal band that used to meet every Sunday at a place on Fifth Avenue, between 134th and 135th. In that group were some unknowns, most of them from Florida—I never heard of them after that. The way they played reminded me of my uncle's circus band.

We'd usually have eight or nine guys: trumpet, trombone, clarinet, saxophone, piano, banjo, tuba, and drums. Maybe a violin or a bandolin—half banjo, half violin. Since there weren't dance arrangements then for saxophones and trumpets, the pieces we rehearsed were mostly pit orchestrations. We'd pull out one clarinet part, one sax part, and on like that. The piano player had a part, as a rule, and the bass player faked. In fact, most everybody faked, since none of us could read that well. The style was very much what you hear on the early records—we called it "ragtime jazz."

One day we decided to play over at the trombonist's house, on 107th Street between Second and Third avenues. That neighborhood was composed of Negro men who had married Jewish women and had families. It had the most beautiful girls in Harlem. We used to go over there Sundays and sit in the ice cream parlor to try and pick up girls. Because we were from the west side of Harlem, the Jewish and Italian boys tried to keep us out, and we had several bad fights. Our band never went back to rehearse there after that one time, since we had too much trouble.

MUSIC IN HARLEM, 1919–21

I used to go hear some of the big Negro dance bands that played at places like the New Star Casino on 107th Street and Lexington Avenue and at the Manhattan Casino, which later became the Rockland Palace. These bands often had thirty to fifty pieces. Sometimes twenty men would be playing bandolins! Among the leading conductors were John C. Smith, Allie Ross (who later conducted *Blackbirds*), Happy Rhone, Leroy Smith, and Ford Dabney. John C. Smith was a trumpeter who had a typical Harlem big band. It played more of the ragtime and syncopation that Harlem liked. Leroy Smith had an orchestra with excellent musicians. About the best soloist Leroy had was Emerson "Geechie" Harper, who was from the Jenkins' Orphanage Band of South Carolina. He played oboe, also jazz clarinet. But Ford Dabney's was the band we most liked to go see. Dabney had played the Amsterdam Roof for many years. He had a high standard of entertainment, since his work included playing for the ultra-rich of New York.

Some of these dances were very formal affairs sponsored by a club or a lodge. There was one group that sponsored dances, the Boys of Yesteryear, made up of guys who had been around New York for a long time. They later moved their headquarters to the Renaissance Ballroom, upstairs over the Renaissance Casino, at 138th Street and Seventh Avenue.

These big bands played pop and show tunes. The saxophone was not very prominent as a solo instrument, but the trumpet, trombone, and clarinet were. The soloists improvised—especially the trumpet players, who used a whole series of buckets and cuspidors for effects. The bands played foxtrot rhythm and still adhered to the two-beat rhythmic feel. The jazz bands that I'd heard in Springfield, however, played in four. The Creole Band with Freddie Keppard and George Bacquet had come to New York about 1915, and I was told they played in four. In fact, Tony Spargo with the Original Dixieland Jazz Band was about the only jazz player I heard playing in two. I remember going to hear that group at Reisenweber's. I had to stand at the back door with the dishwashers.

I wasn't so impressed with the bandleaders, per se. The individuals were the ones who impressed me, especially the trumpet and clarinet players. Usually there wouldn't be more than two clarinets in these bands; often they'd be bucking each other, fighting and cross-firing their lines. But one important clarinet player would take the solos. Ed Campbell did a lot of that. He wasn't much of a jazzman, but he was a very good reader.

I began listening to the Original Dixieland Jazz Band around 1920–21, when I heard their record of "St. Louis Blues," also "Skeleton Jangle" and "Barnyard Blues." I thought Larry Shields was great, and I was influenced by a lot of things he did. Then Ted Lewis came around with his flutter tongue and all. Since I was impressed with Ohio musicians anyhow, I copied some of Ted's things.

Wilbur Sweatman was a clarinetist with a lot of technique who could do things the rest of us couldn't do. He had a bad sound, but he was a great showman. He'd come out and do "Hungarian Rhapsody No. 2" and play "The Rosary" on three clarinets. I'd always go see him.

Sweatman lived at about 143rd or 144th Street, between Seventh and Eighth avenues. I first met him when my friend Junk Edwards took me up there; Junk's father had drummed with Sweatman. Sweatman was my idol. I just listened to him talk and looked at him like he was God.

The top trumpet player around 1919–20 was Jack Hatton. He was a member of the Clef Club who had been in New York most of his life. Hatton lit up Ford Dabney's orchestra. He was very exciting, and played with a lot of power and flutter-tonguing. He also used buckets and plungers, slop jars, chambers, and everything. It was a lot of comedy. But he was sensational, and his impact on audiences was as great as Johnny Dunn's was on record.

Hatton's playing, and that of other New York musicians of the time, was different from the playing of men in Chicago, St. Louis, New Orleans, and

Texas. New York jazz was nearer the ragtime style and had less blues. There wasn't an eastern performer who could really play the blues. We later absorbed it from the southern musicians we heard, but it wasn't original with us. We didn't put that quarter-tone pitch in the music the way the southerners did. Up north we leaned toward ragtime conception—a lot of notes.

Most of the Negro population in New York then had either been born there or had been in the city so long they were fully acclimated. They wanted to forget the traditions of the South and were trying to emulate the whites. You couldn't deliver a package to a Negro's front door. You had to go down to the cellar door. And Negroes dressed up to go to work, then changed into work clothes when they got there. You usually weren't allowed to play blues and boogie woogie in the average Negro middle-class home. That music supposedly suggested a low element. And the big bands with the violins, flutes, and piccolos didn't play it either.

You could only hear the blues and real jazz in the gutbucket cabarets where the lower class went. The term "gutbucket" came from the chitter-lings bucket. Chitterlings are the guts of a hog, and the practice used to be to take a bucket to the slaughterhouse and get a bucket of guts. Therefore, anything real low down was called gutbucket. So far as I know, the term was used in St. Louis, Kansas City, New York, Kentucky, Ten-nessee, and many places.

They improvised in the cabarets and what they played had different timbres from the big dance bands. What the white man in New York called the blues, however, was just more ragtime. The real blues used a special melodic line together with a way of playing that combined Irish cadences and Indian quarter-tones together with the Negro's repetition of melody. (By the Irish cadence I mean a chord sequence that was some-what like the blues.)

I think the influence of the American Indians on jazz has been under-estimated. There were plenty of Indians back of our house in Springfield, and part of my family is Indian. There were Indians throughout the South, Southeast, and Southwest. When the slaves ran away, Indians often took them in because Indians hated the white man, too. How do you think there came to be so many Negroes with Indian blood?

Gradually, the New York cabarets began to hear more of the real pure jazz and blues by musicians from Florida, South Carolina, Georgia, Loui-siana, and other parts of the South. What they played was more ex-pressive than had been heard in New York to that time.

Most cabarets had a five-piece band and seven or eight singers. The singer would sing one chorus at each table and go around to every table in the joint. If you didn't know the song when she started, you would by the time she'd completed her rounds. The pianists could improvise very well; for one thing, they got a lot of practice, working from 9:00 P.M. to 6:00 A.M. After each singer-entertainer was through, the band would play a dance number.

PIANISTS

Harlem was filled with good pianists in the early 1920s. Among the first who impressed me was Carl Edwards, a good jazzman who played with the bunch of guys I used to rehearse with over on Fifth Avenue. At the time he would have been called a ragtime pianist—the word *jazz* was just beginning to be exploited.

Another good player was Alberta Simmons. She was in her thirties, and was one of the first pianists I'd heard who played a style that sounded a little different. (I hadn't heard James P. Johnson yet.) She seemed to use fewer notes, was more expressive, and had more drive. It was ragtime, but it was definitely her version of it. She played a swinging bass line—tenths seemed the dominant pattern; it wasn't a walking bass.

Eventually I came to hear Willie "The Lion" Smith, James P., Willie Gant, Abba Labba, and Fred Tunstall. Willie "The Lion" played more ragtime than James P. Johnson. James P. was cleaner and more inventive, as those early QRS rolls demonstrate.[3] He played things that were very close to what pianists in Ohio and the West were doing. He was getting away from the ragtime of Joplin, adding to what he retained, and expressing *himself.*

Fred Tunstall was a pimp. He had immense fingers, and he dressed better than any musician in Harlem. He played like James P., though not as well.

The major influence on all of them was Abba Labba. I just got to hear him one time, down at the Royal Garden at 135th and Lenox Avenue. He and Fred Tunstall never took a steady job. Abba Labba would come in and play thirty minutes, cut everybody, and go out. He used tenths in the bass, and he could swing. They called it "shout" in those days, from the church when the Baptist minister would start preaching and the congregation would get all worked up emotionally. Negro church music had a great influence on jazz. They sang the blues in church; the words were religious, but it was blues. They often had a drummer and a trumpet player there. The Negro carried his troubles to church and talked to God about them.

James P., due to the influence of Abba Labba and his own capacity, was one of the few great pianists in New York. Later, Fats Waller came to be another. When you heard James P. at his best, you were hearing Abba Labba's style, except that James P., who had studied, played with a little more finesse and taste. When Ellington came to New York with Elmer Snowden's band, he was playing like James P. Apparently he'd heard the QRS rolls.

An important piano influence came out of Baltimore. Players like Eubie Blake, Madison Reed, and Edgar Dowell were early exponents of ragtime who came to New York. They played modified ragtime—technically and musically more complex than what Joplin had done.

Being in big-time vaudeville with Noble Sissle, Eubie Blake was way above the rest of us then. You'd never find him in the cabarets; the people he hung out with were Victor Herbert and Jerome Kern. James P. and Willie "The Lion" were just performing musicians, but Eubie was a composer and considered a great pianist in those days. Maybe in Baltimore he played in the clubs, but when he hit the New York scene, he was way above that, as far as I know.

MAMIE SMITH AND JOHNNY DUNN

Small dance bands in Harlem played in places like the Orient, on 135th Street between Lenox and Fifth avenues. It was a characteristic gutbucket joint, and it was there that Mamie Smith found her band. The instrumentation in the place was trumpet, trombone, clarinet, piano, drums, and sometimes saxophone. The trombone player, Dope Andrews, was Charlie Shavers's uncle. He had the style they called tailgate later on, but there was more beauty and control of tone in his work than in George Brunis's, for example. All of Harlem had bands like that; if they couldn't get a clarinet, they used a saxophone.

I began to work with Mamie Smith in 1921, as part of her band called the Jazz Hounds. I lived back of Perry Bradford's house; he heard me practicing one day, and asked me if I wanted to make some records. He was Mamie's manager. Up to then I'd been doing vaudeville and had played in *Ol' Kentuck,* a book show, at the 14th Street Theater. We did three shows a day, and before each show we went out front to ballyhoo. We played on the stage and improvised. We didn't have any saxophones, but we did have three clarinets, tuba, three trumpets, two trombones, two baritone horns, and two drums (bass and snare).

Mamie Smith wasn't a real blues singer like Bessie Smith. She didn't get in between the tones the way Bessie did. Mamie was what we called a shouter. But the white people called it blues!

Mamie was a very fine-looking lady, had a nice personality, and was a bit higher cultured than a lot of the singers. She wasn't a low, gutbucket type of singer that they were wanting on records. I admired her talent very much, and I looked up to her. She usually had a husband who was a big bruiser, taking all her money.

Perry Bradford used to direct those sessions with Mamie. He'd stand on a big platform and make motions for what he wanted the instruments to do, moving his hands up for high notes, down for low ones. We knew so little about recording in those days. Compared to today's technology, it was like the difference between hitching a horse to a rig and having a Cadillac. If we'd just used common sense, we would have done things much different.

There were usually three pipes or tubes with bell-shaped ends coming out of the sound room. Each horn player sat on a high stool, right close to the tube, and played into it. The piano would be picked up by another overall pipe. There were no drums or bass on these early vocal recordings; apparently these instruments made large indentations into the wax they used for recording, so we couldn't use them. Later on they began to use wood block and snare, but no bass drum.

The first time I ever worked with Johnny Dunn was on a record date with Mamie Smith. I'd seen him before when he was featured with W. C. Handy's orchestra at the Lafayette Theater.

Johnny Dunn was an individualist. He's the guy that made double-time famous, and he introduced wa-wa effects with the plunger. He had a lot of drive, and his sound was dynamic. Lew Leslie later used him in the pits to drive the ensemble. He came from Memphis, and he played the blues so it moved you, but not as soulfully as those blues players out of Louisiana. (Charlie Creath, from East St. Louis, was the only non-Louisiana player I heard who played that style as well as they did, even better.)

Johnny didn't know too much music, but he was a good creator, and he played a saxophone-style trumpet, different from any other trumpet player. He was a stylish guy who dressed well and thought a lot of himself. He carried a cane and wore a big diamond ring, and he always kept three or four fifty-dollar bills in his watch pocket, which most of us had never seen in those days.

Johnny was good behind singers. He created another melody under the singer's melody. A lot of times he'd cross-fire, but his basic style was to answer the beginning of the cadence.

What you hear on those early Mamie Smith sides was the prevailing style around Harlem at the time. Harlem was a melting pot, and many styles from different parts of the country were introduced by musicians who came to live there. Johnny Dunn brought his style from Memphis. The clarinet style I played was something I just concocted there in New York. Dope Andrews was also a New Yorker, like his nephew Charlie Shavers. He hadn't heard Jonas Walker yet, or Honore Dutrey in Chicago. His was more or less the New York trombone style—also similar to what they played in the circus bands.

One time they hired the Jazz Hounds to play a picture at the Lafayette Theater. It was called *Over the Hill,* and we had the score for the whole film. Well, we couldn't read a thing. Johnny was sitting on a high stool, conducting with a trumpet. We just got lost, and kept playing, "Over the hill / Over the hill." When the train was coming we played it fast, and when the hero and heroine were making love, it was "Over the hill / Over the hill," a little slower. That's all we played for the whole picture! They fired us after the first show. They thought because we were Mamie Smith's Jazz Hounds we could play anything. My God, it was pathetic.

I recorded with many different singers in 1921. On one date with Daisy Martin we had Gus Aiken on trumpet and Jake Frazier on trombone. For the two sides, I remember we were paid thirty dollars; we had to wait months to get it. In those days you'd receive a set amount for a single record session, no matter how long it took. It could take all day to make two sides because of the problems of playbacks and blending.

I also did some things with Shep Edmonds. He and his wife were from Columbus, Ohio, and they rented the third floor of our house on 130th Street, where we moved in 1921. Shep was a detective, but also a composer. He had written some tunes, and I did a date with Lillyn Brown where she sang them.

ON TOUR WITH MAMIE SMITH

I soon went out on the road with Mamie, in the winter of 1921, I believe. Bubber Miley replaced Johnny Dunn in the band. We had a fellow on trombone named Carpenter. Charlie Summers was the piano player, a little fellow, a hunchback. And we had a drummer named

Horace from some other town—he came from out West. We didn't have a
bass—bands didn't use bass too much in those days. Ocey Wilson,
Mamie's husband, was our manager.[4] He'd make sure the stage was set
up and run the whole show. He also injected discipline in the group,
more or less.

Our tour was arranged by a Jewish firm in New York. Ocey and Mamie
paid us fifty dollars a week—how much they got for the whole unit, I
don't know.

We broke in the new band at the Pershing Theater in Pittsburgh, where
we were the closing act of a vaudeville bill. Mamie had these new costumes. She used to wear these spangled, form-fitting costumes with big
head plumes, but there were no zippers in those days, everything was
hooks and eyes.

We opened up with "Bugle Call Blues." Then Mamie sang one of her
big numbers, "It's Right Here for You, If You Don't Get It, It's No Fault of
Mine." She went back to make her change and these hooks and eyes got
tangled up and she couldn't get them untangled, so we played the "Royal
Garden Blues" while she was making the change. We vamped the next
song after we finished, the audience applauded, but no Mamie. So Ocey
said play it again, the introduction. Still no Mamie.

So we're getting nervous. Bubber's mouth is leaking—his lip's weak
anyway, since it's his first time onstage. So Ocey said, "She ain't ready!
Something's happened to her costume! Play the 'Royal Garden Blues'
again." We started to, and people yelled, "You just played that!" We
played it through, though, and Bubber's lip is getting weaker all the time.
When we finished, the people went, "Boo! Boo!" Ocey says, "She ain't
ready! Play it again!" So we're about to hit the introduction, and I look
over and see Bubber putting his horn to the side of his mouth, and going,
"pfft, pfft." He knew he couldn't find his mouthpiece, so he starts backing
away.

The piano's vamping, waiting for him to come in, and Bubber's backing
off the stage. Ocey took his foot and literally booted him back onstage.
When the people saw that foot, they screamed. Bubber came on holding
his behind, and they had to drop the curtain.

Bubber and I roomed together occasionally on the road. Often I had to
wake him up and bring him to the theater. We had trouble when we had
to get up early to make a train. You couldn't get Bubber out of bed. And a
lot of times, when it was time to go on at night and do the show, Bubber
had been out somewhere all afternoon and just stayed there. Later James

P. and Fats used to do the same thing when we were doing *Keep Shufflin'* at Daley's 63rd Street Theater.

From Pittsburgh we went to Cleveland, I believe, or Columbus, and later Detroit. I remember in Detroit I got paid fifty dollars in one-dollar bills. That night I went out to the Lyric Park with Horace, our drummer. I had a brand-new suit on, and when the girls saw this big roll of money they went, "Whooo!"

When we got to Chicago, Bubber and I went to hear King Oliver and his Creole Jazz Band at the Dreamland every night.[5] It was the first time I'd heard New Orleans musicians to any advantage, and I studied them for the entire week we were in town. I was very much impressed with their blues and their sound. The trumpets and clarinets in the East had a better "legitimate" quality, but the sound of Oliver's band touched you more. It was less cultivated but more expressive of how the people felt. Bubber and I sat there with our mouths open.

I'd never heard anything like that, even in the circus, because the circus musicians were from Florida, and they played ragtime. But when you went to hear a band out of New Orleans, you heard a different feel. The harmonic line was the same, but the rhythm of the solos was different. You heard the trumpet doing a different thing, half-cocked with a tin mute. That's where Bubber got his growling, from Joe Oliver. Before hearing Oliver, Bubber was trying to play like Johnny Dunn. (That's why Mamie had hired him to replace Johnny.) He had picked up the plunger mute thing from Johnny, but he never growled or used the half-cocked silver mute. It was in Chicago, after hearing Oliver, that Bubber changed his style and began using his hand over the tin mute that used to come with all cornets.

Bubber and I talked with the Dodds brothers, Johnny and Baby. They felt very highly about what they were playing, as though they knew they were doing something new that nobody else could do. I'd say they regarded themselves as artists, in the sense we use the term today.

Freddie Keppard was in the band at the Sunset. There were about twelve men, including Flutes Morton on flute and piccolo. He had a big, loud, powerful sound on the flute, and he was improvising jazz on the instrument back then. The band had two trumpets, and even though they were twelve, they often improvised collectively. They could read— or some of them could, the ones who played the Vendome Theater. Chicago jazzmen had the advantage in those years of having a crack at theater music before the New York jazzmen did. They improved their ability that way, and so could read a little better than jazz musicians in the East.

Fats Williams played first trumpet and Freddie did most of the jazz solos. They played a lot of things together, but not unison breaks the way Louis and Oliver later did. Fats and Freddie were a more dynamic team, though.

Joe Oliver never had the power of Freddie Keppard. Freddie could make the glasses on the bar move—they'd bet money on that. Freddie was more exciting than Joe. He played spells of intricate passages. High notes. Screams. Tongue flutters. But Joe was gutbucket jazz and blues. He played things that hit you inside. Joe also had that lip shake or trill— New Orleans trumpeters created it—that could make people jump out of their seats.

In Chicago we played at the Avenue Theater with Mamie, and I lived with a family on Indiana Avenue. One night, on my way home, I passed a carnival ground there and went in to hear a New Orleans band that was playing. It was the Thomas New Orleans Jug Band, and it was more primitive than Oliver's. It included trumpet, clarinet, trombone, jug, bass, drums, guitar. It had the same beat as Oliver's—what we called in Ohio the "shimmy" beat. They played mostly blues, and they played four beat, as did Oliver.

As I was standing there watching the group, I noticed a great big guy with red lips who kept edging up behind me. I moved away, and he moved closer. I found my way to the gate, and headed for the place where I was staying, but he came out of the gate after me. I walked fast, and he walked faster. So I took off. I ran down Indiana Avenue in the middle of the street, straight to my house. It so happened that the folks were sitting out on the porch where I lived. When I tore into the yard, they said, "What's the matter?"

I said, "Open that door! Look, this man is behind me!" And wouldn't you know, he ran up in the yard after me?

The owner said, "Don't you come another step." They say he stopped and turned around and went on back. Thank God I could outrun him. They said he'd been chasing boys around for years, in Chicago.

We went to other cities in the Midwest, and then pulled into Kansas City, where we were supposed to do a whole show at the 12th Street Theater. Up until then we'd just been doing concerts on the road, and it was billed as Mamie Smith and Her Jazz Hounds. Now it was Mamie Smith and Company, and we had a comedian, a magician, a dance team, and some singers. The band played in the pit during the first half, then it would just be Mamie in the second half. We did two shows a day, each about two hours long.

Since we had to accompany acts from the pit we had to expand our five-piece group. We brought George Bell from Detroit—he was a violinist—and our advance agent sent ahead to get an extra musician in Kansas City. When we got there for the first rehearsal we met this youngster on saxophone who played all his parts and didn't miss a note. When we told him to take a solo, he took a tremendous one. We said, "What's your name?"

"Coleman."

"Coleman who?"

"Coleman Hawkins."

He'd come over for the job from St. Joe. That was the first time I heard him play, and he never made a mistake—we had to read our parts when we played in the pit, and Hawk never hit a bad note. I believe he was playing C-melody saxophone.

The 12th Street Theater was a white burlesque house, but they booked Mamie in there because she was at her height then. Besides, it was summer, and burlesque houses were usually dark that time of year. We used to do a lot of Sunday concerts in burlesque houses in the summer.

After Kansas City we went to Tulsa, but they'd just had a race riot and burned out the whole black neighborhood, so we couldn't play. Mamie contributed money to the people there.

We had a few days layoff in Tulsa, then went back and did a concert in St. Joe. After the concert we went out to Coleman Hawkins's house, where they had a party for us. That's where I talked with his grandmother. We asked her to let him go with us to New York, but she told us he was "just a baby," and too young to go off on his own.[6]

From St. Joe we went back to Detroit. There were two theaters in the Negro neighborhood on Gratiot Avenue. One was the S. H. Dudley, the other the Copeland. We played the S. H. Dudley, a small theater. They'd have a movie, then the big attraction went on.

LEROY'S

After I got off the tour with Mamie Smith I started working at Leroy's, at 135th Street and Fifth Avenue. The place had been owned by

Leroy Wilkins, Barron Wilkins's brother, then it was taken over by Harry Pyles, who kept the name. Harry didn't allow white people in Leroy's. He said, "They'll come in here and trouble is liable to start, so we'll just keep them out." They were allowed in other Harlem places, though.

The band at Leroy's was sensational. We had Jake Frazier on trombone, Gus Aiken on trumpet, Charlie Jackson on violin, Willie Gant on piano, Bill Benford on tuba, and Joe Banks on drums. At different times we also had Buddy Aiken or Geechie Fields on trombone, and Steve Wright on drums. Willie Gant was the boss of the band; the pianist was always the leader in cabaret bands, because he had to play behind the singers.

A lot of these guys had come out of the Jenkins' Orphanage Band from South Carolina. They were schooled on their instruments, and they could *play*. At the time, I didn't like what I did; I wasn't practicing too much. But those Jenkins boys were thorough.[7]

By this time we were certainly influenced by New Orleans players. We played "Shake It and Break It" in typical New Orleans style.

Sunday night was when everybody in Harlem got dressed up. That was the only time at Leroy's we wore tuxedos, and at eleven or twelve o'clock we'd have a special concert and play overtures like "Poet and Peasant" and "Morning, Noon, and Night." Gus and Buddy and all the Jenkins boys knew these pieces, so what parts I couldn't play, they'd hum to me. But I'd take my part home and work on it.

Often when we played blues at Leroy's, each instrument would be in a different corner: the trumpet at the far end, the clarinet in the back room, and so on. You'd take a solo from where you were in the room, then when it was time to start the ensemble you'd come back to the bandstand.

I first saw the Charleston done at Leroy's. Russell Brown came from Charleston, and he did a Geechie dance they did on the Georgia South Sea Islands. It was called a "cut out" dance. People began to say to Brown, "Hey, Charleston, do your dance!" That's how the Charleston came to be introduced to New York.

It was at Leroy's, too, that I first saw piano battles with players like Willie "The Lion," James P., Fats, and Willie Gant. They'd last three or four hours. One man would play two or three choruses, and the next would slide in. Jimmy was on top most of the time. Fats was the youngest, but he was coming along. They played shouts and also pop tunes. You got credit for how many patterns you could create within the tunes you knew, and in how many different keys you could play. You had to know how to play in every key, because all those players had been baptized in cabarets. You never knew what kind of key the entertainer wanted.

There'd be more controversy among the listeners than the participants. There was betting, and people were ready to fight about who'd won. James P. played with the most originality. He'd create things the other guys hadn't thought up.

Our clientele at Leroy's were mainly Negroes from the South who had migrated. They lived in the 130s, off Fifth Avenue—that was one of the toughest parts of Harlem. There was a small dance floor in front of the bandstand. The dancers were our inspiration. Men and women danced close together in the cabarets. When they got high, they just did one step: the slow drag. You just grabbed your gal to have the confidence to go out the back door with her. The closer it got, the better. So slow music would provide them with a chance to do that.

Leroy's was one of the most sensational joints I've ever been in in my life. There were at least three shootings a week there, and a murder once a month. One night they threw a guy out who started a fight. They took him upstairs and beat him up. A little later he came back. Before he got downstairs, he killed the doorman. Then he came down and stood at the foot of the stairs and just started shooting all over the place. Bullets were buzzing and flying everywhere! I remember hearing those bullets whizz past the bandstand. There were six of us in the band then, and we pulled the piano out and everybody dove behind it. Fortunately, nobody got killed down in the bar.

There were always big fights in the Harlem cabarets in those days. It was during Prohibition, and the stuff people were drinking made the people wild and out of control—they'd fight and shoot and cut and break up the place, and we were used to it. But for the first few months, I'd come home a nervous wreck. We played 'til five or six o'clock in the morning. It was good experience, though.

I met Marie Roberts, my first wife, down at Leroy's. She had red hair and blue eyes. Everybody thought she was white, but she wasn't. She had Negro blood in her. She was a chorus girl, and all the chorus girls were light-skinned. At the time she was working in the revue at Reisenweber's.

Marie was friends with Harry Pyles, the owner of Leroy's. When I took her away from him, I lost my job.

NOTES

1. Walter C. Allen cites conflicting sources that present Henderson's first name as either "James" or "Fletcher" in *Hendersonia* (Highland Park,

N.J.: Walter C. Allen, 1973), 2. It seems likely that "James" was in use early on, as Bushell states, but was dropped soon after Henderson's arrival in New York.

2. "Independent time" refers to bookings in theaters not affiliated with any of the major vaudeville circuits, such as the Keith Albee, Columbia, Orpheum, Loew's, Pantages, and others.

3. Based in Chicago, QRS was one of the leading piano roll manufacturers in the 1910s and 1920s.

4. In *Who's Who of Jazz,* John Chilton refers to Ocey *Williams* as a director of one of Smith's groups, but mentions as her husband William Smith, who died in 1928.

5. Mamie Smith and her band appeared at the Avenue Theater from Sunday, 27 February 1921, through Sunday, 6 March. The *Chicago Defender* (26 February 1921, p. 4) advertised this as Smith's "First, last, and only local engagement."

6. Hawkins was born 21 November 1904, so he was sixteen at the time.

7. For more on the Jenkins' Orphanage Bands, see John Chilton, *A Jazz Nursery* (London: Bloomsbury Book Shop, 1980).

3

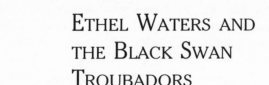

ETHEL WATERS AND THE BLACK SWAN TROUBADORS

Perry Bradford took on Edith Wilson after Mamie Smith got out from under him. As I said, Perry lived right behind us on 129th Street, and I first met Edith and her husband Danny Wilson the same way I met Mamie—right over my backyard fence. I don't know if Perry had sent for Edith or whether she'd already come to New York from Louisville, Kentucky. But Edith and I became very good friends and remained so down through the years.

Perry coached Edith and had her trying to sing like Mamie Smith. Edith had a good voice, sounding like a combination of Mamie and Ethel Waters. Edith's diction wasn't as clear as Ethel's; a lot of her words you couldn't understand. But she sang well, and when she hit on a pitch, she stayed there.

I played on a few record dates with Edith in 1921. That same year, Fletcher Henderson introduced me to Ethel Waters. Fletcher was then working as a song plugger and arranger for Black Swan, the record label started by Harry Pace after he left W. C. Handy. Black Swan had its offices on 46th Street for a while, then it moved uptown, to the east side of Seventh Avenue between 134th and 135th. I never saw Pace; he had nothing to do with recording. But Lester Walton used to come in all the time—he was one of the other partners in Black Swan.

Fletcher was in charge of the record dates. He might pick the numbers in the office, present them to the vocalists, then we'd have rehearsal and get it together. Often there were only two pieces of music, one for the piano and one for the trumpet (or violin). Sometimes everybody had a part.

Ethel had been in cabarets all her life. She didn't sing real blues, though: she was a jazz singer. She syncopated. Her style was influenced by the horns she'd heard and by church singing. She literally sang with a smile, which made her voice sound wide and broad.

Ethel turned out to be an important influence. Mildred Bailey had some of her style, Lena Horne has a lot, and there were others. I'd say the three major influences in jazz singing have been Ethel, Louis Armstrong, and Billie Holiday. (Of course, in Ella Fitzgerald's case, Connee Boswell was the major influence.)

Fletcher never wrote out anything for Ethel, since she didn't read music. Very few singers could read in those days. Ethel had a great memory for lyrics, though, and a great ear, like Ella Fitzgerald.

Since we couldn't use a bass drum or a bass the rhythm tended to get ragged. Also, we'd be in awkward positions and scattered all over the place, which made it hard to keep together. But when Fletcher was in charge it was usually a little more organized, and we'd have good musicians who were concerned about what they were playing.

The records we made were called "race records." The record companies wanted original tunes by black composers which would appeal to the Negro population. The white market didn't know anything about them. A composer like Maceo Pinkard was an in-between; his tunes weren't usually so black-oriented, but were ones that whites would accept—like "Sweet Georgia Brown," "Give Me a Little Kiss," and "Drafting Blues." Pinkard's and Handy's tunes weren't as crude as those of Perry Bradford and some of the others. You'd never hear white audiences singing "It's Right Here for You" or "He May Be Your Man (But He Comes to See Me Sometimes)." This music was strictly confined to the race catalogue until, for the most part, the time of Louis Jordan.

ON THE ROAD WITH THE
BLACK SWAN TROUBADORS

In the fall of 1921 I went on tour with Ethel, opening in Washington and then going on to the Standard Theater in Philadelphia.

Our band had Gus Aiken, trumpet; his brother Buddy, trombone; Charlie Jackson on violin; Bill D. C. on baritone saxophone; Joe Elder, tenor; Raymond Green, xylophone and drums; and Fletcher, piano.[1]

Like any band then that got on stage, we had to do a specialty of some kind. So we had an act in which I was a cop and Green was a preacher. He'd be standing there on the street preaching at what looked like an altar, but it would be his xylophone, covered up. I'd come out in a cop uniform and chase him off the street. Ray Green was a very funny character, and a good drummer, too.

At the Standard Theater, the heavyweight champion Jack Johnson was on the bill with us. He'd just gotten out of Leavenworth. He did some shadow boxing and some talking. People just wanted to look at him.

Jack also did a mock fight with Sandy Burns, a blackface comedian. Burns was a light-skinned Negro who played the Apollo, the Harlem Opera House, the Lafayette, and TOBA theaters all across the country.

For that appearance at the Standard we also had Slick White, who had one of the most fabulous tenor voices I've ever heard. He sang blues, also arias from operas.

We stayed at the Horseshoe Hotel, where all the toughs lived. While we were there someone tried to rob me, but I pulled my gun and ran everybody out of the room. In those days a Negro didn't have much protection from the law and so had to protect himself. You were supposed to have a license to carry a gun, but nobody ever did—all the old-time performers had pistols. Charlie Jackson kept a .45 in his violin case, and Buddy Aiken had a .25 automatic under his derby. When Buddy took off his hat, he meant business.

In Philadelphia I got full of that Prohibition gin and accidentally shot a girl who was trying to frame me. I was fooling around with two girls, and one of them didn't know it was supposed to be on the Q.T., so she told the other and they both jumped on me about it. I was half-drunk, so I said, "Who do you think I am? I'll show you who I am!" I shot down at the floor but the bullet glanced up and struck one in the heel. That quieted everyone down. And nobody bothered with the little clarinet player no more, either.

Another time I cut Charlie Jackson. He did something, so I lunged at him with this big pushbutton knife I had and cut a big chunk out of his arm. That hurt me, because he and I were so close. Oh, I was mean, then. I had a short temper and was going in the wrong direction.

From Philadelphia we went to Baltimore. Tom Delaney was on the bill with us there. He had a comic act with a partner. That's where I first heard "Jazz Me Blues," which Tom wrote.

Baltimore had a great variety of jazz and many excellent performers. They came to New York in droves, and a large proportion of the significant figures in early New York jazz turn out to have come from Baltimore or nearby. Besides Eubie Blake and Edgar Dowell, whom I've mentioned earlier, there was Bobby Lee, piano; John Mitchell, banjo; Percy Glascoe, clarinet; and Pike Davis, trumpet. Later Chick Webb came out of Baltimore.

There was good jazz in just about every cabaret, no matter how low or cheap. Baltimore musicians had more technique than the New York players, I don't know why. They were very fly, smart, creative improvisers. But they didn't play the blues the way the musicians from the South did. Their jazz was based on ragtime piano practices, and piano ragtime influenced the way they played their horns. They also had the best banjo players in the world.

New Orleans musicians, of course, were not the first to improvise. Perry Bradford went from Georgia to New Orleans in 1909. He claimed there were no technicians to speak of there then, and they didn't know much about ragtime. He said ragtime came up the East Coast from Florida and Georgia and that when they brought it to New Orleans, the musicians there put the blues to it.

After Baltimore we did one-nighters in and around Pennsylvania for about a month. I heard Joe Smith for the first time at the Grape Vine in Pittsburgh. He was out of New York, but I hadn't heard him until then. His style was similar to that of Johnny Dunn, but he had a much better sound. Joe actually played more like some of the white trumpet players. By that I mean he was more lyrical and had a finer sound. Joe played for beauty rather than drive. He was a trained trumpet player and had the right embouchure. You see, 90 percent of the Negro musicians were self-taught. Since opportunities for training were mostly for the whites, that's why generally they had a better sound. Several Negro musicians of the time, however, had the talent and capacity to become first-rate classical musicians—if there had been openings for them. There was Joe's brother, Russell Smith, for example, who was one of the best legitimate trumpet players in the business. Anyway, Fletcher Henderson was very impressed with Joe's sound, and he never forgot it.

When we got to St. Louis, I heard the greatest blues player of his time: Charlie Creath. He played at Jazzland, a huge place with the bandstand up in the balcony. The bandstands in the dance halls at that time were usually near the ceiling; the musicians felt safer there. Gene Sedric, a big, fat kid, was playing clarinet in his band. We were the invited guests and were asked to play.

Creath had a Joe Smith-like tone, but with more blues feeling and drive. He had beautiful sound and soul, and his forte was the blues. He had command of the high register, too; most New Orleans players couldn't go above B-flat. Tommy Ladnier, for instance. Louis Armstrong was an exception. He went up to C and D and later to F and G whenever he wanted to.

Creath was a phenomenon. I once heard Tommy Ladnier say: "When Charlie used to hit certain notes, the whores would just fall out and throw up their legs." He made his biggest impression on women—not so much his looks as his playing. The way he played the blues mellowed you; people threw their glasses in the air. He'd hit a seventh chord and sustain it, and the people fell out. Later he committed suicide; a woman was involved in some way.

Creath didn't get to New York except maybe for a visit. Even then there was a myth about the place. A lot of groups were afraid to go there, because everything big seemed to come out of New York. Look how long Joe Oliver stayed in Chicago before he came to New York; and Louis Armstrong and Tommy Ladnier wouldn't have come if they hadn't been sent for. Anyway, New Orleans people believe in security; they don't usually take chances. And they're clannish, they prefer to be where other New Orleans people are.

There was great music in St. Louis then. New Orleans influences had come up the river, especially blues playing. The St. Louis musicians had a lot of originality and a great desire to broaden their music. There were many places to play, and they slept and ate music. By contrast, the bands just out of New Orleans seemed more limited.

We had a battle of music and a lot of people said we outplayed the Creath band. In our band, Gus Aiken was a good trumpet player and his brother, Buddy, played somewhat in the style of Jimmy Harrison. He was a good legitimate trombone player and whatever he thought of, he could play.

A lot of traveling was on the TOBA. "Take Old Bailey's Advice," some of us called it. A man named Bailey ran it with headquarters in Atlanta. We also called it "Toby" and another way of spelling it out was "Tough On Black Artists."[2]

There were Negro theaters all over the South and Midwest. Many were very small former nickelodeons. They were often dirty, with dressing rooms in the cellar—except for the biggest in Baltimore. Memphis, incidentally, was headquarters for a lot of Negro performers.

If a Negro musician or entertainer on the circuit was good, he came to New York, auditioned, and was put on the Independent, Keith, Loew, or Proctor circuits.

The Negro theaters remained because Negroes couldn't go to white theaters in those towns. When I came to New York there was only one theater in Harlem where I could sit downstairs, and that was the Lafayette. Wherever there were whites, we couldn't sit downstairs until 1927. That made us bitter. In some white theaters a Negro could go through the alley, up five or six flights, and sit in the gallery, above the balcony. But in those theaters you didn't see many Negro entertainers, and no Negro singers.

There were local bands in the pits of the Negro theaters. They played jazz and had to improvise behind the singers. Bad notes didn't mean anything if the tempo was right.

The tent shows played the theaters in the winter time. These all-year-round revues carried a comic, singer, dancer, piano, drums, and maybe one horn. There were maybe thirty or forty stops for the season.

I never saw a white person in the TOBA theaters. The kind of music played there hadn't yet been accepted by the whites, and the "higher class" Negroes didn't want to hear the blues—the blues were "low class."

The top pianist of that day in the South, by the way, was Eddie Heywood's father in Atlanta. He played in a TOBA theater there, the 81 Theater. He was modern, I was told. They said Eddie played just like his father.

We didn't play any white theaters with Ethel, only ballrooms or TOBA theaters, and then, naturally, we went on after the movie. We made about fifty dollars a week, I guess. Conditions of traveling didn't bother us too much. If you had to walk the streets all night or sleep in a church, you did it. Sometimes we couldn't get a room and we'd have to call up the black preacher.

He'd say, "Well, you can sleep over in the church. I'll send the janitor down and he'll open it up. You can sleep on the benches there until you get ready when your train comes in."

We also stayed in black hotels and in people's houses. In Dayton we stayed in a rooming house, I remember. Or they'd have a family picked out, and say, "You can go to 24 Dearborn Street." Accommodations in Negro neighborhoods could be lousy—with bad food and a lot of bedbugs. But being young, we didn't care. We were having a ball on the road.

In Louisville, where we went next, the music was like the kind we'd heard in Peoria: good, flexible, moderate-tempo ragtime. They used a lot of tricks, but it wasn't corny. The usual instrumentation had three horns in the front line—trombone and two saxophones. The saxophone—not the tenor, though—was very popular in Indiana, Ohio, Kentucky, and Tennessee. There wasn't too much clarinet.

It was in Louisville that I ran into another kind of hazard you could meet on the road.

At this theater we were playing a woman came backstage and said, "I'm going to have a party for all of you. Make sure you come." She invited Ethel to her house. But it turned out that this Tiny Tally ran seven buffet flats—whorehouses—in Louisville. The mayor, the chief of police, and everybody else were her clients. Tiny was about forty years old, and she had so much money she didn't know what to do with it. She had a big Packard, and when you had a Packard, you had the same as a Rolls Royce.

Tiny Tally fell desperately in love with me. She'd put $500 or $600 in my pocket every day to go down to the track and bet on horses. She wouldn't ask me how much I'd spent. She'd say, "Bouchand, how'd you do?"

"I lost everything."

The next day she'd put another $500 in my pocket. I just kept packing the money up; I'd spend a little at the racetrack. She told me, "Baby, if you stay in Louisville you won't have to work another day in your life. You know I got money. You got nothing to worry about." She loved the ground I walked on.

Every night was a party. She'd bring her various hookers in, but I know she threatened them: "Don't you bother with that one. That little young one over there, that's mine." She was too big to get in bed with a man. She must have weighed over two hundred pounds.

The fellow she went with before I came to Louisville was a captain in the army. He came back one night during the week I was there. When he arrived, Tiny said to me, "Bouchand, you sit right there." They went in the front room and argued. Pretty soon I heard chairs being turned over and bottles being broken. I pulled out my gun—I always carried a pistol then—but the maid said, "Don't you worry. Tiny will handle him." And she did—she whipped this guy, knocked him out! They put water on him, and he finally staggered out the door.

So it was the night of our last performance in Louisville. When she called up the hotel, I told her I wanted to go some place else after the show. By then I had maybe $2,000 in my pocket, and my God, you were a millionaire if you had that much money back then. Well, as I was getting ready to leave the theater, there she was: she had backed her Packard right up to the stage door, and she was sitting at the exit with a razor in her hand. "Bouchand," she said, waving her razor at me, "You're going to stay with me." The Packard door opened, and I walked in, and we went back to her house.

At about five or six in the morning—it was daylight by now—she went out in the kitchen to fix some ham and eggs. I had my clarinet and handbag there, because it was closing night. When she went out, I picked up my bag and my clarinet and went out the side door.

I ran about fifteen blocks to the railroad station, right down the middle of the street. (If the cops had been there, they'd have shot me.) When I got there, I went directly into the men's room, and I gave the porter a five-dollar tip. I told him, "If you see Tiny Tally, you didn't see me."

"Oh?"

"Tell anybody else who comes in here. Split that with him. You come back and let me know when my train for Chicago comes in."

Sure enough, he came in later and said she'd been there looking for me, but that she was gone and I could board my train for Chicago.

When I got to Chicago, I met Gus Aiken, and we went to a buffet flat and stayed until four in the morning. (They called it a "buffet flat" because they served all the liquor and food from a buffet.) Afterwards we stopped at a restaurant to eat. As we were leaving, these three big white fellows crossed the street toward us. I pulled my gun and Gus took out his knife.

They said, "Leave it right there! Drop it!" I never saw so many guns in my life. They were detectives. I told them that we were just going to our hotel, but they didn't listen. They took us down to the jail, then transferred us to the Clark Street station. The night was cold—it hit eighteen below or so, the coldest night in Chicago, they said, in forty years. The nickel of the handcuffs froze to our skin, and for many years after I had the mark where they'd put the handcuffs on.

They never booked us, but they kept us in jail for three days. Fletcher didn't know where we were, and Buster Bailey and Raymond Woodson, who were in the Grand Theater pit orchestra, had to get up and play our parts. Buddy Aiken was all over town looking for us. It turned out a lot of cops had been killed in New York that year, and when they found out we were from New York, they held us until they communicated with the New York Police. Buddy and Charlie Jackson, our violinist, finally found us and we were bailed out. It took all the money I had to pay Policy Sam (he was a bondsman in town) and the lawyer.

But all this trouble saved me from Tiny Tally! She had come to Chicago looking for me intending to kill me. She finally left after two days, while I was still in jail.

Getting arrested shook me up a lot. After that, I knew I had to be smarter. I couldn't emulate those old-timers in show business. I couldn't get by that way.

From Chicago, Ethel was going South. In those days you went South at the risk of your life. It would be very uncomfortable, very miserable touring the South then. So many incidents occurred; you weren't even treated as a human being.

Four of us—Gus, Buddy, Jackson, and I—gave notice and left the band in Chicago. (I think Buster Bailey and Raymond Woodson went with Ethel down South.)[3] We had just enough money to get to Pittsburgh. But they knew us at the Bailey Hotel, on Wiley Avenue, and old man Bailey—after we told him what had happened—said, "Well, I can feed you and put you up for tonight. But maybe some of the other musicians can help you. They know you around here."

"Who?"

"Earl Hines has a band down at the Duquesne Gardens and there's a dance tonight. Why don't you go down there?" So we went, taking our instruments along. We talked to Earl, told him what had happened and that we were trying to go back to New York. He said we should play, and they'd pass the hat. So we played "Tiger Rag," the four of us, with the rhythm section. Strangely enough, when we counted the money there was just enough for our train fare to New York, to the penny. When we went back and told old man Bailey the exact amount we'd made, he didn't believe us!

While on the train to New York we started practicing. The sandwich man heard us, and we were told by the steward that if we'd play in the diner, they'd feed us for free. Life on the road was like that. So we went in and played for lunch, and afterwards they gave us chicken à la king, fried chicken, steak, anything you'd want. They asked us if we wanted to do the same thing that night for supper, and we said sure.

We rode into New York on a full stomach, but I had to borrow a nickel from a porter to telephone my father to come down and pick us up at Pennsylvania Station.

NOTES

1. For more on the tour, see Allen, *Hendersonia,* 24–31. The baritone saxophonist identified by Bushell only as "Bill D. C." may have been the bass saxophonist listed as "C. Mosby" in the 2 December 1921 *Baltimore Afro-American* (*Hendersonia,* 26).
2. TOBA stands for Theatre Owners and Booking Association, an organization formed in 1920 to hire and promote black entertainment acts in theaters across the country. Eventually the TOBA Circuit included eighty theaters. For more information see, Thomas L. Riis, "Black Vaudeville, the TOBA, and the Morton Theater" (Athens, Ga.: privately published, 1987).
3. Allen lists the replacements as Joe Smith, cornet; George Brashear, trombone; and Clarence Robinson, clarinet (*Hendersonia,* 28). The last-named is presumably a different man from the well-known dancer and show producer.

ON THE VAUDEVILLE CIRCUIT

After returning from the Ethel Waters tour in February, 1922, I went back into Leroy's for a couple of months. Then an act called "A Modern Cocktail" sent for me, so I traveled out to St. Louis and joined them.

"Modern Cocktail" was a headline vaudeville act that played the Keith Circuit. A man by the name of Norma Thomas—we called him Tom—was the pianist and owner of the act. There were five in the band, the singer was Naomi Hunter (Tom's wife), and they had a dancer, Arthur Bryson. Addington Major was our trumpet player, Lew Henry, trombone, and Sonny Thompson on drums. I took Jimmy O'Bryant's place on clarinet.

"Modern Cocktail" did very high-class, sophisticated jazz. We played "Carolina in the Morning," "You're in Kentucky Sure as You're Born," and "Bugle Blues." Tom would do a piano solo on "Listen to the Mockingbird"—he had some tricks he used on that—and we played some blues.

Being on the Keith Circuit was the big time. At Leroy's I'd been getting thirty dollars a week plus tips. Now I was making seventy-five dollars a week. I had to pay for my meals and lodging, but that was minimal, because you could get the biggest meal in town for $1.50. Breakfast was always less than a dollar. And your room was never more than $2.00 a night, in most cases $1.00 or $1.25. So at the end of the week, a lot of times I'd have fifty dollars left from my seventy-five dollars, and I'd put that money in my watch pocket. On the Ethel Waters trip I came home broke. But on the Cocktail trips I used to come home with money, and then I'd go down to Leighton's on Broadway and buy three or four suits. I'd stroll down Broadway sharp as a tack: that was part of my trademark.

We might play a whole week in the big towns and a split week in the small ones. Those were all white houses. We were on the bill with George Burns once—this was the Loew's Circuit—when George had a partner, and he was the straight man! And like all the Keith acts, we'd do the Poli's time up in New England, through Connecticut, New Hampshire, Maine, and Massachusetts.

We were always the only black act on the bill; they'd never have two at the same time. We'd either go on before intermission or close the show. Being the headliner act, we were always the biggest thing on the bill. Since our privileges had been so limited coming up, it sort of went to our head now that we were the main attraction. We didn't handle it too well. Being kids, we possibly overdid it. I'm quite sure we did.

Once we were playing at the opening of a new Poli's theater in Connecticut, and all these movie stars came up from New York to the reception. Rudolph Valentino was there, and Fatty Arbuckle, Mae Murray, and Gloria Swanson. We were sitting with them at this table at the reception, and I pulled the boner of my life. Sonny Thompson, our drummer, was next to me, and I saw him reach over, get the salt, and put some in his cup.

I said, "Look at Sonny puttin' salt in his tea."

And Lew Henry was sitting across from us, and said, "Shut up, fool. That ain't tea. That's boullion, that's soup!"

Valentino, Mae Murray, and Fatty Arbuckle laughed, and I'd never been so embarrassed in my life. Here I am sitting at a table with the biggest people in movies, and I have to open my big mouth and say, "Look at Sonny puttin' salt in his tea."

Being on the road and away from home so much, I'd lost a lot of the things I should have had. I was boisterous, just going all over. It's a good thing I caught myself.

My character and attitude came the hard way, through trial and error. I made mistakes, I was embarrassed, and I even went to jail for some of the things I did wrong. But what I know today, and what I've become, I learned mostly myself. That's why I developed so late, and why it took me so long to do what I've accomplished, because I had to find out things for myself. Experience has taught me.

Another incident occurred as we were traveling up in New York state by car. Addington Major and I were riding with Tom and Naomi, and Sonny

Thompson and Lew Henry were in another car. Earlier that evening, Sonny had had some words in the dressing room with Naomi. Now Naomi told Tom what Sonny had said. When Tom heard this, he pushed on the gas and began to accelerate to catch up with Sonny, who was ahead of us. He kept honking and pulled alongside of them. When he stopped, Naomi said, "No, Daddy, don't get out of the car, don't get out of the car!"

Sonny was a bad guy, rough. He said, "What's the matter with Daddy?" He was also a comedian.

Here we were blocking the road at about two or three in the morning. Tom was fumbling with the door to get out, and Naomi was trying to hold him back. But Tom couldn't find the lock. (Major and I thought he did it on purpose.) Meanwhile Sonny's saying, "All right, let Daddy out of the car, let him out."

It's a good thing Tom didn't get out, because Sonny probably would have shot him. He always carried a gun.

This meant Sonny was fired. We had to send back to New York, to the Touraine Restaurant, for a replacement. Whenever you needed somebody—a musician, singer, performer—and were out of town, you called the Touraine, which was right next door to the Lincoln Theater. It was headquarters for Fats Waller and everybody else. The next day we sent for Ray Green, whose work I knew since he'd been with Ethel Waters.

"Modern Cocktail" went out to the West Coast on the Pantages Circuit. First we started in New York on the Keith time, then went to Cleveland and Chicago. In Chicago we picked up the Orpheum Circuit and played around Illinois and Michigan. Then we picked up the Pantages Circuit in Milwaukee, I believe, and headed west, doing split weeks. When you got to Los Angeles you'd do a full week there.

Jazz on the West Coast was nothing compared to the Midwest, East, and South. They were using tuba and two saxophones—not trumpet, clarinet, and trombone, so far as we heard—and were trying a "symphonic" approach to popular music. It was really ricky-ticky orchestrations, and no blues.

Going west was the same as being in Georgia or Mississippi. It was segregated: you couldn't stay here, couldn't eat there, couldn't go out. You couldn't go anywhere in Los Angeles. Transportation wasn't segregated, but everything else was. At the time, Los Angeles was occupied by white southerners. It was miserable living there.

We always had to go to the black neighborhoods, which we enjoyed because we had a lot of fun. As a matter of fact, we had no *desire* to integrate then. Our culture was something else. We didn't talk the same language, and we didn't eat the same kind of food, and what was funny to whites wasn't funny to us. We were thankful of the fact that they enjoyed what we did on stage. They'd applaud, stop the show, and all that. But when we'd come off the stage, we'd go our way. Because we knew it was a precarious thing. Some drunk might come along and call you a nigger, and you'd either cut him or shoot him or have a fight with him. So we tried to avoid that. Living then, as a black man, you were too uncertain about what could happen from day to day. That's why you were happy to get in your neighborhood and stay there.

But we drew the line on certain of our own people. For instance, I didn't go to the gutbucket joints. If I found out a joint was just a joint, out I'd come. Several of us in the band were like that. We didn't adhere to the lower-class Negro then. In fact, I was taught to shun them. Some of the old traditions of slavery had wiped off on us, because the mulatto Negroes were treated different than the black ones, and we knew that.

It's like some of those New Orleans musicians. Red Allen told me he wouldn't mix with the guys that came from Gretna, down on the lower part of the peninsula. And Albert Nicholas, the clarinet player, told me, "Listen, boy, I'm from a different culture altogether. I don't have nothing to do with that part of New Orleans." It's changed now, because we knew we had to turn it around. We learned that divided there's no strength.

When I first joined "Modern Cocktail," I went with them by myself. But later, when we began playing dates around New York and New England, Marie came along with me. Her red hair and light complexion were an advantage. Whenever we wanted to buy tickets at a theater or get a room in a hotel, she'd go ahead and do it.

One night I brought Marie home to our house on 130th Street. I'd told my father that I was going to get a marriage license. He said, "Son, you haven't married that woman yet. You got the license?"

"Yes, I've got it."

"You're going to marry her tomorrow."

He woke us up about eight o'clock in the morning. We went down into the front room in our bathrobes, and he married us right then and there.

I regret that I didn't spend more time with my father. He was a great man, and he had a lot to offer me. But I rarely saw him since I slept during the day and worked at night. Once in a while I'd go in his study and sit down and talk with him for five or maybe ten minutes. He'd always take the opportunity to give me advice on certain things, and I could have listened. But I figured he didn't really know. Now I realize that you have to have some basic ideas, some good theories to go on, so your reasoning becomes logical. I didn't then. I wasn't saving any money, and I wasn't accomplishing a hell of a lot musically.

LIZA AND HER SHUFFLING SEXTET

By this time I was known as a vaudeville clarinet player; I'd been out on the road with Mamie Smith, Ethel Waters, and "Modern Cocktail." So another act sent for me. Adams and Robinson were a dance team, and their agent talked them into getting a band because they could make more money: put it on vaudeville and make it a big headline act. Bert Adams was the piano player, and Clarence Robinson was the dancer and singer (he also produced a lot of the floor shows around New York). They got Seymour Irick on trumpet, Lew Henry on trombone, Mert Perry on drums, and myself. We didn't have any bass.

Now, one night some fellow fought Bert Adams in the park and shot him. He got killed. So we had to revise the act, and got Fats Waller on piano. We put Katie Crippen into the act as the singer. One of the agents downtown thought up the name: Liza and Her Shuffling Sextet.

At the time, Fats was just another good piano player. He hadn't composed anything then, and he was not seen opening his mouth. He drank as much, but he didn't sing. He was a big, happy, fat wrassler who could play a lot of piano. He used to come waddling down the street to the theater eating a big apple on a stick. Fats was a big baby. He never grew up.

Clarence Robinson took over the act then, and I handled the business. I'd go down and rent the drops for the cyclorama—each act had its own scenery—and I'd take care of transportation and deal with the booking agent. I became part owner of the act with Clarence.

Seymour Irick was an erratic Geechie.[1] He had a good philosophy, and he was a pinchpenny. All he talked about was money. He kept himself clean and dressed well. But Mert Perry set the standard. He was a cocky little guy, like a little bantam rooster: immaculate and sharp, very sophisticated, very articulate. You'd think he was worth a half million or something when he talked with you, with his big cigar. So we all patterned ourselves after Mert. We smoked big cigars, La Preferencia maduro. We thought we were something extra, and that there were very few people like us. We set ourselves apart.

Our act usually opened with a fast instrumental number. Then out came the girl singer. Then the band did something special. After that, Clarence would come out and sing a song, and then maybe Katie would do another one, and join Clarence in one. Next Clarence would dance; he and Bert would do a duet together, like they had done in vaudeville (they'd been a big-time act on the Keith Circuit). To finish, we three horn players would put down our instruments, go out, and do a buck time step, then do "over the top" right along as a finale. We'd use something fast, like "Bandanna Days" or "Runnin' Wild." The pit band would pick it up, along with our drummer, and five of us would be doing the steps together in our tuxedos. It was a big finish. Many a time I sprained my ankle doing that "over the top."

We had so much pleasure. In those days a young musician's ego would just run away. That's why we didn't practice: we were too busy around Broadway. People said, "Oh yes, he's a member of so and so's act. Yes, that's a headline act." Your social value was set according to your rating in show business. If you were a big-time act you came in contact with big-time people. And pretty gals went together with that, too.

We were in Boston New Year's Eve of 1923, on the Poli time. Fats and I were sharing the front room in a brownstone in Back Bay. We'd been out of New York for three or four weeks. Everything was so old and depressing-looking in Boston in those days. This room had old furniture, old dark mahogany wood, dull yellow ceilings, and gaslights. There was also a bed and a piano. It was about quarter to midnight. Fats started noodling around on the piano, very soft. We were talking about being homesick for New York, wishing we were there. All of a sudden, at twelve o'clock the bells start ringing, people began shooting out the windows. And right then Fats came out with the theme to "Squeeze Me." He turned to me and said, "Hey Mackie, did you like that?"

I said, "Yeah, what is it?"

"I don't know."

"Does it have a middle part?" In those days, ninths were just becoming popular in bands, and you did it chromatically. Fats tried something, and said, "How's that?"

I said, "That closes it up. Put that on there." Then he put the whole thing together. He didn't have a title for it, but the next day, he said, "Hey Mackie, you know what I'm going to call that? 'Boy in the Boat.' Didn't have no hat, didn't have no coat." That was how he created it, right up there in that room.

On a trip down to Washington, D.C., a few of us went to hear a band in a little backstreet place. This group was headed by Elmer Snowden, the banjo player. There was a youngster playing piano named Duke Ellington, Toby Hardwick was on saxophone, Schiefe [Arthur Whetsol] on trumpet, and Sonny Greer on drums.[2] After we heard the band, Clarence and I got in a terrific argument, and we decided to split up. So Clarence went to Snowden and said, "I've got a job for you." I kept the original band, with Fats on piano.

In the meantime, we had six and a half more weeks booked with the act on the Poli time. Clarence figured that he could take this new band and do the gigs, but I decided to beat him to the punch. Early Monday morning I went up to the Palace Theater office in New York. I said, "Clarence and I split up, and he's bringing in a strange band. I have the original one. Now, I could get a new dancer, or what do you want to do?" They got leery and canceled the whole six and a half weeks. So when Clarence arrived in New York with Snowden, Duke, and that bunch, they didn't have any work—I'd canceled all their jobs.[3]

Towards the latter part of the act we had various dancers, and finally Bill Basie replaced Fats on piano. Then Seymour Irick was shot. He had a room in Johnny Hudgins's house, in the South Bronx, and a white girl shot and killed him. We couldn't get another good trumpet player.

NOTES

1. "Geechie" refers generally to blacks from the coastal areas of South Carolina and Georgia. Many members of the Jenkins' Orphanage Bands, from Charleston, South Carolina, would be considered (or called) Geechies. Brian Rust, in *Jazz Records: 1897–1942* (New Rochelle, N.Y.: Arlington House, 1978), lists several titles that use the word, including "Geechie Dance" and "Geechie River Blues." (There is an Ogeechee River in eastern Georgia that runs through Savannah.)
2. "Schiefe" was the surname either of Arthur Whetsol's father or stepfather. He was sometimes called by the nickname "Chief."
3. For slightly different versions of how the Washingtonians went to New York in the spring of 1923 (after they'd already made a trip there to work with Wilbur Sweatman), see Duke Ellington, *Music is My Mistress*

(Garden City, N.Y.: Doubleday, 1973), 69; Barry Ulanov, *Duke Ellington* (London: Musicians Press Limited, 1947), 30–31; and the Elmer Snowden interview in Stanley Dance, *The World of Swing* (New York: Scribner's, 1974), 49. The first two accounts have Waller inviting the musicians to New York, while Snowden claims that Robinson wanted a band but no pianist (since Waller was still in the picture).

5

SAM WOODING AND
THE NEST CLUB

In Harlem, all the cabarets used to have what they called breakfast dances. Each cabaret would take its band to another cabaret, and they'd have a jam session. The Goldgraben's band would go to Happy Rhone's, Happy Rhone's would go to Leroy's, and Leroy's would go to Barron Wilkins's. That's how Sam Wooding came to hear me. I went to Barron's one morning with Leroy's band and Sam was there. He had a whopping good band at Barron's; it was a small group, but they cut all of us.

A little later Sam called me up and asked if I'd come to a rehearsal. He knew me as a clarinet player, but he'd heard that I played saxophone, too.

Saxophone was becoming very popular then. The first saxophonist I heard in New York was an old guy in Harlem called Nappy Lee; I heard him at a couple of rent parties. Sam had a good saxophonist with him, Rollin Smith, who had a very fast vibrato and was also a great singer. But what really did it for me was hearing Ross Gorman with Paul Whiteman. This was at the Palace Theater, when Whiteman was playing on the Keith time. Gorman was a great influence on me, and inspired me to go out and get a saxophone—this must have been about July of 1923.

When Sam called me he had left Barron's, and a job was coming up at the Nest, a new place that was opening up on 133rd Street. Johnny Carey and Mal Frazier had put up a building in a vacant lot, and they made the Nest down in the cellar. I remember the opening date: October 18, 1923. They put in a Leonard Harper revue with lots of stars, and Sam Wooding's band.

I played first saxophone in Sam's group. Before that I'd had very little experience on the instrument—none, actually—so I was really learning on the job. I didn't study saxophone until years later, when I went with Cab Calloway.

Sam had hired Herb Johnson as a tenor player. Herb was from Boston and had studied at the conservatory there. He also played bassoon, and I liked that. So when a guy came along and offered to sell me a bassoon, I bought it and asked Herb to teach me. We had a thing at the Nest where we used two bassoons, which was unheard of.

The clientele at the Nest was mixed; we had as many whites as blacks, especially weekends. The revue was built on the theme, "Where do the birds go every night? To the Nest! To the Nest!" They had bird costumes and all that.

At the Nest the band played against the west wall, and the audience sat all around on the east side. In the center was the dance floor, and the revue worked there—there was no stage. The bar was in the back. It wasn't a standing bar, just a place for mixing drinks. The Nest was a big place, decorated very beautifully.

Since this was during Prohibition, people who came to the Nest brought their own liquor, and you could get soft drinks at the bar. If the owners knew you, they might serve you some Chicken Cock, a type of whiskey that came with a tin cover over the bottle and was very popular in Harlem.

Johnny Carey and Mal Frazier were New York boys, born and raised in that area. The police never bothered them, just like they never bothered Ed Smalls. A lot of money was paid to keep lieutenants and captains looking in the other direction. Of course, sometimes the Federal men would get in. But we never had a raid while I was at the Nest.

Big stars like Paul Whiteman, Otto Kahn, and Phil Harris used to come to the Nest. It wasn't a bucket of blood, like Leroy's; the elite of Broadway and Harlem went to the Nest. We'd start playing about 9:00, and the revue would go on at about 11:00 or 11:30. The second show would begin about 3:00 A.M. We'd be finished by 4:30 or 5:00 A.M. Then we'd often go some place for breakfast; Sam, Bobby Martin, and I would sit up and talk about what we were going to do with the next arrangement. It was always daybreak when I got home.

Marie was working at the Nest Club, too. She'd always go home after-wards—or say she was going home! I was glad to get rid of her so I could go out and have a ball. Those were the great days of fun. If we didn't have an afternoon rehearsal, I'd sleep until six in the evening. In the wintertime I never saw daylight.

Our first opportunity to broadcast came while we were at the Nest.

We were rehearsing one day at the club, and talking about a dance broadcast. Radio was in its infancy then. George Howe, our drummer, said, "Man, we ought to go broadcast somewhere."

"Where?"

"Just go down to WJZ, in the Bell Telephone building down on Broadway, and see if they'll let us broadcast." So we did. We packed up our horns, got into two taxicabs, and went down to WJZ. Sam and I went inside, leaving the band out in the cabs.

One of the fellows in the studio said, "Can I help you?"

Sam was always backward, so I had to do the talking. "Yes, we have a band out there, and we'd like to broadcast."

"What?"

"We'd like to broadcast."

"What you got out there?" he said.

"We got a good band!"

So he turns to some other guys, laughing, and says, "So these guys want to broadcast."

I just said, "Yeah, We want you to hear us."

Finally he said, "All right. Bring 'em in."

We went out and got the other guys, and everybody comes in grinning.

"All right boys," he says, "set up and let's see what you sound like." We played one tune, and then suddenly a guy runs in and says, "The U.S. Navy band can't go on. Would you like to go in their place on a hookup?" That was it. We went in and did the broadcast.

THE CLUB ALABAM

Because we were drawing attention at the Nest, we started doing vaudeville dates around New York on the Fox Circuit, also the Loew's time out in Brooklyn. In the summer of 1924, I believe, we were playing the Audubon Theater up in Harlem (that's where Malcolm X was later killed) and a couple of guys from the Club Alabam came to hear us. Fletcher Henderson had been playing there, but he had put in his notice since he was going to the Roseland. That's how we came to get the job at the Club Alabam.

Clarence Robinson was doing the shows at the Club Alabam, and we rehearsed the new one that was coming in. Sam said we had to get rid of our old tuxedos and get new uniforms. We got dark blue bolero jackets at eighty dollars apiece. But Herb Johnson wouldn't have any of it, and said he'd rather quit than pay for his new uniform. That was his biggest mistake. I never heard him play again with anybody after that. He just drifted off.

We had some great people in the show with us at the Club Alabam: Al Moore and Ruth Cherry, both ballet dancers, also another dancer, Lida Webb, the Three Eddies, the comedian Johnny Hudgins, Eddie Rector— who had originated various tap steps, and who was greater, I think, than Bill "Bojangles" Robinson—also the great singer Abbie Mitchell, who had been with Williams and Walker. We also had Bobby and Baby Goines, who were contortionists; they could tie their bodies up in knots, and also had a tumbling dance routine.

Like the Nest Club, the Club Alabam was downstairs—it filled the entire basement of the Little Theater, which had been renovated. It was one big room with two levels—the lower one was where the dance floor was, and then there was an elevated tier with tables, which gave people a little better view of the show. That's where Gloria Swanson and Nora Barry would sit when they came. The bandstand was on the lower level, and they made it look like the front porch of an old southern colonial mansion, with pillars.

The show at the Club Alabam was similar to the one at the Nest, although on a more elaborate scale, and with twice as many people. The choreographers—Clarence Robinson and Leonard Harper and Addison Carey—all had about the same routine. The revue would start about 11:30, after the theaters let out. We didn't leave until 4 in the morning. Often we were tired from doing things during the day—seeing agents, rehearsing, or just checking things out on Broadway—so we'd fall asleep on the stand. You'd fight it, but you just couldn't help it. Afterwards we'd sometimes walk uptown, and maybe we'd get tired at 85th or 90th Street and take a cab from there to Harlem. I was in good shape then.

When Herb Johnson left Sam, we got Gene Sedric to take his place. We also added a third sax, first Eugene Mikell, and later Willie Lewis. We had Bobby Martin and Maceo Edwards on trumpet, and we brought in Te Roy Williams on trombone. Te Roy was a great trombone player, a good cellist, too. But he always drank a lot of whiskey. There used to be a cesspool in the dressing room where the dirty water went from the washing in the basement. One night Te Roy got drunk and fell in there in his uniform. We had to fish him out, take off his clothes, and dry him off.

We had numbers where we used woodwinds and cello: I had an alto clarinet, and there'd be two bass clarinets, and with cello playing the solo we sounded like a huge organ. Then we had a thing with bass saxophone, two baritones, and cello. Or our two trumpet players would double on mellophones. We had all sorts of combinations. The reed section was featured on "Mandy, Make Up Your Mind." On each chorus the reeds would switch—we'd have a trio of oboes, then bass clarinets, then sopranos, clarinets, and bassoon, flute, and oboe. People would just stand up and applaud.

Sam and Willie Lewis didn't get along too well. Willie was a better musician than Sam gave him credit for being, but because he was obnoxious and in Sam's hair all the time, Sam wouldn't feature him much. Willie was the kind of guy, if you gave him an inch, he'd take a yard. You had to be careful there.

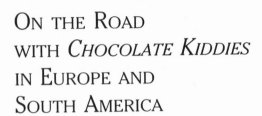

6

On the Road
with *Chocolate Kiddies*
in Europe and
South America

After we'd been playing at the Club Alabam for a while, we had an opportunity to go to Europe. The year was 1925, and at that time there hadn't been any major European tours by a black jazz orchestra, so we were anxious to do it.

Arthur Lyons was a theatrical agent in New York. He was Russian, and he got in touch with some other Russians who came to New York and put up money to create a large Negro revue to tour Europe. A few years earlier they'd sent a similar revue to England from the Plantation Club—Florence Mills was in that one—so I think they wanted to expand on the idea.

They chose Sam Wooding's orchestra to play with the revue, which they called *Chocolate Kiddies.* Duke Ellington and Jo Trent wrote some of the songs for the show. We rehearsed for a few weeks in New York and then left for Germany in May, 1925, aboard the SS *Arabic.* There were eleven of us in the orchestra, and more than thirty chorus girls, dancers, and comedians. Several of the acts had appeared with us at the Club Alabam.[1]

On the way over we kept rehearsing. One day a wave hit the boat and water came through the open portholes. A lot of the chorus girls had bought their dresses on time, and the salt water ruined them. So eventually they sent over to collect money for the dresses and the girls had to pay.

GERMANY
(May–August, 1925)

I got off the boat in Hamburg with a wife, a trunk full of horns, and twenty-five cents in my pocket. I hadn't adjusted to holding money back, and just spent it on everything I wanted. We had to wait around the station all day for our train, and didn't get into Berlin until that evening.

We arrived in Berlin May 18, but the show didn't open until the 25th, so we had some time to pull it together. In New York we'd rehearsed the numbers in Bryant Hall—that's where I saw Duke and Jo Trent, who came a few times and played their tunes for us. Now Arthur Lyons had to stage the show, and Charlie Davis had to adjust the choreography to the theater. The scenery had already been made, but we had to put it up. We rehearsed day and night for a whole week getting it ready. Even then, it wasn't exactly ready.

Opening night at the Admiral's Palace the reception was very good. The audience whistled and hollered "Bravo." At first we thought they were screaming at us, "Beasts, beasts!" Then we learned they were calling out "Bis! Bis!" for encores. Most of the numbers had to take several encores. "Mit Dir" ["With You"], sung by Lottie Gee, took about three, and "Jig Walk"—they just couldn't get over that.

The show was in two parts with sketches, dance numbers, and comedy bits.[2]

At the beginning of the first act it was twilight on the plantation. Arthur "Strut" Payne came out and sang, "Gone are the days when my heart was young and gay, / Gone are my friends from the cotton fields away." He was a great bass singer, and a good cello player, too. We had the same opening at the Club Alabam. Black shows on Broadway often began with a plantation scene, like, "Pickin' cotton, pickin' cotton, down on the O-hi-o!" It was the part of our heritage that they saw was viable, and people would pay money to see it.

There was always a jungle number in the Negro shows. In New York Florence Mills used to do one called "Hawaiian Night in Dixieland" that featured trumpeter Johnny Dunn. In *Chocolate Kiddies* we had "Jungle Night in Dixieland." They'd always give the same reason to have some jungle music: tom-toms and hoochie-coochie.

The second scene was set like the interior of a Harlem cabaret. Adelaide Hall sang—she was a soubrette then, more or less, not a leading lady. Bobby and Baby Goines did an Apache dance. (It was supposed to have been Ruth Cherry and Al Moore, but they didn't go.) They threw and slammed each other around, and tumbled and stood on their heads.

Chocolate Kiddies was built around [Rufus] Greenlee and [Thaddeus] Drayton. They were a big-time vaudeville act here in the States, and they'd been in Europe before World War I. They had an international act where they'd come out dancing and talk in all these different languages. They'd start with Hungarian, then they'd speak Russian, then French, Yiddish, English, and finally wind up in German.

Willie Robbins and Chick Horsey did "Two Happy Boys" in blackface. They sang a song, then they went "Wah wah, Wah wah," and Bobby Martin emulated their speech with his trumpet. That was a big hit. They were trying to do Johnny Hudgins's act. (Johnny wouldn't go to Europe with us.)

The Three Eddies (Shaky Beasley, Tiny Ray, and Chick Horsey) would come out and do a comedy routine. They wore bowler hats, round-rimmed spectacles, white gloves and spats, and worked in blackface. They had an act like the Redcaps, very fast and funny, with great singing and dancing. Back at the Club Alabam they used to break up the show nightly.

For "Jim Dandy," Jessie Crawford did a strut dance and drill with a chorus line. Charlie Davis used to do the same routine at the Club Alabam. But in Europe, Jessie and Chick Horsey did it together. Jessie was an excellent dancer.

The band was in the pit for the first half, then played the second half onstage. We opened after intermission, did our specialty, then the rest of the show went on behind that. Often we'd switch pieces around on the program. We learned that from vaudeville. We'd evaluate numbers as to what response we got, so we always knew what to give the people onstage.

We never had any music when we played onstage. All our stuff was memorized. Sam conducted from the piano, which was off to the side. He only stood in front of the band after we came back from Europe, because that was the style then.

One problem in Europe was that pits were deeper than they were in America. You couldn't see the stage unless you were sitting on the outer rim. In Europe the actors followed the music. But since we had to follow the actors, we had platforms built across the pit that elevated us.

One of the band's specialty numbers was "O Katharina," a German tune. They loved it in Berlin. Sam had arranged it before we went over, and we rehearsed it on the boat.

In the reed section, we'd change horns a lot, but Sam always gave us time in his arrangements. On those records, when you hear a modulation, the brass and rhythm are making it, and we'd be changing from saxophones to three clarinets or sopranos. We even did a thing with three oboes (although Gene Sedric and Willie Lewis couldn't do very much on the instrument).

If the saxophones were playing a triad on our own, the lead voice might be on top. But if we were supporting the brass, you might have your first alto doubling the second trumpet part, the second alto doubling third trumpet, and then, to strengthen the lead, the tenor doubling first trumpet.

Sam was somewhat of a genius. He made his own arrangements, copied them and all. And he didn't have any training. He heard something, imagined what it was, and experimented until he got what he wanted.

Sam admired Paul Whiteman and his style of symphonic jazz. At that time Whiteman had the premier orchestra in the States. No question about it. It's like when Muhammad Ali was champion: it was undisputed.

Towards the end of the show we did "Jig Walk." That's where we got to do the Charleston. Charlie Davis staged that. He'd been a lead dancer in *Shuffle Along,* and he did a lot of staging at the Club Alabam. He was also choreographer for the Lafayette, the Apollo, and all the Negro shows in New York. "Jig Walk" turned out to be the big hit of the show.[3]

After opening night at the Admiral's Palace there were people out front crowding around the performers and musicians. Everybody was commenting on how well we'd performed, how much they loved our work, and what a great show it was. But one German evidently had had too many drinks. He came right up into the crowd and tore open his shirt, saying in German (which I spoke), "I'm a German to my heart. I don't understand why the government allows these black people to come to our country. During the war they cut off our noses and our ears." He was speaking about the Senegalese, you know. The Senegalese didn't take prisoners: when a German went down they just cut off the end of his nose or an ear and put it on a string. That way when they went back home they could show how many men they'd killed. So this guy went on, saying, "I have not forgotten what they did to us, and I won't stand for it. They should run them out of Germany."

He turned to Rufus Greenlee and grabbed him by the coat. Greenlee just clipped him on the chin and down he went. Now, this man was so drunk that he could barely stand up. But after Greenlee knocked him down, he got up, shook himself off, and walked out of the crowd down Friederichstrasse. That punch straightened him right out.

In July we made some recordings for Vox.[4] We did "O Katharina," "Alabamy Bound," "Shanghai Shuffle," and "By the Waters of Minnetonka." The arrangements were good, but since we had a lot of self-taught musicians in the band, a lot of them weren't played as well as they could be.

I took a few bassoon lessons while we were in Berlin, but my instrument was so bad, my teacher told me to get another one. "Oh yeah, I'll get one somewhere," I told him. But it didn't matter much to me. In the back of my mind I wanted to be a good bassoon player, a good oboe player, and a good clarinet player. But I just didn't get around to it then. A little later, though, when we got to Paris, I started taking the clarinet more seriously.

In Hamburg I bought Ajax, a Great Dane that had been on police duty. Oh, he was monstrous, like a horse! Many of the theaters we played in Europe had stables, and I'd often have to leave Ajax in one of the stalls.

At the hotel in Hamburg I started bragging about my dog. "He'll bite anything I tell him to." So somebody says, "Yeah? Tell him to bite that chair." It was a big leather chair in the lobby. So like a fool, I say, "Ajax, fasselberg!" And he lit into that chair with his teeth and just ripped it to shreds. I couldn't stop him, because he weighed more than I did. It cost me a hundred some dollars.

After we left Hamburg there was an incident on our way to Stockholm. We took the train to Stettin, Germany [now Szczecin, Poland], where we had to wait for a ferry to take us to Malmö, Sweden.

Now, Strut Payne was a big fellow with an enormous appetite. He was also very shrewd. He'd been at Reisenweber's and played with a lot of bands, so he knew all the tricks.

When we got to the dock in Stettin, Strut ordered five hot dogs, put them in his hand, then stood there and just fooled around. He timed it perfectly. When they called "All aboard," he just ducked out to keep from paying for the hot dogs. Well, the vendor ran after him crying, "Wo ist mein Geld?" He didn't see Strut, so he grabbed one of the handbags they'd set down in front of the boat. He thought it was Strut's or belonged to one of us, so at least he'd get something for his money.

The police and soldiers met us in Malmö. Turns out there was a diplomatic emergency. Someone had stolen the bag of a Swedish diplomat that had important papers from Berlin. They'd searched everybody's cabin but couldn't find it. Then somebody checked back in Stettin and found this hot dog man with the attache case and all these important documents that the king of Sweden was supposed to sign. Strut was laughing so hard his big belly was shaking. "Well, I fouled 'em up, didn't I?" Oh, that knocked him out.

In Malmö we had to sit in the train all night, right on the water's edge. They hooked up our train at eight o'clock the next morning.

SWEDEN AND DENMARK
(August–September, 1925)

Stockholm was a beautiful city, although the people were a little prejudiced. Some of the Swedes had been to the States, and they proceeded to enact some of the things that went on here. But the women were fantastic, and we made the most of it.

I was with my wife Marie, but that made no difference. Remember, I'm only twenty-two years old, and I ain't gonna miss nothin'! Every day I went to the Swedish bath and massage. They have these big blondes with beautiful shapes, and they're nude. After you go through the steaming process you jump in the pool, then you come out and they soap you down. You get on a table—you're naked, she's naked—and she looks down and says, "Ach, du schön!" Don't you know, I almost got pneumonia from going every day to bathe and then coming out in the cold. It was worth it, man.

The Swedish men were crazy about the girls in our show. A guy would give one of them an American hundred-dollar bill just to go and sit at the table with him. Yes, the girls made money while they were there.

Marie and I stayed at a pension in Stockholm. In different cities, people stayed where they wanted to. The agent would give you a list of places, or sometimes they'd arrange to get us in a hotel where we could all be together.

Once I was invited to go out to the palace and play saxophone for the crown prince of Sweden. Sam went with me, and we played selections from the show.

After a few weeks in Stockholm we went to Copenhagen and played the Benneweis Circus. A lot of theaters we performed in were called circuses, since they featured horse and animal acts.

In Copenhagen some of us we went to a cabaret and the girls working there just flocked to our table. Here were all these rich guys who would have bought them champagne, and we were just buying beer. The owner came over and said, "I'm asking you, please don't come back to my cabaret! Not that I don't like you, but my girls won't work."

One big blonde took a liking to me and sent a bouquet of flowers to my hotel. When I got there, Marie had torn it all up. On another occasion I met the blonde at the hotel when Marie came in. Marie was a little fighter—she'd fight like a tiger if you bothered her. When Marie saw us, the blonde got up and panicked, and Marie came up and hit me over the head with a vase or something. Since most of the band was staying at the hotel, a lot of journalists were there. The next day there was a cartoon of this incident, with the heading, "Will Copenhagen Be Able to Keep Sam Wooding?"

I was always broke from buying dogs, diamond rings, and fancy clothes. In Copenhagen I ran out of money. Marie and I went without food for three days, but the dogs got their meals. I took a bag and went around to various rooms of the hotel and collected scraps from plates people had left outside their doors.

I went to the telegraph office to cable my father for more money, but I didn't have enough even for that. And I was too proud to let Sam know I was broke, while all the time I was strutting around with my cane. Marie and I were down to a can of string beans. We ate a little for dinner, and a little for breakfast the next day. I knew I wasn't going to hold out much longer.

That afternoon we had rehearsal, and I couldn't blow.

Sam said, "What's wrong with you?"

"I don't feel good."

"You don't look good. What's wrong with you? You sick?"

"Yeah, I don't feel good in my stomach."

So he says, "Drink some water."

"Sam," I said, "I'm hungry."

"What? You're hungry and you didn't tell me?"

"Well, I don't tell you everything."

He said, "Rehearsal's off. We'll meet tomorrow." He handed me ten dollars in kronen and Marie and I went down to the dining room and ate it all up. Sam was like a father to me.

Just about that time the show almost broke up, but Leonidow, the promoter, and Sam came to an agreement. Sam must have gotten a raise, and we continued the tour to Hannover, Magdeburg, Dresden, and Prague.

EASTERN EUROPE
(October–December, 1925)

Our reception in Prague was good, although we had competition with a dancing bear act. For me the most important thing was being engaged to play with a Czech dance band the whole time we were there. Every night after the show I went to this beer house and played alto with the band. They had three or four violins, cello, piano, and drums. A lot of aviators and Czech soldiers used to come in and request numbers.

This band played American dance music—that's why they hired me, since they were interested in knowing how American jazz musicians played. They were a few years behind our things in New York. Rudolf Friml's "Indian Love Call" was very popular then, also "Whispering," "Avalon," and "St. Louis Blues."

The piano player, I remember, was terrible; to him the piano was a solo instrument instead of a rhythmical thing. But I didn't mind the musicians, as long as I got paid. I made a lot of money, something like the equivalent of fifty dollars a night. George Howe, our drummer, used to play with this band, too. We'd come home every morning at six o'clock, full of champagne, and fall into bed.

Marie finally left me in Prague. I had started fooling with Allegretti Anderson—another dancer in the show—and staying out. (I knew what Marie had been doing back in New York, that's why I did it!) So Marie went back to the States by herself. I didn't see her again until two or three years later.

I didn't marry Allegretti, but I called her my wife. Actually, I never had to divorce Marie. I later found out from a girl that lived in our house that my father had never registered our marriage license at City Hall. So nothing ever happened when I eventually got married again.

You see, in those days I didn't have much regard for such things. Let hell come whatever way, I did what I wanted to do. Later I found out this was a big mistake—that you have to conform to some sort of routine, some organized system, in order to enjoy your life.

In Budapest I heard Palmer Jones and his band, a group of black Americans playing at the Moulin Rouge. That's also where I was introduced to the music of the gypsies. It was the most impressive music I'd ever heard. Fantastic! The gypsies, I think, are among the greatest and most creative musicians in the world, although they don't get credit for it.

There was an old man there who was king of the gypsy violins. Every night I'd sit up and listen to him, get drunk, and cry.

Some of the tunes I heard there stayed with me. Later I made a dance arrangement of "Hejre Kati" and used it as my theme song. Eddie South used it also. He lived in Budapest for a while, and they even called him "The Black Gypsy."

One night at the Hotel Britannia, as we were listening to the great Hungarian violinist Bela Kis, [Maceo] Eddie Edwards got mad at his girl, Rita Walker. He'd had two or three drinks, and she did something he didn't like. So he said, "I'm gonna take her upstairs and whip her butt!" This was about 4:30 in the morning. "I'm gonna kill her!" Later, about break of day, I heard a knock at my door.

"Hey, Bushell!"

"What?"

"Open the door!"

It was Bobby Martin. He had Eddie with him, who was bleeding, blood running down everywhere. I said, "What happened? You beat her up, didn't you?"

Bobby said, "No, she beat him." Rita had taken glass and cut him all over the head. There wasn't a scratch on her.

I did quite a bit of sightseeing in Europe. In Hungary I went to the Roman village in Pest, right across the river. In Vienna I toured the catacombs underneath the city with Adelaide Hall. There was row after row of skeletons, thousands of bodies on tiers in copper caskets. Adelaide got scared because an old man about eighty or ninety years old was leading us around. She said, "Suppose he drop dead? We'll never get out of here!"

Vienna was where I first saw and heard Arthur Briggs. What a beautiful trumpet player! He was in an orchestra with some Austrians, some French, and a couple of Senegalese. His trumpets made ours sound like beginners.

I also went to concerts in Vienna and became interested in Mozart there. I went to the palace and stood on the same platform where Mozart had performed. I sat down in his chair. They had a painting of him on the same bandstand, a little boy six years old.

Traveling is a liberal education. They can tell you about it, or you can read it in books, but you don't realize how it is until you see it yourself. In New York there were things I didn't experience because I didn't have time. Either I was sleeping or working at night in the clubs. I knew Broadway show business, vaudeville, and cabarets—I was well seasoned in that. But my knowledge of the world enlarged when I was in Europe.

SPAIN, FRANCE, SWITZERLAND
(January–March, 1926)

We took a train from Mannheim to Paris, and from there to Barcelona, where we played the Olympia Theater. When we got there it was very chilly. I'll never forget the first day in the pension. We lived on the Palermo in Barcelona. The food was bad. They had some soup that had a little white thing that looked like a worm. It had two little black eyes. They said it was a fish, but I wouldn't eat it. I said, "That's a worm. You can call it a fish, if you want to."

We played this circus in Madrid, and appeared at the palace two or three times. The queen came to hear us in the theater a half-dozen times. She made it a habit to come in late, towards the end of our opening number. The girls are dancing, the band's playing, the cymbal's flying, and suddenly you had to stop everything right there and play the national anthem so everybody could stand up when she entered. It was sort of foolish. When she'd sit down, we'd pick up where we left off.

The Circo de Price in Madrid had fights after the show. Since it was a circle and we played in the middle, they'd just take out the seats and put up a ring. One time a boxer didn't show up for an exhibition bout. George Staton, one of our dancers, had been telling them he could box. George was a bantamweight, maybe a featherweight. He was a tumbler—squat and muscular.

They said to him, "You want to box this kid? We've got to have another bout."

George sort of looked over and said, "All right. I'll put on trunks."

One of us said, "Come on, George, the man will kill you, he's in training."

"I'll fight him." George hadn't been training, but he'd been dancing every day, doing his knee drops and Russian dancing.

The kid was saying to George, "Now, don't hit me in the stomach, because I just ate." George agreed not to punch him there.

So the announcer introduces him: "In this corner, George Staton, the sensational boxer from New York! He's also appearing in the show." George stepped into the ring.

Now, George was a clever fighter. He had almost been a champion, but they didn't know that. The people got excited when they saw the way he maneuvered round, ducked, hit the kid, and ducked again. Finally George got cute, and the guy clipped him and knocked him down. But when George fell he did a complete flip over backwards, came up on his feet, and chilled the kid: knocked him out cold in the second round! The crowd went wild. Afterwards they begged George to stay in Spain and fight. He could have stayed and made big money.

Another time we were playing the small ballroom in the palace and Herb Flemming and Willie Lewis almost got into a fight. Willie was noodling during Flemming's solo. Flemming was sensitive. You never knew which way the wind was blowing with him. If you said, "Hello," he might say, "What are you saying hello to me for?" So when Willie started interfering with Flemming's solo, Flemming put down his horn and went over and took a swing at Willie. We had to part them right then and there. Sam almost died. In all the years I knew Sam, I never saw him so thoroughly disgusted.

After Madrid we went to Paris, and were slated to go to Russia. That's when George Howe and his girlfriend Mamie Savoy left us. George wouldn't go, saying that they'd do this and that to you in Russia. So we picked up Percy Johnson in Paris, who had come over with Josephine Baker. Percy was a good show drummer. He used to stand up and drum—he had to, otherwise he'd go to sleep. He was a clown, and a very nice person. You could call him anything, do anything you wanted to him, and he'd always smile. But those are the kind of people you have to watch. Percy wound up killing a guy in Washington who'd taken advantage of him.

We had a week's layoff in Paris before we went to Switzerland. We went around to nightspots and saw the different guys who'd left New York years ago. "Subway" Johnson was our guide. He was an ex-musician, now a con man in Paris. He took us around to all these joints and charged us a fee. I lived on Rue Fontaine, not far from the Moulin Rouge.

In Basel we had one bad incident. Three of us were sitting in a bar, and a guy on the other side of the room started bothering us. Every time he smoked a cigarette down, he'd flip the butt over at our table. Now, Sam was there, and he's a funny guy. If he says he's going to hit you or shoot you, he'll do it. So Sam casually said, "If he flips another one of those cigarettes over here, I'm going to throw this ashtray at him." I thought Sam was kidding.

Sure enough, the next cigarette butt hit Sam right on the forehead (the others hadn't hit anybody). And as the guy picked up his glass of beer to drink, Sam threw the ashtray and cut that glass of beer off right in his hand! The guy stood up and froze, scared to death. The manager came over and said to us, "Nobody's going to bother you now." We just got up, paid our check, and walked out.

Later Sam said, "I'd never be able to do that again in my life." He'd aimed at the guy's head and missed!

After Switzerland we headed for Berlin, where we had another bad incident. One night five of us were sitting in a backroom place drinking beer when six or seven students came in. (You could tell they were students, because they all had scars on the left side of their faces from dueling.) They locked the door, saying, "Now we're going to run the Schwarzes out tonight." Then one asked, "What are you doing in Germany?"

I answered in German, "We're here playing in the show. We're entertaining."

"We don't want you here. Why don't you get out?"

"We don't have anything to do with that," I said.

Then, as Bobby Martin picked up his beer to drink they dumped the glass out of his hand. Now, we had Chick Horsey, one of the dancers with us. Chick was tough, an ex-fighter. We also had Jimmy Boucher, an English Negro, about six-foot-two and 190 pounds. Then there was Bobby Martin, Herb Flemming, and myself.

When they knocked the beer out of Bobby's hand, we stood up and started slugging. I didn't weigh but 140 pounds soaking wet then, and I got knocked down real quick. But the other four guys cleaned up. We unlocked the door, and Boucher stood outside with his cane. Chick would push them down and shove them out, and Boucher flattened them with the cane. They had to carry some of them out that night. They threatened to bring the whole school back the next night, but they never showed up.

From Berlin we took a train to Russia.

RUSSIA
(March–May, 1926)

When we got to Moscow it was cold. Even though it was March, it was something like twenty below zero! You couldn't see the sides of the streets for the snow. For sixty kopecks you could take the droshky from the hotel to the theater.

The people loved us in Russia. It was just like being in heaven. They'd come to the theater after every performance and pick out different band members, saying, "I'd like for you to meet my family," or, "You and this fellow over here, come to my house for dinner. I want you to meet my daughters." We'd take a sleigh out to somebody's house and stay there until four or five o'clock in the morning, singing songs, dancing, drinking vodka, and eating shish kebab. It was a great time.

Every Monday night after the show we'd go the Artist's Club. That's where all the girls were, and that's where I saw Sidney Bechet playing with Frank Withers's band. We hung out together and got drunk on vodka.

Herb Flemming got sick in Moscow and we had to leave him there. He ended up staying a month. When he came back and joined us in Berlin he was speaking Russian like a native. Herb was very apt in languages—he also spoke Spanish and French.

While in Moscow we picked up a valet who ran errands for us. He'd go to the grocery store for us and take us downtown. He dressed in the simplest, crudest clothes. When we left to go to Leningrad, he said, "Mr. Wooding?"

"What do you want, Harry?"

"I am happy to send in a marvelous report."

"Report about what?"

"About you and your people in the show."

"What?!"

Then Harry pulled out his credentials, and they were in English. He was an official of the secret police, and he'd been assigned to watch us the whole time we were there, all the while posing as a simple errand boy.

We also met a guy in Russia who must have offended one of their laws, possibly narcotics. When they found the evidence on him, they just disposed of him, without so much as a trial. We found out how swift justice was in Russia.

I wouldn't say I adhere much to Russia's politics. But Russia was the first country I'd ever been in where I was considered a human being—a person like anybody else. In France, you were "la Nègre." In Germany, "ein Schwarze." But in Russia I was accepted as a *man,* and treated like an artist.

GERMANY, ENGLAND, FRANCE
(June, 1926–March, 1927)

We played with the show in Leningrad, Riga, Königsberg, and Danzig, but when we got back to Berlin the band split off from the company. We played the Ufa Palace by ourselves. It was around this time that John Warren, our tuba player, left to join another show, so we sent for Leslie "King" Edwards.

Sidney Bechet came to Berlin with a band—I'm not sure if it was with Frank Withers. Sidney had an undersized Doberman he thought was part bulldog. And I had Caesar, a huge harlequin Great Dane I'd bought in Königsberg.

So one night, about four o'clock in the morning, Sidney and his dog came around to my room in the Darmstadterhof, on the Friedrichstrasse. He knocked, and said in his deep bass voice, "Hey, namesake." (That's what he always called me, since our last names were so close.)

"Sidney, what you want? It's four o'clock in the morning."

"Just open the door, I want to tell you something."

I opened the door, and he had this squatty dog with him.

"I brought my dog 'round here," Sidney said, "and I really want to let you know just how much dog you don't have, and how much dog I've got. So come on out in the hall and let 'em fight."

By now Caesar's clawing in the back, trying to get me out of the way to get to this Doberman. I said, "Would you take your dog and get away from here?"

"No, we gonna fight 'em out here this morning in the hall."

By this time people are getting up and knocking on the doors. I heard someone say, "Rufen sie die Polizei!" I closed the door on Sidney's face. Don't you know they got Sidney and locked him up that morning, not for drunkenness, but for disturbing the peace. But when they found out it was Bechet, the great musician, they let him out.

Sidney was an idol of mine. He was a funny guy, and he had unusual values. I don't think his education had gone too far. But he had phenomenal musical sense. As far as I'm concerned, no one ever played a horn like Sidney.

After performing at Barberina in Hamburg, we boarded a ship for England.

I didn't like England at all. Accommodations were bad, and they closed up the restaurants at eleven o'clock at night, so when you came out of the theater you couldn't eat. It was always raining, and the rooms were cold. In Birmingham you had to put a shilling in the meter to get gaslight. Then there was the left-hand traffic. Tommy Ladnier was almost always getting run over. One day he was crossing the street and didn't know which way to go, so he just laid down right there in the middle of the road.

England in those days wasn't too good for black musicians. But the

NEW YORK SOCIETY LIBRARY
53 EAST 79 STREET
NEW YORK, NEW YORK 10021

people would listen to you. We went over big in Manchester but were an absolute flop at Holborn's Empire in London. We couldn't understand it, since we'd been a sensation everywhere else. Maybe we were a little bit too classy. We dressed in striped trousers, and Oxford gray coats and ties. I think the British audience would have accepted a black orchestra doing comedy and slapstick. But we had a classy organization, and Europe had rubbed off on us. So we didn't do well in London at all.

Early in November of 1926 we crossed the Channel and went to Paris, where we played the Apollo Theater. The Apollo was a beautiful place, a theater that had been turned into a nightclub. They had a big floorshow, and we were part of it. By 11:30 every night we were back up in the Montmarte. Then we went to Bricktop's, Zelly's, and the Flea Pit—that's where all the black musicians used to hang out with the Arabs, Algerians, and Africans.

Things were always happening in the Montmarte. Leon Crutcher was a famous piano player who had left New York to live in Paris. I remember being with him at Bricktop's one night until six o'clock in the morning. I went home, and Allegretti woke me early in the afternoon and said, "Crutcher was killed last night." Seems his girlfriend had shot and killed him in Bricktop's place.

I knew Bricktop from Barron Wilkins's, in Harlem, and Sam knew her very well. When we got to Paris she received us with open arms. We also saw Josephine Baker. She and Allegretti were good friends from *Shuffle Along,* and she visited us after we moved into a place on Rue Laferrière.

Right around the corner from us lived Henri Selmer, the head of the Selmer instrument company, and I began taking clarinet lessons from him. (Buster Bailey studied with him too, I believe, when he was in Paris.) The old man couldn't speak English, so his son, Maurice, interpreted. Every morning at eight o'clock I was up there, on Place d'en Coeur.

I was playing a Selmer instrument but it was an Albert system, and the old man disapproved. As Maurice told me, "My father say you will never play clarinet until you change systems."

"I don't want to change," I replied. "Teach me what you can now with this, and I'll decide."

Henri Selmer changed my embouchure and taught me about the "cushion" you have to have. But he was most concerned with the interpretation of etudes and the quality of sound you got. Some of the things he taught me I still teach today.

Louis Mitchell acted as our go-between in Paris. He handled us while we were there and tried to get us to stay. But we wanted to move on. Louis must have gotten Sam a booking in Nice, and from there, one in South America.

In Nice we played in the big ballroom of the Hotel Negresco, on the Promenade des Anglais. We'd do a tea dance in the afternoon and another dance at night. I remember this little kid who came up to the bandstand and looked at my horns. It was Prince Rainier of Monaco, who was only about four or five years old. At the time, his grandfather was prince of Monaco, and they'd bring this little bitty runt to afternoon tea. They had some American dance acts at the hotel, too, and we'd play for them. We were learning to read pretty well by then.

We took a train to Marseilles, then got on a French ship, *La Floride*, to go to Argentina.

SOUTH AMERICA
(April–July, 1927)

It took us seventeen days to get to Buenos Aires. The voyage was fine until we got off the coast of Africa. Then there was a terrific undertow and the boat started pitching back and forth. Everybody got sick, including me and my two dogs I had with me. Things smoothed out when we crossed the Atlantic.

On the ship we rehearsed about every other day. We didn't play for dancing, but we did entertain a little for dinner a couple of times. Jessie Crawford was with us—she was Willie Lewis's girlfriend—and she did a little dance routine with Allegretti.

We got off at Rio, which is a very impressive town. It's like the States, with so many different types of people there: black Africans, Portugese, Spanish, and mulattoes. I could live in Rio and enjoy it, if I could speak the language. But they had segregation there. We went to a fun house once, and they wouldn't let us in.

Our first date was in Buenos Aires, where we played at a cabaret called Ta-Ba-Ris, and also did a vaudeville act at the Variety Theater. We also gave an afternoon concert at Teatro Maipu—that's where I forgot my solo.

We were doing a number from *La Bohème* that featured a saxophone quartet: two altos, tenor, and baritone. (King Edwards played baritone.) I was playing lead, so I stepped forward to make the first eight bars, and Sam hit the arpeggio. The pit orchestra is just sitting there staring, you know, at the great American band that has come. I looked down at them and my mind went blank. Sam said "Hit it!" I don't know what to play. He hit the arpeggio again. I still don't know what to play. Pretty soon Sam sang the beginning of the phrase, and all of a sudden it came to me quick. But I was so excited that I played it too fast, and they couldn't follow me on the saxophone. By this time the guys in the pit were laughing and the audience was screaming. I must have looked so shocked. Afterwards the man just said, "Keep that number in, it's a sensation." And every time we'd do it, I'd pretend to forget. It was the biggest hit we had in our show.

There was a hypnotist playing the Teatro Maipu. He lived in the same house that I lived, and he kept a big python in his room. In South America the hallways are outside, on the sides of the building, with little tin roofs over them. So once Allegretti was preparing a meal back in the kitchen and she called me to come and eat. As I walked down the hall, suddenly I heard "hhhsssss." I turned around and there's this big python's head sticking out the transom, looking right at me. Well, if you want to make me run into the river or jump off the Empire State Building, just shake a snake at me: I'm gone. I'd picked up garter snakes in Ohio, but this one was twelve or fifteen feet long. I guess I just froze from the shock. I backed up against the wall, hit my head, and knocked myself out. They came and got me back in the house, and the next thing I remembered I was in bed. They said the snake had been only a few inches away when they found me. He probably would have licked my face, and I guess I would have died.

Buenos Aires was a fast town with a lot of activity. The guys would come in from the pampas with a lot of money and spend it all in the cabarets. They lived and drank hard. They were short on women, so every ship that went down there used to take English and French girls. Some of them had the fortune to meet rich Argentines: that's why the population is so mixed.

I met the Pensacola Kid, the great clarinet player from Florida, down in the Argentine. He took me around his ranch in a car. He had so much land down there, I never did get to see it all. He'd bought it for two dollars an acre. That's what encouraged me to try and buy some land. I was going to purchase 500, maybe 1,000 acres, return to the States, and later go back there and sell it. But when the authorities heard that I was just going to leave and not stay there and develop it, they wouldn't let me buy.

We stayed several months in South America, but by now we'd been away from the States over two years. We'd played for the royalty of

Europe—for the crown prince of Sweden, the king and queen of Spain, and the president of Russia. It was time to go back home and rest on our laurels for a while.

NOTES

1. Several articles about Sam Wooding and the *Chocolate Kiddies* revue have appeared in the English periodical *Storyville.* See Horst J. P. Bergmeier, "Sam Wooding Recapitulated," *Storyville* 74 (1977–78): 44–47; Bernhard H. Behncke, "Sam Wooding and the Chocolate Kiddies at the Thalia-Theater in Hamburg, 28 July 1925 to 24 August 1925," *Storyville* 60 (1975): 214–19; and Björn Englund, "Chocolate Kiddies: The Show That Brought Jazz to Europe," *Storyville* 62 (1975–76): 44–50. See also J. and H. Larsen, "The Chocolate Kiddies in Copenhagen," *Record Research* (April 1965): 3. Contemporary articles on the tour appear in *Variety,* 17 June and 19 August 1925, and the *Pittsburgh Courier,* 16 May 1925, 10.
2. Programs indicate that the structure of the revue changed over time. The version Bushell recounts, beginning with the plantation scene, resembles the show in Hamburg (28 July–24 August 1925) described by Behncke; however, in Sweden (25 August–13 September 1925), according to the program included in Englund's *Storyville* article, the first act opened with the Harlem cafe scene.
3. "Jig Walk" had the longest life of any of the *Chocolate Kiddies* tunes written by Ellington and Trent. It was recorded as late as 1941 by Pee Wee Russell, Joe Sullivan, and Zutty Singleton. The other Trent-Ellington songs known to be used in the *Chocolate Kiddies* revue are: "With You," "Love Is Just a Wish (for You)," "Jim Dandy," and "Deacon Jazz."
4. Horst Bergmeier believes the date to have been 6 July 1925. See Bergmeier, "Sam Wooding Recapitulated," 46.

7

Back Home Again

   I decided I wanted to save money, so I bought third-class passage on the steamer *Vauburn* leaving Buenos Aires. Everybody slept together down there in third-class, and when water got through the roof, you felt it quite a bit. I stood it for two days. When we got to Santos, our second stop (after Montevideo), I changed to second-class. We also stopped at Rio, Pernambuco [Recife], Trinidad, Barbados, and some of the other islands.

  In Barbados we got off the ship in our white suits and the women had on big hats. We passed some people sitting on the front porch—they lived under very poor conditions there—and one old lady said, "Well, mon, I can die now and go to heaven. I done seen some of my folks dressed up like white folks."

  The trip took us twenty-three days from Buenos Aires. Percy Johnson slept the whole time. I had along two dogs I'd brought from Europe. They only had room for one in the kennel, so I got permission to put the other in the hospital. The crew had been slipping off, while they were on watch, to go into the hospital and sleep. One guy reached in, opened the door in the dark, and the dog grabbed his arm and just tore it to pieces. So I went down to talk to the crew, and one of them said, "Well, mon, we slowed down the ship because the captain wouldn't let us stay in Barbados another day, and now we're going to slow it down more, because your dog chewed up the mon, and you're going to pay."

  I said, "No, I'm not going to pay. I'm sorry for what happened, but I paid fifty dollars to bring this dog up here, and that's where they assigned him to go. I have nothing to do with it." But that slowed us down a bit.

  We had rough weather off Cape Hatteras, but finally made it back to

New York harbor. After two years, I was glad to see the Statue of Liberty again. We docked in Brooklyn, and my mother was there to meet me.

My parents were no longer living on 130th Street. I had gotten a cablegram in Russia from my mother saying that she and my father had separated. (Because of the separation, the people at Walker Memorial Church asked my father to resign—that fall from grace eventually killed him.)[1] So I got a room in my mother's apartment building. When I saved up a little money I found an apartment on Fifth Avenue at 127th Street. That was a nice neighborhood; a lot of Swedes still lived there. I had five rooms: Bobby Martin had one, Allegretti and I had one, and my mother and sister Mildred had another.

When we got back to New York, we found out that stage orchestras were using violins. So we expanded the Sam Wooding orchestra by adding two violins, Louis Metcalf on trumpet, and a pianist, since Sam started conducting. We considered our group an orchestra, not a great jazz band, like Fletcher Henderson's.

We made the rounds in Harlem to hear what was going on. Everybody was glad to see us. We were the first good big band to go across and have a successful tour. I went to Smalls' and heard Benny Carter—I hadn't heard him since 1922, when he was a kid, trying to play. Charlie Johnson had a tremendous band there, and Benny was making a lot of his arrangements. In fact, all the bands sounded better. They'd gotten away from symphonic jazz, so we had to change our style a bit and put in more jazz. Sam made some arrangements, but he was not a great jazz arranger—his was strictly the Paul Whiteman style. His jazz arrangements had a bit of ricky-ticky in them, but they were acceptable.

We rehearsed every day up at Coachman's Hall, on 138th Street and Eighth Avenue. After four or five weeks we got our first vaudeville date. We went right into the theaters—we didn't want to play in the dance halls any more.

Sam made one big mistake after we came back from Europe. Herman Stark, manager of the Cotton Club, sent Sam a telegram that read: "Call at your earliest convenience if you will accept Cotton Club engagement at $1100 a week." That's more money than we usually made. But Sam turned it down, saying "No, I'm not coming back to Harlem. We started in Harlem, and we've been playing on Broadway and for the royalty of the world. We don't come back to Harlem." It was the biggest mistake he ever made. Duke Ellington took the job, he got that radio hookup two or three nights a week, and the rest is history.

Whoever dreamed that the Cotton Club would turn out to be like that? Jack Johnson had had it, and it had been a failure. Sam might have been a very big man, because he was brilliant musically and had a lot of creative ideas. But he blew it.

We had some vaudeville jobs around New York, in New England and Pennsylvania. But they petered out to nothing, and in February of 1928 I left the band to join the pit orchestra of *Keep Shufflin'.*

KEEP SHUFFLIN'

James P. Johnson wrote most of the music for *Keep Shufflin',* and Fats Waller contributed some numbers, too. Some of the comedy bits in the show were like *Shuffle Along.* Two of the big songs were "Willow Tree" and " 'Sippi." In the band we had tenor saxophonist Al Sears, who later went with Duke Ellington, also Jabbo Smith on trumpet. Allegretti was a dancer in the chorus, and Blanche Calloway was in the cast, too.[2]

Jimmy conducted the pit orchestra, and Fats played piano. They had a two-piano thing where they played some of the same things they did down at Leroy's. The show could hardly go on after they got through.

Some Monday nights we'd have to send someone out to find James P. and Fats, since they'd have been out at parties since Friday night, playing piano, spending money, buying liquor. They'd just close the places up. Monday night they'd be ossified and you couldn't get them on. That was living in the fast lane, then.

In March I went down with James P., Fats, and Jabbo to record in Camden, New Jersey. Victor had bought this church there which had a great-sounding organ, and used it as a recording studio. The organ pipes were in one room and we were in another. Fats played organ on this date. The piano and the organ manual were together, but since the pipes were in the next room Fats had a real job, because the organ always sounded a fraction of a second late. It was quite a thing. And it was hard keeping time because we had no drums or bass. That morning, Fats didn't drink his fifth of gin until *after* we got through recording.

We did two songs from *Keep Shufflin'*—"Willow Tree" and " 'Sippi"— also "Persian Rug" and "Thou Swell." I played some of the first jazz bassoon on those recordings. My sound was terrible then. I was fasci-nated by Adrian Rollini's style on bass sax, and my bassoon playing just came out that way, even though I wasn't trying to imitate him. On the record they called us the Louisiana Sugar Babes—I have no idea why, maybe Fats created the title. He always looked at the humorous side of things.

Keep Shufflin' started out at Daley's 63rd Street Theater, then moved down to the Eldridge Theater on 42nd Street. In the fall of 1928 we went out on the road, going to Michigan, Ohio, and as far west as St. Louis. In Chicago, Arnold Rothstein, the gangster who owned the show, was murdered in the barbershop of the Park Central Hotel. So the union closed the show, and everybody was stranded. I stayed a while, because that was Allegretti's hometown. Jabbo and I worked at the Dreamland with Charlie Elgar's big band.

But then Allegretti and I had a falling out. On Christmas Eve she didn't come home, and I drove around looking for her until six o'clock in the morning, my .45 next to me on the seat. I was hoping to find her coming out of those streets with somebody; I'd made up my mind to shoot her. But I never found her. Christmas Day I called Charlie Elgar and said, "My mother's sick and I have to go home." So I caught a train back to New York.

BESSIE SMITH

I free-lanced around when I returned, and did a show called *Bamboula* at the Hudson Theater. That's where I met Hilda Perleno, a dancer from St. Louis whom I married a few years later. There was no ceremony; we just went down to City Hall.

Hilda and I went out on the road with the number two *Blackbirds* company. Johnny Dunn was with the band for a while, and Lorenzo Caldwell conducted—the violinist I'd played with on some of those early blues dates.

Lew Leslie owned both *Blackbirds* shows, and his brother Saul toured around with us. Lew was a vicious disciplinarian: that's why his shows were so perfect. He knew his show from the pit to the backdrop, knew the lights, and could get in the pit and demonstrate how the music was to be conducted. He was very successful with black shows, and a shrewd businessman—although he cut everybody's throat in order to be one.

In the spring of 1929 I was called to do a couple of dates with Bessie Smith. I think this was my first opportunity to work with Clarence Williams, who played on both sessions. I went to a rehearsal once at Bessie's house; she lived on Seventh Avenue about 118th Street, on the second or third floor. Bessie was a rough sister. She used to get drunk all the time and fight like a man. But when it came to singing the blues, there was nobody like her.

I had fun on those sessions, although I couldn't play much. In those days I enjoyed everything. I didn't know there was more to life than pleasure. Only recently have I tried to sit down and accomplish something, to be analytical enough to contribute something for the privilege of being here.

NOTES

1. J. D. Bushell died in 1937. Effie Payne Bushell later ran her own beautician's business, remained active in the church as a pastor's aide and leader of women's groups, and wrote a booklet on parliamentary procedure. She died in 1968.
2. Anderson played a character called "Grit." Blanche Calloway may have joined the *Keep Shufflin'* road show when it came to Chicago.

8

Tough Guys and High Society

In 1930 Elmer Snowden invited me to join his band down at the Hot Feet Club, in Greenwich Village. Snowden was from Baltimore, where many of the best banjo players came from. He had eight pieces, but the lineup was unusual: four saxophones, piano, banjo, bass, drums. There were also four waiters who made up a quartet and four girl singers, so we split the money sixteen ways. I was coming home with $10–$15 a night.

The Hot Feet Club was owned by Harry Lyons, one of the toughest gangsters in New York. Mobsters used to come in all the time. One was Boston Blackie, who had the most handsome teeth of anybody I've ever seen and was always grinning. He'd paste $1,000 bills on the waiters' heads and let them run around all night with them. He'd take them off before he left. A lot of Uncle Tomming was done that way, because so much money was involved. Gene Tunney used to come in there, too, with his brother, and everybody would try to outspend each other.

It's too bad Snowden's band never recorded. We didn't rehearse, but everyone in that band had tremendous ears and a good sense of harmony. Otto Hardwick was lead alto saxophone, I was second alto, Crawford Wethington was third, and Bingie Madison was on tenor. We played four-part harmony to everything without music and we broadcast that way. Our theme song was "I'm Confessin'."

Otto Hardwick was a sensational performer. He never tuned up, he never cleaned out his mouthpiece. I saw him change a reed one day, and I swear, I think worms were in his mouthpiece. He just pushed it back again and he never sounded better. One night I heard him go out there and play string bass. He was gifted.

We were doing pretty well for 1930, because things were rough that year. At least we had a steady job. But we wanted a raise, and Snowden told Harry Lyons about it. Lyons said no, so Snowden gave him notice.

That night, as it was approaching quitting time, Lyons threatened Snowden: "You'd better not take those instruments out of here tonight. If you do, you'll find yourselves in the gutter."

"All right," Snowden said, "you'll see."

Snowden had already told us, "When I give a signal, have your horns packed."

When it came time to stop we all got up to leave. Lyons kept at us, saying, "Youse won't get uptown. I'm going to dump youse in the river before you get uptown!"

Snowden said, "Well, start dumping." Snowden had more nerve than anybody I've ever seen. He had the guts of a mountain lion. We just walked out of there and nothing happened.

I also played with Snowden in Harlem at Smalls' Paradise, seven nights a week. I was straw boss in his big band there, and rehearsed it and conducted shows. We were such good friends we bought an automobile together, a Chrysler roadster. He couldn't drive, so I'd go pick him up and take him out riding.

Around this time, in the early thirties, I got calls to do a lot of different gigs. I conducted some shows at the Lafayette Theater and put together bands there. I also did some arranging at the Apollo. It was a rough period, though, because the biggest gig you could get only paid ten dollars. We worked at Smalls' for fifty dollars a week. That was a big salary.

I left Smalls' to go back with Sam Wooding in vaudeville. We had new uniforms made. I think we had four saxes, three trumpets, two trombones, two violins—a bigger band than before. We did about four dates, then the thing collapsed. I'd spent all the money I made at Smalls'. I had a period of nothing.

I recovered some of my losses by going out on society dates with Luckey Roberts. Luckey was a favorite with the rich people. He took some of the gigs that Ford Dabney used to have.

There'd often be four of us—Luckey, Sam Speed on banjo, a drummer, and myself. Luckey probably got $500 for the group, and I'd make maybe $20 for the date. I used to get $75 and $80 a week with Luckey for four or five gigs. We'd work that much. With Luckey I went outside of New York to Boston, Philadelphia, Virginia, the Carolinas, and as far south as Georgia.

In South Carolina they conditioned a lot of race horses. We might go there to play a New Year's dance, or a Christmas party. One time down there we were met by a Negro who was about my complexion. His name was Post. So in driving us out to the plantation, this Post says, "You see that fellow over there? That's my brother. He's the finest son-of-a-bitch that ever lived." This guy was white, Post was a mulatto. These two had the same father but different mothers. Our driver lived in another house on the plantation, and he couldn't even go in the front door of the main house. There was so much of that in South Carolina, also in Mississippi. The prosperous white men would have two families, both living on the same plantation.

But with Luckey we were treated as artists, and as guests, down South. They let us use the front door. Luckey was just like a little king. He was polite, but he was also powerful on that piano and a great exhibitionist. People would crowd around him, just listening to him play.

You see, these rich whites, the Stokesburys, Goulds, Wannamakers, and all, would come to New York for parties. We'd be playing, and Luckey would hand out his card. That's how he made his contacts. Someone would come up and say, "Ahm from Gowgia. Lahk to have y'all come down sometime."

Now, Luckey was one of the ugliest guys you've ever seen; he looked like a little gorilla, and had a steeple head and big thick lips. But when he opened his mouth you'd hear a very articulate man. Luckey would say, in this very dignified voice, "We'd be happy to oblige," and give them a card. The first thing you know, we had a trip down to Atlanta.

I enjoyed that atmosphere, learning about the rich people and how they lived. That's where my firsthand information about millionaires came from, without ever having been a servant.

Through Luckey I even made contact with the Vanderbilts. One particular afternoon W. K. Vanderbilt himself called me up.[1]

"Bushell, what're you doing?

"Nothin'."

"Can you come out to the house?"

"Yeah, sure."

"Be sure and bring that fat one with you, the one that plays the organ."

"All right," I said.

I took along Fats Waller and Mert Perry. We hired a car and took it out to the Vanderbilt estate on Long Island. After you go through the gate it takes about six minutes to reach the house.

When we arrived, W. K. said, "I'm just lonesome and wanted to hear some music today." We played about two numbers and he said, "All right, come on, sit down here and let's talk." He wanted to know what we did, what made us tick. I'd been to Russia, and he wanted to know all about that. Then he said, "All right, play another tune." A little later, "Come on, let's drink." By that time a big dinner was ready.

W. K. loved Fats. He even had an organ in his house, and Fats played it. Vanderbilt said, "I'd give anything in the world if I was just free to do like you guys." I remember his exact words: "I don't know how to have fun."

So Fats stood up and said, "Mr. W. K., you give me some of your money and I'll show you how to have some fun!" That knocked him out. Then he went on, "You know, it's a curse being a Vanderbilt. Everybody yesses me, it's not genuine. Even my wife. I can't trust anyone."

A few years later he died. What did he die from? A broken heart, frustration.

NOTE

1. William Kissam Vanderbilt II (1878–1944) had an estate on the north shore of Long Island called Eagle's Nest. In his music room was a $150,000 pipe organ with player piano attachment.

9

WITH FESS,
FAT MAN,
AND FLETCHER

By this time I had a pretty good reputation as a first alto man, so Fess Williams sent for me in 1933. I went to New England with him, and we also worked the Rosemont in Brooklyn. That was a steady job that paid about $37–$38 a week, not much more. We did the Lafayette Theater as well, and went down to the Standard Theater in Philadelphia.

Fess had a good, well-rehearsed band. Columbia wanted to put us on radio. We were going to have a weekly show on WOR called "The Devil and His Imps." Different members of the band would have talking parts. They auditioned us, and both Fess and I read the part of the Devil. After I finished, the man said, "That's the voice and tone and phrasing that I want for the Devil."

Fess said, "What part do I play?"

"Well, you have a voice that fits one of the imps."

Fess was a shrewd businessman. When he heard this, he said, "This is Fess Williams and his band. If I don't have the principal part, there won't be no part." So we didn't do the program. Fess was like that.

Fess was one of the pioneers in jazz and presentation. He was a good showman, a good clown, and a better musician than Cab Calloway. Fess was a black Ted Lewis, although he could play more clarinet than Lewis ever played. He wore a high hat and a tuxedo with rhinestones on the lapels. He also set tempos better than any bandleader I've ever worked under. He could feel the pulse of the people dancing and know just what they wanted. What determined his success as a conductor was how much he could show off. It wasn't how an orchestra interpreted what he did with his hands—it was the impression the audience got, if he could wave his hands in time, jump around and clown, or do certain tumbles. He could sell a band, sell a number. He'd had experience in Chicago as an emcee at the Balaban and Katz Theater, on the South Side. That's where he formulated his act.

Fess did some of our arrangements, so did Lloyd Phillips, our pianist, and I did a few. Fess liked to put the classics in dance form, such as "Poet and Peasant," the *William Tell* Overture, and "Russian Rag," which is based on a Rachmaninoff prelude. He was qualified; he'd taught school down in Louisville. That's where he got the name "Fess," from Professor.

We also improved on stocks, just as Sam Wooding had done in the twenties. You'd put in your own introduction, then play the first chorus as it was arranged on the chart. Then you'd put in a rhythmic modulation and go into another key for solos. Then you'd come back, and if there was a good ensemble chorus, you'd play that. If not, you made your own. A lot of bands did this, since you didn't have too many arrangers.

I worked as straw boss under Fess. We took pains every day to rehearse each individual section, to check each man's vibrato and make sure it was the same as the next man's. That's how you'd get a section to blend. I got the trick of blending horns from James P. Johnson, back when I was in *Keep Shufflin'*.

We had a whopping good act with Fess. Clarence Wheeler would come out and do "The Sheik," singing and playing while standing on his head. Clarkie [Emanuel Clark], our second trumpet player (he was West Indian), would come out and sing "The Peanut Vendor" in Spanish and dance a rhumba. I used to sing songs in three different languages, French, German, and Russian. I'd learned them in Europe. Then we had a railroad imitation called "Hot Town." Little Stoney [Perry Smith], a small bald-headed guy, was a comedian in the band. He'd call out the names of different towns—Hot Town, Swing Town, Stompburg. He'd call out Gutbucket Junction, and we'd start playing the blues.

Fess ran his band with a good system, until it came to money. He never made much and couldn't afford to pay much. We traveled around in three old broken-down cars—two Lincolns and a Cadillac—that used to skid all over the roads in the wintertime. But Fess created a camaraderie between the men in the band. It was like a family. We'd stop by the roadside, and if there was a field we'd go out there and wrestle each other or play touch football. If one of us got in trouble, we all got in trouble.

In those days on the road, all you had to do was be black and you'd get accused of doing something. Once we were driving between gigs in Massachusetts, and they stopped us because someone had turned in a false alarm and they thought we did it. They handcuffed us and put us in jail, so we missed our gig in Old Orchard, Maine, that night.

Another time we ran into some trouble in New Jersey. We were playing in the dance hall at Columbia Park, an amusement park, and taking a percentage of the door because they didn't guarantee us anything. We stayed, though, because Columbia gave us a radio hookup, fifteen minutes three times a week.

During our second week there, some little punks came in and walked up to the bandstand. "Fess Williams!"

Fess turned around, looked down, and said, "Yeah?"

"We're here to do you a good deed. We're going to give you protection while you're here."

"Listen, we don't need no protection."

"Oh yeah, you do. These kids over here are pretty tough. They're going to come up and clean you. You need protection."

Fess said, "No we don't, we'll protect ourselves."

"Well," the punks said, "that's the way it is over here in Jersey. You've got to have protection, otherwise you can't stay here."

"We'll stay, all right," Fess replied.

"Well, we'll be back tomorrow. You make up your mind."

Fess said, "You can come back anytime you want to, but we don't pay for no protection."

After the date, Fess said, "Now see what we're up against?" In the first place, the New Jersey musicians didn't want a black band over there, they wanted the job themselves. They were trying to scare us off. Fess said, "We need this spot, we need this hookup, and we don't let nobody run us off."

So Little Stoney spoke up and said, "Well, let's bring our artillery in." All those guys had guns. Saxophonist Craig Watson was a marksman. Every time he went into a shooting gallery he won all the dolls and everything. (Eventually he wound up killing two guys in Toledo.)

So Fess says, "We'd better bring something in and at least scare them. If we have to shoot, we have to."

The next day, Stoney brought in two guns and Craig brought in three, and everybody in the front row had a gun behind his seat. Wheeler, Clarkie, and Jelly[1] had revolvers back there behind their stands. We opened at 2:00 in the afternoon, and these guys came back at about 2:30. There were three of them.

"Well Fess, here we are! You got what we were talking about?"

Fess says, "What?"

"You got that? You know, what we've come to collect."

"Have we got it, boys?" And we moved back the racks, and everybody came up with a gun: there were .45s, 30-30 rifles, .38s. You should have seen the expressions on those punks' faces! Fess said, "That's what we got. And if you make a move out there, we'll let you *have* what we got."

"All right, if that's the way you want to play it, we'll be back."

That was the last we saw of them.

Fess was a good showman but a bad businessman. His theory was to keep working regardless of how much money he got. This might have been good, but the guys were always dissatisfied because we were always going out on the road and coming back with nothing. I had to have money, and needed a steady job.

CHARLIE TURNER

I left Fess to play with Charlie Turner at the Arcadia Ballroom, in midtown Manhattan. Our salary there was something like forty-seven dollars a week. Charlie was our bass player, and we had Eddie Mallory, Jack Butler, and Bobby Stark on trumpets; Al Washington, Wayman Carver, and myself on reeds; Hank Duncan on piano (we called him "Potatohead"); Slick Jones on drums; and Emmett Mathews was our conductor. We called our guitar player "Abe Lincoln." Charlie, of course, was "Fat Man."

I took Jerry Blake's place in the band, and had to sing some of the things he had done, like "Hurry Home." I also did my foreign-language specialty songs.

The boss of the Arcadia was very prejudiced. When we'd go in, we had to stay close to the wall and go upstairs to the dressing room. We could never venture out on the floor of the ballroom. The same thing was true at Roseland. The white musicians would come off the stand and go across the dance floor and sit down in the lounge. But we weren't allowed to do that. Nothing you could do about it, if you wanted to work.

By this time I was living on 138th Street and married to Hilda. I'd bought a used twelve-cylinder Cadillac, but the gangsters wouldn't even let me park it on my own block. They had an after-hours spot and didn't want the cops to see a car like that there. Many times I'd park it in front of the Cotton Club, and the cops would say, "How's Owney?"

I'd say, "Fine." They thought I was the chauffeur for Owney Madden, who ran the Cotton Club.

In January of 1934, the Apollo Theater started a new policy of featuring name bands. Benny Carter was the first band to go in there, and Charlie Turner and his Arcadians had the second band. I did some arranging at the Apollo then. I remember doing "The Peanut Vendor," a Victor Herbert song, and an arrangement of "Stormy Weather" with bassoon. Clarence Robinson was the choreographer, and when they had a production number he'd say, "Hey Rev, we want to do this number, come upstairs." We rehearsed next door, over the Apollo. He'd say, "Listen to this, and watch that." Then he'd give me a score and I'd go arrange it for the band. I usually did one production number—that's the big ensemble number with the chorus, soubrette, and featured soloists. Tom Whaley was the rehearsal pianist. Later he left and went with Duke.

FLETCHER HENDERSON

After I was at the Apollo with Charlie Turner we laid off, and I had nothing else to do. I couldn't pay for my apartment, so I lost it. Hilda and I bundled up and got a big front room on 139th Street—that's the same street Fletcher Henderson lived on. Things got so bad that I had to go find Rudy Powell and make him pay fifty cents he owed me! I threatened to fight him if he didn't pay me back. That's how tough things were.

Around this time, Fletcher and his brother Horace had a kind of falling out. Horace managed to take some people from Fletcher's band, and Fletcher had to get some of us who'd been playing with Charlie Turner. Fletcher hired Cecil Scott, Benny Waters, "Jobetus" [Theodore McCord], and myself. He also had George Thigpen, Max Maddox, Fernando Arbello, Herman Autrey, Billy Taylor on bass, and Slick Jones on drums. The reed section went and rehearsed over at Fletcher's house. (Leora, Fletcher's wife, used to do the copying for the band.)

This was the first time I'd been back with Fletcher since the Ethel Waters days. Our first date was at the Harlem Opera House. A movie would be shown in the morning, then we'd come on about 11:00 or 11:30.

The second show was around 2:00, the third show at 5:00. The fourth show was 8:00 or 9:00. There were chorus girls, comedians, dancers—we had a whole stage show. But Fletcher's was never a great stage band. It was a good dance band, not a stage band.

I went with Fletcher on dance dates around New England, also down to Philadelphia, Baltimore, and the Eastern Shore. Eventually we went into Roseland, where we got fifty dollars a week. That was a big salary.

But the pay wasn't always consistent with Fletcher. Once we were playing in Philadelphia and the guy didn't pay us at intermission. So Fletcher said, "Well, the man ain't gonna pay, so we're gonna have to stop playing." This was in North Philadelphia, the black section.

One by one we eased off the bandstand. I got off real soon. I wasn't going to get my horn broken up. That happened every time there was a fight in the dance hall, they'd rush in and knock my horns over. So I had my horn with me. Fletcher stayed on stage 'til the end, though, since he was such a big coward.

In the meantime, the guys were out in the alley packing up the bus. But they beat up Slick Jones, our drummer, and broke his drums. We had to patch up his eye and get him a new set of drums. We never did get paid.

Another time we rode down all the way to South Carolina and I didn't get paid, even though I was straw boss. Fletcher had a second alto player named Leroy Hardy, who figured I was complaining about him since I was straw boss. (Fletcher had complained about him, but I never said anything about him.) So we're in this dressing room one night in South Carolina, down in Leroy's home town. His grandfather was an undertaker there. I saw Leroy standing on the side with a handkerchief in his hand. He said, "You know, I ain't two minutes off of you."

"What are you talking about?"

He had this sneer on his face, and I looked and saw that he had his knife wrapped up in his handkerchief. In South Carolina, you could kill a man and just pay ten dollars and costs for disorderly conduct. On a Saturday night, Leroy had shown us five or six bodies down in his grandfather's funeral parlor. If there were only two bodies it was a very slow Saturday night.

I said, "What's wrong with you?"

"You complained about me."

I said, "No, man, I didn't say nothin' about you."

"Yeah?" He's getting ready to cut me with his knife.

I said, "Hey! What do you want to do, hurt your best friend? Shit, if it wasn't for me, you wouldn't be in this band. I'm the one that keeps you in!

What you want to cut me for?" I had to talk my way out of it, because he was a Geechie boy and I knew what they'd do: cut first and ask questions later. And it worked, but it was a close call.

Fletcher was a nice mama's boy, like a baby. There wasn't much fight in him. That's why the guys in his band did whatever they wanted. There was no discipline. If someone came to the stand late, they were just late.

Once we were scheduled to follow Benny Goodman at the Savoy Ballroom. But Goodman's book was the same as Fletcher's; every time Fletcher made an arrangement for Goodman, he'd keep it for himself. So we couldn't go on after Goodman and make fools of ourselves. What good would it do, since Goodman had better musicians than we did, and could play the arrangements better?

Fletcher was never accepted by blacks as much as Duke. I don't think the blacks of Harlem bought many of his records: they were too sophisticated, not racy enough, and sounded like a white band.

One night I got tired of not being paid and said, "Just give me ten dollars or twenty dollars or something." We'd just finished playing the set.

"I don't have the money," Fletcher said. He had the money in his pocket so he could reach in and peel off two one-dollar bills, or a five, anything he wanted. So he reached in and I pulled his hand out, before he had a chance to separate the bills, and out come these ten- and twenty-dollar bills on the floor. Now, Fletcher was a milquetoast. "Garvin," he said, "that ain't no way to treat me. You know how long we've been friends."

I said, "That's why you should pay me sometimes." But he didn't. He figured he'd try and pay the rest of them, because I would tolerate it. He died owing me $2,000 or $3,000.

I finally got fed up in Chicago, when we were playing there in the winter of 1936. We were appearing at the Grand Terrace Ballroom, and I hadn't gotten paid for the first week. He always came up with a lame story. So on a Sunday night in February I got a call from Cab Calloway, and I left Fletcher the next day, just walked out without giving notice. Benny Goodman came up and did the broadcast for Fletcher. One of the world's worst saxophone players!

NOTE

1. Clarence Wheeler and Emanuel Clark, trumpet, and David "Jelly" James, trombone.

10

CAB CALLOWAY

Things picked up when I joined Cab. He was the biggest attraction in the country in 1936. To go with him was to go a step higher, and conditions were better. I started getting $100 a week.[1]

My first appearance with Cab was in Indianapolis at a Balaban and Katz presentation theater. Milt Hinton and I joined at the same time. Eddie Barefield—who had quit the band—had written most of the arrangements, and there were a lot of hard saxophone parts. At first I had a little difficulty, but it finally threshed itself out.

We started doing one-nighters in the Midwest, traveling by Pullman. When we got to Chicago I bought a new alto and clarinet. Cab seemed interested in me then. I had a big raccoon coat on, and Cab had a raccoon coat, so he figured, "Oh, this guy's all right." Foots [Walter Thomas] was also very helpful. The guys in the band accepted me.

To my mind, Cab never had a great dance band. Cab didn't set good tempos, even when we were at the Cotton Club. He forgot how people wanted to dance. There were some good musicians in the band, but nobody every rehearsed us to pick up the loose ends. Also, the rhythm section was sluggish and backing up all the time. Bennie Payne and Leroy Maxey were very heavy on the four beat. And you could never hear Fruit's guitar.

Nearly everyone in the band had a nickname; some, like Doc Cheatham, Shad Collins, and Keg Johnson, had theirs before they went with Cab. Lammar Wright was "Slop" because he used buckets and slop jars for mutes. Walter Thomas was "Foots" because of his big feet. Irving Randolph was "Mouse," I'm not sure why. De Priest Wheeler was a fine baseball player so we called him "Mickey," after the great catcher Mickey

Cochrane. Claude Jones was "Wiggy" because he wore a wig. Andrew Brown was "Flat" because his voice was so high-pitched, way up there around E-flat. Ben Webster was "Frog" because of his big, round, pop eyes. Milt Hinton was "Fump"; he didn't weigh but 135 pounds when he came into the band, so "Fump" meant "next to nothing." (Bennie Payne named him that.) Morris White was "Fruit," maybe because he always had a bag of fruit nearby. Leroy Maxey was "Cash" because he was always talking about it: "How much cash am I gonna get? How much cash did you spend? Well, I got the cash! Cash is what counts!" My nickname was "Butch."

Foots Thomas was more or less the straw boss. He'd been in the band when it was the Missourians. Every now and then he'd arrange a number, and he started the band up when Cab was offstage.

When I joined Cab, I didn't notice Ben Webster's playing too much because he wasn't as good as he became later on, in the 1940s and '50s. He was still developing. Besides, there weren't many solo opportunities in the band; Cab took up all the extra space in an arrangement, and every number always featured him as a singer or dancer. Ben may have had an unusual style, but it wasn't enough to upset anybody in those days. Chu Berry would upset you more than Ben when he came on the bandstand and played. On records, though, you can hear what kind of artist Ben really was.

I got to know Ben very well. He was an unusual character, very humorous, also very tough. He didn't get along with the girls at all because he'd knock them down if they said the wrong thing to him. He was a typical product of Kansas City at that time. Kansas City was a fast town where the people were on top of everything—in the line of music, gambling, hustling, and all that. Some of the sharpest characters in the world came from there. I think Ben was influenced by the hustlers and pimps—he had their mannerisms.

Ben wasn't the most brilliant in thinking. You'd talk with him, but he didn't discern much of deep inner thought. His whole life was impressing people.

Ben and Cab were buddies. But Ben wasn't too happy in the band, so when he had an opportunity to leave in 1937 he did. Cab got drunk when Ben left, and cried, "My man is leaving. I don't know what happened."[2]

Cab was only about thirty years old when I was in the band. Many times he acted his age, while other times he tried to be mature by showing how much he knew. He was quite intelligent and articulate. But he was a little rougher than he should have been on musicians. On the stand he was a tyrant. He ran his orchestra with an iron hand, not giving much room for your decisions, your concept. We began calling him Simon Legree. At rehearsals he'd scream and holler at you into submissiveness—he thought by acting that way he could make up for his limited knowledge of music. That was a mistake.

Cab couldn't really conduct, but in those days there were a lot of phony conductors. Lucky Millinder was one, but he was the best of them. At least he had a good concept of conducting and gave the audience the impression that he was a real, legitimate conductor. Emmett Mathews, in front of Charlie Turner's band, was nothing. But he could dance across the stage and sing, so he was good in front of a band. Conductors usually weren't conducting the music; they were an image in front of the band; they just put a lot of motion into the scene, introduced numbers, and acted as emcees. They were clowns, more or less. The same was true for Bardu Ali with Chick Webb's band.

ON TOUR WITH CALLOWAY

It was a pleasure traveling with Cab, because you had all the conveniences. When you stopped you had a chance to go to a hotel, or you could wash up in your Pullman car—take a birdbath, as we called it. We always carried extra performers. Avis Andrews was our singer, Nicodemus used to do comedy things, and Dynamite Hooker was a dancer. On one trip to Canada we took a tramp band with us.

I was generally happy being on the road with Cab. The only thing that bothered me was playing in the South. Even if it was a black dance there were always white spectators who'd try to create trouble for Cab. They loved Cab's ability, but they were jealous of him.

I was always very nervous in the South, but I got along this way: I approached the southerner with an air that I was his equal, if not better. When I spoke I used the best English that I knew. I had confidence in myself. I never backed up.

Once we were in Longview, Texas, a small town in the eastern part of the state. In the afternoon, after we'd arrived, we were in our railroad car, lying in the upper berths, resting.

A fellow came aboard and said, "I'm running the dance here tonight. I wanted to warn you that this town can be a little rough. Everybody's rich, since we just had a new oil strike. So you may have a little trouble. But I'm going to have the sheriff and six deputies there tonight to protect you, so don't worry."

We looked at each other and thought, "Oh my God, what we gonna have here tonight?"

That evening, the bus came to the yard, picked us up, and took us to this roadhouse. Sure enough, there was the sheriff and about six or seven deputies. The sheriff said, "How you doin', boys?" You know, down South you're always a boy, even if you're ninety years old.

During the first set, the sheriff said, "These folks are gonna fight, because they're drunk. They've got a lot of money." He and his men lined up in front of the stand to keep the people moving. One guy came up to him with seven hundred-dollar bills and said, "Sheriff, if you'll just move out the way and let me hit that nigger in the mouth, you can have this $700."

The sheriff replied, "What you want to hit him for?"

"He's too damn good anyhow. He's pretty. I'm liable to hit him anyway."

Cab was scared to death. Many times in the South, guys would pull knives on him and say, "Play 'Minnie the Moocher,'" "Play 'Jim Jam Jump' ["The Jumpin' Jive"]." To them that was an achievement, to have a celebrity like Cab do their bidding. That was the greatest thing in their lives.

So when intermission came, the sheriff said, "Y'all go down to the cellar." The cellar was right off the bandstand. "Y'all go down, don't stay up here on this stand."

Our valets were in the habit of always staying on the stand during intermission, to keep people from bothering and taking the horns. But we went downstairs, commenting on what had gone on so far. Soon we heard a rumble overhead. The sheriff poked his head down the stairs and said, "It's on up here. Don't come up now!"

So I'm sitting near the cellar door that goes up the steps to the band-stand, and I heard this expression I'll never forget: "Take yo' black-ass hands offa me!" I looked up and saw Harold, our valet, trying to keep a guy from coming downstairs. Harold said, "No, you can't go down there."

"Take yo' hands offa me!"

I rushed upstairs real fast. "Hey," I said, "what's this? What's wrong?" I'm trying to con him with my best New Yorkese con. "What does he want?"

"Well, this nigger here doesn't want me to go down and see Cab. I want to see Cab." He was a big cracker, must have been about six-five. He was drunk, too.

"Sure you do," I said, "I know that. But you know how hard he works. He's down there, completely winded. He's exhausted. So give him a little more time, and then I think you can see him."

He said, "Looka here, I can do this?"

I say, "Yeah, sure, you can do it. Just give him a little more chance." In the meantime I noticed Harold going downstairs.

The cracker said, "Where you from?"

"I'm from New York."

He said, "Yeah? Looka here. You know what they tell me? They tell me y'all mixes up in New York."

I said, "No."

"Y'all have white women up there."

"No, man," I said, "don't believe that propaganda. We got the most beautiful women in the world."

"Is that right?"

"Absolutely."

"You talk like a pretty smart fellow, look here." He went in his pocket and pulled out his card. He was editor-in-chief of the *Longview Times*. He said, "Do you think old Cab would come down and see me tomorrow?"

I said, "He'd revel at the opportunity to come down and talk with you."

"Well give him my card. You too! I want you to come down with him."

In the meantime, everyone's downstairs listening to what's going on—Cab and the rest. So I said, "See you tomorrow," and went downstairs.

"Well Bush," they said, "you did it. You saved the situation."

The next day we had a layover and Cab and I went down to see the guy. He turned out to be polite. He put out his cigars and whiskey, and just wanted to sit down and talk with us. He wasn't a bad person, just a dyed-in-the-wool Texan who had been raised like that. It was an incident that had very peaceful results.

The southerner has some prejudices that you can't get out. But he also has principles that you can respect, for frankness and saying what he means. You can depend on that. If he says he doesn't like you, he doesn't like you. If he says he likes you, he'll stand by you. That's their creed down there.

Cab was at the peak of his popularity then. He drew huge crowds. In New Orleans we played under the grandstand at the racetrack for 11,000 people. It was some kind of attendance record for the city.

Even so, it was hard to be in a black band on the road. Maybe the white bands had trouble, too, but in a different way. Some of the people who insulted us would insult anybody. But they didn't have to go through the racial aspect of it. There's nothing more bitter than that. Things that involve a racial standpoint—you can't explain them, hardly.

For example, we were in Dallas, Texas, on June 19, 1936, which is Emancipation Day.[3] That night Joe Louis fought Max Schmeling, and Schmeling finally knocked Louis out. Now, Joe Louis was our idol. In Minneapolis, when he was in training for Jim Braddock's fight, he had even umpired our baseball games. Cab came out on stage and said, "I regret to announce that Schmeling knocked out Joe Louis in the eleventh round." And the crackers stood up and said, "Here! Here!" The Negroes just slid down in their seats. You could hardly see them. They were so stunned they almost disappeared.

I said, "Do you see what I see? Here a foreigner beats an American champion, and the crackers stand up and applaud." The Negroes just scrunched down in their seats, their heads were dropped. You can't imagine the human reaction to that extent over an athletic event, but it happened.

Later that same week I was downtown in Dallas, shopping for a sports jacket to wear as a uniform. I was with a young lady whose husband was head of the Texas Centennial Exposition. So we come to a store, and I said, "Let's go in here."

"Oh no, no."

I started in the door and had her in hand. "Come on," I said. I wasn't going to back out then.

I walked right in and said, "Good afternoon."

The guy said, "Where are you from?"

"I'm from New York. Why, does it make a difference? I want to buy something."

"What would you like?"

"Well, I saw one of the jackets out there in the window and it reminded me very much of what I had in mind. If you have it, I'd like to see it please."

"You from New York? What are you doing in Texas?"

"I'm here with Cab Calloway's band."

"Oh, with Calloway?"

"That's right."

"Well, come on in. What's that you wanted?"

Then they brought out the jacket, and I tried it on. I said, "This is the one. What do you want for it?"

"It's $150."

I didn't want to pay that, I wanted something for $50 or $75. So I said, "This is for a band uniform. Do I need a $150 jacket to sweat up?"

"You're right," he said.

"I thought of something a little cheaper."

"We don't have anything less than that." This was one of the biggest stores in Dallas. $150 for a sports jacket in 1936 was unheard of; it was like buying something on Park Avenue.

So I said, with my dignity and loud voice, "All right, let me see one of those Meerschaum pipes." I thought I had better buy something to carry the act out.

In the meantime, they said, "How's old Cab?" The crackers loved Cab, you know.

"He's fine, just fine."

"Well, tell him to come on down to the store. We'd be glad to have him. Maybe we've got something he wants."

The pipe was fifteen dollars. That wasn't bad, so I said I'd take it.

They smiled all over and said, "We haven't sold one of those in a long time."

When we got outside, this woman's hands were shaking. "Give me air so I can breathe." Then she told me that in that particular store, they'd thrown out Negroes who'd come in to ask for a job as a porter.

But I had been taught, by working with Luckey Roberts, how to act around millionaires. I knew how to show that you had class. That always superseded anything else. I had learned in New York that when you want something you show no fear, no doubt as to your qualifications or your reason for coming into an establishment. You talk loudly and keep walking.

I also learned this lesson from my father. He'd lived in Texas with his Bible in one hand and his .45 automatic in his hip pocket. He said, "Son, you can always disarm a cracker with intelligence. Don't forget that." It stood me in good stead all over the South.

One other bad incident on the road comes to mind. In Johnson City, Tennessee, we were on the bandstand playing when I heard this remark: "If you move I'll pull your goddamn head off!"

I looked up and saw this black man had a knife on this white man's throat. Evidently the white man had provoked him in some way. This was a black dance, with white spectators. In the South, as a rule, there was always an alloted space for white clientele at black dances. There'd be a spot roped off on the side, or they'd have them stand in front of the bandstand.[4]

Suddenly, before I could blink my eyes, the white man grabbed this Negro and threw him over his back. When he hit the floor, all the whites around him started kicking him. They beat this poor guy to a pulp.

When the cops came they picked the black man up off the floor and took him out the side door. Then they came back in and said, "That's enough, Calloway. You're through for tonight." This was 11:30, and the dance was supposed to go until 12:00 or 1:00.

"That's all," a cop said, "We're gonna kill all these niggers in this place tonight. When you get off the stand, go out the side door, don't go out the front door." After we packed up, that's what we did. Our bus was on the side.

But we saw what happened. As the Negro clients were coming out the front, the cops were there beating them with clubs, one by one, women and all. I'll never forget, Bennie Payne started crying, and we had to hold him back. He said, "We got to stay here and witness this? C'mon, let's get away, I can't stand it. Otherwise I'm gonna have to do something."

The cops came up to our bus and said, "Y'all get 'em on out of here, 'cause we're gonna finish 'em up tonight." The bus took us to our Pullman, out on the side tracks. We stayed there all night. We heard shots.

Finally, the railroad detective came through and said, "They're shooting up all the Negroes in the neighborhood." They just went through and shot up people in all the houses.

All this happened because one Negro stood up to a white man at a black dance.

Now, I should say that the black crowds we played for in the South and Northeast could be quite rowdy. I had figured the purpose of going to a dance was to have fun. But I found out that there were certain people who went in order to create a disturbance. Ignorance proves itself in many ways. It comes out in being vicious and resenting somebody for no apparent reason at all.

One night in Connecticut a black guy was so vicious that he grabbed another fellow and bit the end of his nose off, and spit it on the floor. It took six cops to subdue him. Baltimore was always bad; I hated playing dances there. You'd be a nervous wreck, because you knew there was going to be a fight and somebody would get cut.

Another time we were playing the Howard Theater in Washington. Claude Jones and I were coming around the corner in front of the theater when we saw Ben Webster backed up against a wall, and a guy getting ready to throw a ball at him. It turns out Ben had been throwing the ball back in the alley with someone and it had missed and hit one of the thugs that was hanging around. The guy was telling Ben, "You hit me, now I'm gonna hit you!"

Ben was frightened—but if you turned Ben loose, he was vicious, very vicious. At that moment, Keg Johnson came down the alley with his .45. He said, "Don't throw that ball, you motherfucker," and he shot up in the air. That cleaned everybody out. But then someone called the cops. The manager of the Howard took Keg's gun and put it in his office, so the cops never did find it.

When you were a star attraction, you were protected. You could do a lot of things that normal people couldn't do.

With Cab there were always a lot of women hanging around, both black and white. You had to shoo 'em off, and avoid them as much as possible. Sometimes you didn't avoid them.

I remember a night we were playing an auditorium in Toledo. During the next-to-last tune before intermission, somebody said, "Hey, look at this!" We looked, and there's a white woman standing in the wings with her dress up, saying, "When you get through, come and get it." Well, we got through the last tune, and we made a beeline to where this gal was standing behind the curtain. Ben Webster was the first one there. There was also Foots, Doc, Mouse, Keg, Wiggy, Mickey, Cash, and Fump. Frankly, I never did get to it because I was last in line. After four or five guys had it we went back on the stand, and she took on all four of our valets.

But we usually avoided such contact, because it was easy to say that your attraction was causing a nuisance on the road, especially mixing with white women. They'd cancel you out and refuse to book you.

THE COTTON CLUB

When we got off the road with Cab we'd always come back to New York. In the fall of 1936 we opened the new Cotton Club downtown.[5] Our first rehearsal for the show was called for eleven in the morning, which is when I got there. Cab was already on the stand. He turned to me and said, "How do you do, Mr. Bushell? Did we disturb your time?" The chorus line was there, too, and everybody laughed. I was bewildered and didn't know what to say. Then it hit me quick what had happened.

"Well, I'm sorry," I said, "I had car trouble. My car stopped in Central Park and I had to wait until the mechanic came to get me out, or I would have been here sooner." I could lie pretty fast then. "I know you called eleven, Fess, but I had car trouble." All the leaders were called Fess, you know; it came from the days when the leaders were professors.

"Well," Cab said, "eleven o'clock doesn't mean you come in at eleven, it means we start *playing* at eleven."

That was the last time I was late in Cab's band. I didn't know any better, because with Fletcher and Fess Williams nobody was that punctual.

We rehearsed two weeks for that Cotton Club show. Will Vodery had written many of the arrangements, also Bennie Payne. Vodery had given me some parts for oboe and bassoon. There was a bevy of beautiful girls—eight ponies (or small girls) and eight show girls (tall ones). We had stars like Broadway Jones, Anna Lewis, exotic dancer Kaloah, and the Berry brothers. It was a terrific show, and Clarence Robinson staged it.

During my time with Cab I developed more as a saxophonist, mainly because of Foots Thomas. Foots had studied with Merle Johnston, and he got me to start taking lessons, too. Johnston was the premier saxophone teacher in New York. He made me conscious of quality of tone, maintaining pitch, embouchure, the "cushion," and other principles that are still important to me today.

Ben Webster once went to Merle, who told him: "Ben, you do everything wrong, but you sound great! I'm not going to touch you." He wouldn't teach him.

Merle Johnston opened my eyes to the requirements of first alto player. Prior to joining Cab, I thought I was great. But I found out I wasn't nearly as good as I thought I was. So in a way, this was the beginning of a turnaround in my musical career. It took me many years, but from Cab on I began to change my whole routine, knowing that I had to practice technical things, and finding out there was much I couldn't do that I should be able to do.

NOTES

1. By way of comparison, the top salary for a member of Duke Ellington's orchestra in 1933 was $125 a week, according to an article in *Fortune,* August 1933, p. 95.
2. Bushell believes that Calloway and Ellington—both managed by Irving

Mills—had a formal agreement not to take men away from each other. So Webster apparently gave Cab his notice and left before joining Duke two weeks later. In July of 1937, Leon "Chu" Berry filled Webster's vacancy in the Calloway band.

3. This day, also known as Juneteenth, commemorates the emancipation proclamation for slaves in Texas, 19 June 1865.

4. Bushell recalls one black dance in South Carolina where three sections were roped off for dancers: one for whites, one for mulattoes, and one for dark blacks. There were policemen present to make sure no one crossed over into the wrong section.

5. The original Cotton Club in Harlem closed its doors 15 February 1936. The new one opened on Broadway 24 September 1936.

CHICK WEBB

One night before a show at the Cotton Club, Cab complained to me about the saxophone section, accusing me of not playing my part. I knew the charge was trumped up. Chu Berry would just sit there with the horn in his mouth and go to sleep during the show. But Cab let Chu do anything he wanted to do.

When we got on the stand that night I wouldn't even look at Cab conducting. I just turned my head on him, since I knew how the show went anyway. The next day one of the valets handed me my notice.

I went to see Cab and asked him, "What is this all about?"

"Well, Butch, you don't cooperate, and you don't pay attention to direction." He had a lot of excuses.

"If that's how you want it, O.K." I didn't argue with him or beg for the job. Partly he was right. But I had done what I'd intended to do, and it was up to him: if he didn't want to go along with me, then he had to get rid of me.

Actually, I think Chu was behind all of this. I'd been getting on Chu for not playing when Cab was off the stand, and he in turn went to Cab and complained about me. At the time, Chu was rated the top tenor saxophonist in New York; whatever he said, Cab listened to.

But the very same day Cab gave me notice, I got a call from Wayman Carver. "Chauncey Haughton's going to leave, and Chick wants you to come take his place." The next day I went to rehearsal with Webb, and that night we played the Savoy.[1] Our first theater date was at the Apollo with Ella.

When Clarence Robinson saw me, he said, "Rev, you in this band now? What happened?"

"I just changed orchestras," I said.

"Oh, man."

He couldn't understand why I'd leave Cab to go with Webb, since Chick and Ella weren't anything then. My feathers were really cropped. My ego was deflated. But it turned out that Chick's was the better band, and later I felt as though the move was a good one.

When I joined Chick in 1937 it wasn't the first time I'd played with him. He'd hired me some years before, in the early thirties, to do a few weeks with him. Big [Charlie] Green was in the band then, and Bobby Stark. We went out on the road, but we weren't getting paid. We went out to Pennsylvania, playing in Pittsburgh, Hershey, and Harrisburg. In Harrisburg we stayed with a woman named Caroline, who had a large boardinghouse. Nobody had any money. But Caroline was nice to us, because Chick had been through before. Caroline served liquor and had women there; you could go upstairs with a chick anytime you wanted. So Caroline let us sleep on the floor of her living room, all sixteen of us.

The next morning the valet woke us up and said we had to leave, since we were supposed to be on Long Island that night. Caroline said, "You got any money, boys?" I don't think there was two dollars between the whole sixteen of us. But she gave us bacon and eggs and coffee, and sent us on our way.

When we got to the dance way out on Long Island, we said, "Webb, we get paid tonight or we don't work no more."

"I'll do the best I can," he said. But we didn't get paid that night, either.

So we were heading back to New York in our two Cadillacs, and the chauffeurs hadn't been paid, either. One of them pulled over on the side of the road, and said: "Webb, you've got some money, and you're going to pay me. I don't care about the damn band, but give me some money for gas."

Chick said, "I ain't got it."

The chauffeur opened up the car and started taking out all the music stands and books. We got out to help him. There was Chick with his drums and books and stands way out on Long Island, at four o'clock in the morning. We left him sitting there in the woods by himself.

He just said, "It's all right. I don't give a damn."

We figured he might come through with some money, but he didn't. He called our bluff!

We started to drive off, but after a while turned around to get him. It had started to thunder and lightning.

"Y'all didn't have to come back," he said. "Don't make no difference to me. I ain't got no money. That's it."

We told him to get in the car, and took him back to New York.

Now, when I joined Chick for the second time, I said, "Don't you want to pay me what you owe me?"

He said, "I didn't make nothin'. I ain't gonna pay you."

He may have been right about making no money. His band wasn't pulling well then. Before Ella came in, it hadn't got far.

Musically it was much more pleasurable with Webb than with Cab. The arrangements were better, and featured the band more. The sections had a better quality of sound. And in order to feature Webb, we had to play some uptempo tunes. But there were other inconveniences, such as transportation—no more Pullmans, now we traveled in buses. The salary was lower, too, something like $47–$50 a week. And work was less consistent. We'd go in and out of the Savoy.

Touring the South with Chick was better than with Cab. The black people accepted Ella and Chick more than they did Cab Calloway; the whites went for Cab. Therefore, with Chick we had more social activity— we were invited to parties and social affairs. With Cab, sometimes blacks didn't even know we were in town: "You guys playing downtown? Didn't know that."

Occasionally we'd have "battles of the bands." I remember we couldn't win when we faced Jimmy Lunceford. He was too powerful, and had a unique band. Sy Oliver's arrangements had a different style, a different concept from ours. They could swing a band right off the pickup. People would just coattail. They could dance to that. Webb's band wasn't quite as low in tempo, and Jimmy Crawford could put in a certain feel that Chick never could do.

When you had to play opposite Ellington's band, you'd stand off to the side and say, "I haven't had breakfast yet. I feel funny, I haven't eaten." Ellington just washed out everybody.

With Webb, as with Cab, I mostly played alto. But I took some clarinet spots, too, though I never liked them. When Eddie Barefield took over the band after Webb died, he made arrangements that had better clarinet solos and more things to work on.

Webb was an uneducated cripple, and those people are sensitive. I don't think he could read or write his name. I never saw him try to read a paper. He didn't know 1 percent, 2 percent of nothing. But he had a fantastic memory. The band would go through an arrangement once, and he could come up on the stand and play it.

To my knowledge, Chick was the first drummer that became publicly known to drum the arrangement. Gene Krupa got a lot of his style from

Chick. Even so, Chick didn't inspire soloists in his band, because his beat always lagged when he wasn't taking a solo. You'd get up there and lose all the fire you had. But his solo drumming was sensational.

Chick also had a good concept of what a hit would be. He's the one that picked "A-Tisket, A-Tasket." Everybody said, "I don't want to hear that garbage."

"Oh," he said, "you can never tell." It turned out to be the biggest hit Ella ever had.

Ella was about seventeen when we put her on the bus. It was pretty lonesome for her, because none of us paid her any mind. She was big and gawky. She never made an impression on anybody.

Wayman Carver and I would usually bunk together or stay at the same house. I always considered him more intellectual than most of them. I stayed away from Taft Jordan. He was noisy and loud. Nat Story was in everybody's business. He'd always talk and talk and talk. I might hang out with Beverly Peer, the bass player. Teddy McRae was a loner who never associated with anybody.

Hilton Jefferson was easy to get along with. He lost his eyesight for a time when he was in the band. We were playing in Pittsburgh, and I had to take him every day and put him in the cab. "Jeff" was a loner, too. It was never too straight in my mind just what Jeff and his life philosophy was. He was a very peculiar-acting person—intelligent, though, and a fine artist. I think he was a troubled sort of man. His mind was never clear. You could feel that there was always something that worried him, something that kept him from doing much talking. I had been with many men who didn't know what side of the fence they were on, and they were a very troubled lot of people. I discovered that in Ben Webster, and also in Hilton. Their minds were in turmoil. But I never let that bother me. They were great artists, and I loved them both.

Bardu Ali was our conductor. His father was Egyptian, and he looked it. He had been part of an act with his brothers, the Ali brothers. They were tumblers, and did one of those fast Arab acts. Chick had him stand in front of the band because he was so handsome. He couldn't sing. He couldn't dance. But he could move around and had a conception of how to conduct.

For some reason, Chick wanted his band to sound like a first-class white band, so he used these white arrangers like Al Feldman that he thought were great. But they didn't arrange for colored bands, they didn't write the things we played. They knew the voicings, but not the rhythmic patterns, the placement of ideas and riffs. So consequently Chick didn't have the Negroid interpretation that Sy Oliver or Jimmy Lunceford or Duke Ellington had. Chick had no original ideas to draw on for his concept of what the band should be like.

What really made the band, though, was Ella. Chick was smart enough to see that. But Ella's one problem was that she didn't have a tremendous amount of personality on stage. She couldn't put over a number like Louis Jordan, who was in the band when I joined. Louis would go out and just gas, break up the show. Nobody could follow him. Louis was overshadowing Ella, so Chick decided to fire him.

In the summer of 1938 we were at the RKO in Boston when Chick decided to get rid of Louis without giving notice. Louis was always hollering, "If you don't like what I do, fire me!" I heard this down the hall, after the show.

I remember Chick said, "Well, that's exactly what I'm going to do."
Louis said, "You're going to let me go? Why don't you fire Bushell?"
"I'm firing who I *want* to fire," Chick replied.

And that was the best thing that ever happened to Louis, because he got a job at the Speedway in New York—that's where he started his Tympany Five—and that was it.

On the last tour with Chick, in June of 1939, we played a job on a boat on the Potomac. It was a white dance. Chick was pretty sick, and the next night they put him in a hospital in Baltimore, and we went on down South. We were playing at a black Masonic Temple in Alabama, and Tim Gale—our road manager—said, "Everyone come back here in the room during intermission." When we went in there, we weren't surprised to hear that he'd died. We knew he couldn't last that long.[2]

While we were talking about what to do, some of the Masons wanted to get into the lodge room. Tim Gale had forgotten that there were certain times when being white was a disadvantage in the South. He hadn't let these people know that we were having a private meeting. A big guy outside said, "Don't you lock this door and prevent me from coming in, because I have to pay for every crack of wood and stone in this building."
"Well," Tim said, "we got bad news."
"I don't care."
"All right, we'll come out."

We went back on the stand, and it was a very sorry last half we played. Chick had his faults, but we liked him.

Afterward we went back to Baltimore and waited there for his funeral.

Early in the morning the day before, I went out to the little house where Chick often had stayed with his uncle. The casket was on view there, and Gene Krupa—who was playing in town then—was sitting by the casket and sobbing. He idolized Chick Webb. Later I came back and Gene was still sitting there. He stayed all day.

The following day they stopped traffic all across the city for his funeral procession. They hadn't even done that for the mayor, but they did it for Chick and paid their respects.

After Chick died, I stayed with the band a little while. Then they got rid of Bardu and were going to bring in Eddie Barefield and put him in front of the band. They wanted to emulate a Benny Goodman setup. When I heard Barefield was coming—so they wouldn't need me as a clarinet player—I put in my notice, and beat them to the punchline.[3]

NOTES

1. According to John Chilton, in *Who's Who of Jazz,* 4th ed. (New York: Da Capo, 1985), this was November of 1937. Bushell's first record with Webb was 17 December 1937, and Haughton's with Calloway was 10 December 1937.
2. Webb died 16 June 1939.
3. Eddie Barefield's first recording with the Webb band, under Fitzgerald's nominal leadership, was 15 February 1940, so presumably Bushell left in January or early February of that year.

12

ON MY OWN

After I left Chick Webb I began free-lancing. In the fall of 1939 I did a record date with trumpeter Eddie Mallory, whom I had known in Charlie Turner's Arcadians. Ethel Waters sang on that one. Then I did a brief stint with Teddy Hill—a week at the Savoy, and a week at the Orpheum Theater in Memphis with the singer Maxine Sullivan. We didn't draw flies in Memphis. They couldn't care less about "Loch Lomond" down there. The theater owner was disturbed because he wasn't making any money. I remember in the second show, Teddy announced Maxine as "Miss Maxine Sullivan." The theater owner sent word backstage to change it for the next show. He said, "Folks down here aren't used to introducing a Negro woman as Miss. Just call her by her name." It was a white theater, but they allowed Negroes up in the gallery.

I suppose Maxine wasn't singing a Memphis type of music. Bessie Smith would have packed them in. But anyhow, I could never see why they tried to make Maxine Sullivan into a big record star. She was cute and looked good on stage, but she didn't have much of a voice. She was an average singer. Since I'd worked with Ethel Waters, Mamie Smith, and Bessie Smith, you had to do better than that to impress me. And Cab impressed me because he was something different.

I also played with Edgar Hayes's big band around New York and on the road in Pennsylvania and New England. Since I had just come off the big bands, I had the reputation as a first alto player, so both Hill and Hayes used me for that.

I had known Edgar Hayes back in Ohio in 1918, and played with him in a band at Wilberforce. He was glad to have me in the band, and treated me wonderfully. I was more or less the straw boss, and he allowed me to arrange. He was a marvelous pianist, and a good arranger himself.

We played opposite Jimmy Dorsey once, who was a favorite in those days. Black bands sounded so different from white ones. For one thing, our musicianship wasn't as good as in the white bands. Also, our saxophones and brass played too hard, and we were louder. That's why quite often the white bands would sound better in the record studios.

SLIM GAILLARD

Slim Gaillard was a weird character. Nobody compares with him at all. After my stint with Edgar Hayes I did two months with Slim, mostly in Philadelphia and Wilmington, Delaware. We made some records, too, with Henry Goodwin on trumpet, Loumell Morgan on piano, Slam Stewart or Nick Fenton on bass, and Hubert Pettaway on drums.[1]

Slim was one of the happiest musicians I've ever been around. He was also wild and unpredictable. You could never trust him. He was strong and powerful, and if you asked him too much about money he owed you he'd fight you. He'd always get drunk on payday and you couldn't find him.

Slim was a genius. He just created things, one after another. He spoke another language. When he talked to you offstage, it was "Hey, allright a rooney! How you doin', poppaseeda?" He spoke this weird, jazz patois, all this "rooty toot de toot" and "putty de doot toot." He was a quirk, but a genius.

There were two periods when I was satisfied with my clarinet playing. One was with Wilbur De Paris, the other with Slim Gaillard. I didn't touch the saxophone at all during my time with Slim. I had fallen in love with the clarinet again.

In Slim's group we had some organized patterns and then a certain amount of freedom to do what we wanted. That's what I liked more about getting back with the small groups in the forties: you could interpret things your own way, whereas in a big band you had to play the way someone else wanted it.

Down in Delaware there was an old widow in her sixties or seventies who took a liking to me. She managed the dining room at this black hotel where we stayed. Her husband had been very rich. I figured she still had some money. (I was looking for anything I could get my hands on, in those days.) She let me operate the cash register in the hotel, until the owner came in one day and gave her hell. I shacked up with her the whole time we were down there.

But I could only tolerate playing with Slim for so long. You had to hunt for him every Saturday night to get your money, and then maybe you wouldn't find him 'til the middle of the week.

LEXINGTON CASINO

So in the fall of 1940 I left Slim and started building my own six-piece group. We auditioned at a spot on lower Broadway called The Place—Gene Sedric also had a band there. We got the gig and stayed two weeks. But the third week I was hit by a motorcycle when I was crossing the street at St. Nicholas and 125th Street. I was in the hospital twenty-six days, so the gig fell through.

When I got out of the hospital I started practicing again and reorganized. I got word that a guy in Philadelphia wanted a band at a place called the Lexington Casino. (Bardu Ali had a ten-piece band there, and the owner was getting rid of it.) So he set up an audition in New York and hired my six-piece band. Johnny Russell was on sax, Bernard Flood on trumpet, Herbie Cowens on drums, Kenneth Billings on piano, and a bass player named Turner (everybody just called him "Bass"). They were all free-lancers at the time. I had about ten arrangements ready, and we kept playing these until I got some more made. We went there for four weeks and stayed seven months.

The Lexington Casino was on the road from New York to Philadelphia, about three or four miles outside of Philly. They had shows and vaude-ville-type acts there, and I did a little work as emcee. During the day I wrote arrangements for the group. Every Saturday after we finished I'd take the train back to New York, if I could.

I enjoyed working at the Lexington Casino because I was developing a band there. I did have a little trouble with Herb Cowens. He went to the union and told them we'd been playing two minutes' overtime one night, three minutes the next, and he added it all up and had a couple of hours overtime. He sued me and didn't get a quarter. Herb was pushy, a hustler. He even pushed his tempo ahead and you couldn't keep up with it.

Harry Weinberg was the owner of the Lexington Casino. He was an ex-fighter with a temper. Harry said to Herb, "You don't get a penny out of

me. You played two minutes over? You ought to be ashamed of yourself."
I had to hold Harry to keep him from beating up Herb. But it turned out all
right.

When our contract expired Johnny Russell was drafted and the band
broke up. This must have been in 1942.

USO SHOWS WITH EUBIE BLAKE

For a season I played in an orchestra led by Eubie Blake
for USO shows. Noble Sissle was in charge of the black section of the
USO, and he put Eubie in front of a band that was touring around. It was a
twelve-piece unit—a dance band, more or less. We performed in pits and
theaters all over the camps on the USO circuit.

Since we played down in the South, lots of unpleasant incidents cropped up.

In Columbia, South Carolina, Eubie refused to play because they made
the Negro officers sit in the back of the theater. The officers were supposed to sit in the third or fourth row, but the MPs got up and made the
Negro captains and lieutenants move back. Eubie said, "Wait a minute.
We don't play."

A warrant officer came up. "Mr. Blake, this is scheduled to go on."

"No."

"Why not?"

"Not without those officers sitting where they're supposed to sit. You
don't do that to me." So Eubie turned to us and said, "Come on, out of the
pit."

About five minutes later the colonel came down and confronted Eubie.
Eubie stood his ground, and the colonel had to go and see that the
officers could return to their seats. Eubie played "The Star-Spangled Banner," and it was on with the show.

I hated traveling in the South. I was a nervous wreck. In our Pullman,
we had to wait until people brought food in to us; we couldn't eat in the
diner. One time we were in Texas and there were forty-five or fifty German
prisoners on the train. They marched them at gunpoint up to the diner to
eat. Here we were, starving in our car, and they were feeding *prisoners* in
the diner, but wouldn't let genuine, fourth- and fifth-generation Americans go in there to eat. And we weren't bums—we were the artists entertaining the soldiers. This was the 1940s, during World War II.

I made one whole tour with the USO, but on my second time out, in '43,

I quit before it was over. I left in Charleston, South Carolina, and got on a train to come home. They put me on a Jim Crow car with crates of chickens, cans of milk, and a few black country folks sitting in the baggage compartment. I was miserable there. When the conductor came by he saw my Masonic pin on, and I saw his, and I asked him if he could give me a better seat. He did me a favor, possibly because I was a Mason, and I rode a Pullman all the way back to New York.[2]

PASTOR'S

When I got back I organized a five-piece group, and this time went down to Tony Pastor's in the Village. For the next two years we stayed there six nights a week. I used different guys at Pastor's—Ram Ramirez, Wellman Braud, Louis Bacon, Bobby Stark, and others. Victoria Barksdale—wife of the guitarist Everett Barksdale—played piano for me. She was a good reader. Each player made $47.50 a week, and I made about $20.00 more. The pay wasn't much, but believe it or not, we were happy there.

Pastor's was a cabaret on Eighth Street, with a bar in front and a back section. It was a hangout place for lesbians, and since this was the Village, it goes without saying that there were quite a few peculiar people who came in. Different entertainers would perform there, and we played shows in addition to our own sets. Pat Rossi was one of the singers. At times Tony Pastor himself was on the bill.

One night I was standing outside of Pastor's talking with Pat Rossi. That part of New York was all Italian then, and it was wartime. A young Italian fellow there made this remark, "You know, you colored folks got to make a stand for something. You've got to be proud to be Americans and make it stand for something."

I lit into him, beginning, "You don't know your history." I told him about Crispus Attucks and the Revolutionary War, about Toussaint L'Ouverture and the slave uprising in Haiti, about the outstanding Negro heroes in World War I. I told him about the first heart surgeon, and about the man who invented the third rail and the air brake. I told him about the creation of American music and some of our Negro writers. He stood there and listened until finally someone said, "Hey, Bushell! Your time's up. Time to go back on the stand."

Later, Rossi said, "You gave him a liberal education there."

I said, "I wanted to. These are the kind of people who need it. If they have the nerve to insult people, they need to be told." There were many who were ignorant about who the Negroes were, where we came from, and how long we'd been here.

THE RESTAURANT BUSINESS

I was impressed by two of the cooks down at Pastor's—one woman was Irish, the other Italian—so I asked them, "How would you like to go up to Harlem and open a restaurant?" They said they'd love to.

I had finally gotten $10,000 as settlement of the motorcycle accident case from several years before and wanted to invest the money. So these two women and I bought this place on Seventh Avenue, between 133rd and 134th, and opened up an Italian-American restaurant. All during 1945 and part of 1946 I kept it going. In those days you had food stamps, and if you ran out, you were in trouble. But friends I'd made in the Village helped me get supplies for the restaurant. Many times I had pork chops and chicken in my freezer when other restaurants on Seventh Avenue had run out.

I sold my alto saxophone, which I regretted very much. Because I was making good money, I thought I'd never play again. But I'd miss music when the guys would come in. They, on the other hand, envied me for getting out of the music business.

Hilda and I would split shifts—she'd take the day, and I'd often come in at night. But eventually the strain became too much. All of a sudden I had a nervous breakdown and had to sell the place. My health just blew up on me.

I was out of commission for a long time, and all my restaurant money went to medical expenses. But by the end of 1946 I was pretty well on my way to normal. I went into Pastor's again briefly, but no one was much impressed. So I started teaching at my home, at 574 St. Nicholas Avenue (near Edgecombe), and began practicing clarinet much more seriously.

THE SYMPHONIC SIDE

In the late 1940s, groups like the Urban League and the NAACP were pushing for Negro musicians to be more involved in symphony orchestras, recording, and other aspects of the music field. They were always harping on how there was a lack of Negro participation in major orchestras.

At the time I was trying to broaden myself, looking to other fields. In those days everything had to be a challenge, something that nobody else could do. Not many Negro musicians were playing bassoon. I remember being intrigued by Herb Johnson's sound on bassoon with Wooding's band and the fact that the bassoon was a weird instrument. I began to hear that bassoon was one of the most important instruments in the symphony. You can often hear it all the way through. And it played in three clefs—tenor, treble, and bass—which was also a challenge.

I began studying with Simon Kovar. All bassoon students in those days went to Kovar, who had retired from the Philharmonic and had played with it for forty or fifty years. At the time he was about eighty-seven years old.

Then I took from Eli Carmen, who played with the Ballet Theater orchestra. He knew I was doubling and playing jazz. His idea was to get me to think in a different way when playing bassoon, to practice daily the right posture, the right tonguing, the right amount of air. I used to see Eli every week until he got busy, then I switched to Angel DelBusto, a member of the Goldman band.

Eli recommended me for the American Ballet Theater Orchestra. I didn't have to audition; I just came in and made the first rehearsal, playing third chair. I sat next to Bernard Garfield, who was for a long time bassoonist with the Philadelphia Orchestra. He tried out my reed and taught me some things about making reeds.

There was quite a bit of resentment on the part of white musicians to keep blacks out of orchestras. When I went to the Ballet Theater no one spoke to me for three days. On the third day I had a solo, and one of the oboists said to me afterwards, "Are you new in New York?"

"No, I've been here almost thirty years. Why?"

"I've never heard of you."

"Well, I'm trying to make it so you'll hear more of me."

Another important part of my symphonic training came from Maximilian Waldo, who conducted the Heights Symphony in Manhattan. We rehearsed twice a week. Waldo was very thorough, and explained everything. He showed me that I was coming in too soon, that the downbeat actually began later than I thought. I'd played in concert bands before and wondered why I was ahead, but no one had ever explained it to me.

I also began studying oboe with Al Goltzer and Bruno Labate. As a result, I was able to fill oboe and English horn positions around town, including concerts with the Radio City Hall Orchestra. I never experienced more tension than when I went into Radio City and the opening number featured me on the English horn playing in six flats. I was scared to death, and my knees wouldn't stop shaking. I'd been in show business all my life, and was used to the jitters and nervousness you had on opening day, or when you were the opening act. But there's more pressure in a symphony orchestra than playing jazz, because you can't make any mistakes. Still, the more challenges I had, the more I could endure the pressure, and the more I could make it.

Around this time I faced another incident of discrimination. I had registered down at radio station WJZ that I played oboe, bassoon, clarinet, and saxophone. Finally I got a call from a secretary who worked for the contractor.

"Mr. Bushell, can you come down to the office?"

"Sure."

"How soon can you get here?"

"As soon as the train will get me there."

"Well, there's a job in Paul Whiteman's orchestra. The chair pays $350 a week, play bassoon and saxophone."

I said I'd be right down; I'd never made anything like $350 a week. That was top salary then. I rushed down to the office and the contractor looked at me and said, "Are you Bushell?"

"Yes."

He looked down at my application. "But the chair calls for a flute player."

I said, "But you knew I didn't play flute. I didn't have flute on my application."

"Yeah, but the girl, she make a mistake, the chair calls for flute. I'm sorry."

I walked out and went right over to the musician's union. I told the business agent there that I'd been offered a job, the salary was stated, but the minute I got down there they took back the offer. The agent said, "That's what he did to you?" He came with me straight back to the contractor's office, marched in, and said, "I hope you aren't guilty of what I think is going on here."

"Why?"

"This man says you offered him a job and quoted a salary, then refused to give it to him. Why?"

"But the chair calls for a flute player. The girl, she make a mistake. Let

Ella Scott ("Gram")

*Anderson Penn,
Garvin's maternal
grandfather*

*Dressed up for Sunday
with leather cap, bow
tie, and cowboy gloves,
Springfield, Ohio, 1911
or 1912*

At a Detroit amusement park, on tour with Mamie Smith's Jazz Hounds, 1921. Horace, the band's drummer, is in foreground.

Sam Wooding's band at the Nest Club, New York, 1923. Left to right: Herbert Johnson, John Warren, Garvin Bushell, Sam Wooding, George Howe, Bobby Martin, Johnny Mitchell, Maceo Edwards.

Sam Wooding's Orchestra in the Vox Phonograph Studio, Berlin, July 1925. Seated, left to right: *Tommy Ladnier, John Warren (behind Ladnier), Sam Wooding, Willie Lewis, George Howe.* Standing, left to right: *Herb Flemming, Eugene Sedric, Johnny Mitchell, Bobby Martin, Garvin Bushell, Maceo Edwards.*

"At Curiosity's Expense," Copenhagen, 1925. Left to right: *Herb Flemming, Shaky Beasley, Garvin Bushell.*

Garvin and Caesar, Königsberg, 1926

Madrid, Circo de Price, 1926.

Top: Front row, left to right: *Willie Robbins, Bobby Vincent, Thelma Watkins, Baby Goines, Jessie Crawford,* unidentified. Second row, left to right: *Thaddeus "Teddy" Drayton, Arabella Field, Enid Boucher, Thelma Green, Bernice Miles, Allegretti Anderson, Mamie Savoy, Rita Walker, George Staton,* unidentified, *Rufus Greenlee.* Back row: *Willie Lewis,* two others unidentified. The large papier-mâché head was not used in the show, just picked up backstage at the Circo de Price.

Center: Left to right: *George Howe, Willie Lewis, Eugene Sedric, Garvin Bushell, John Warren, Sam Wooding (seated), Johnny Mitchell, Tommy Ladnier, Bobby Martin, Herb Flemming, Maceo Edwards.*

Bottom: *"Tap drill"* scene from Chocolate Kiddies. Left to right: *Thelma Green, Bernice Miles, Allegretti Anderson, Mamie Savoy, Thelma Watkins, Enid Boucher, Bobby Vincent, Rita Walker, Baby Goines, Jessie Crawford.*

EN EL CIRCO DE PRICE   LOS "CHOCOLAT KIDDIES

Harlem cafe scene from Chocolate Kiddies, *probably Moscow, 1926.* Front row, left to right: *Bobby Vincent, Maud de Forest, Bobby Goines, Baby Goines, Arabella Field, Thaddeus "Teddy" Drayton (standing), Willie Robbins.* Back, left to right: *first two unidentified, Jessie Crawford (standing), Enid Boucher, Allegretti Anderson, Thelma Green, George Staton, Thelma Watkins [?], Rufus Greenlee.*

Arriving at the theater, Moscow, 1926

Sam Wooding's
Orchestra, Hamburg,
1925. Left to right: *Willie
Lewis, Eugene Sedric,
Leslie "King" Edwards,
Garvin Bushell, Sam*
*Wooding, Johnny
Mitchell, Percy Johnson,
Bobby Martin, Herb
Flemming, Maceo
Edwards.*

The Wooding reed
section, Hamburg, 1926.
Left to right: *Willie
Lewis, Eugene Sedric,
Garvin Bushell.*

Buddy Gilmore, "To My
Pals and Friends Mr.
and Mrs. Bushell,"
Hamburg, 30 September
1926

Charlie Turner and His Arcadians, 1934. Left to right: *Emmett Mathews, Charlie Turner, Hank Duncan, Jack Butler, Wayman Carver, "Abe Lincoln," Herman Autrey, Al Washington, Garvin Bushell, Fred Robinson, Davey Martin, Slick Jones, Bobby Stark.*

Cab Calloway's Orchestra on the Vitaphone soundstage for "Hi-De-Ho," 1937. Front row, left to right: *Bennie Payne, Cab Calloway, Morris White, Doc Cheatham, Lammar Wright, Irving Randolph.* Middle, left to right: *Garvin Bushell, Walter "Foots" Thomas, Keg Johnson, Claude Jones, De Priest Wheeler.* Back, left to right: *Ben Webster, Andrew Brown, Leroy Maxey, Milt Hinton.*

Cab Calloway's
baseball team in
Minneapolis, 1936 or
1937. Front row, left to
right: "Mack" (husband
of singer Avis Andrews),
Milt Hinton, Leroy
Maxey, a member of the
"tramp band." Back,
left to right: Bennie
Payne, Claude Jones,
Cab Calloway, one of
Cab's valets, Garvin
Bushell, another valet,
De Priest "Mickey"
Wheeler.

With Ben Webster
backstage at the Loew's
State Theater, 45th and
Broadway, 1936 or 1937

Singing with Cab. Left to right: *Garvin Bushell, Morris White, Andrew Brown, Ben Webster, Milt Hinton, Walter "Foots" Thomas.*

Chick Webb's Orchestra at the Apollo Theater, probably 1938. Left to right: *Mario Bauza, Beverly Peer, Bobby Stark, Nat Story, Sandy Williams, Bardu Ali, Chick Webb, Ella Fitzgerald, George Matthews, Bobby Johnson, Teddy McRae, Wayman Carver, Hilton Jefferson, Taft Jordan, Garvin Bushell, Tommy Fulford.*

Chick Webb's Orchestra.
Foreground right (back
to camera): *Bardu Ali.*
Front row, left to right:
Tommy Fulford, Beverly
Peer, Chick Webb,
Wayman Carver, Teddy
McRae, Garvin Bushell,
Hilton Jefferson. Back,
left to right: *Bobby*
Johnson, Taft Jordan,
Bobby Stark, Dick
Vance, George
Matthews, Nat Story,
Sandy Williams.

Soloing with the Chick
Webb Orchestra at
Loew's State, probably
1939 (after Webb's
death). Left to right: *Bill*
Beason (partly
obscured by drums),
Taft Jordan, Bobby
Stark, Wayman Carver,
Dick Vance, Garvin
Bushell, Nat Story
(behind microphone),
Edgar Sampson, Sandy
Williams, Hilton
Jefferson.

Garvin Bushell's band and other acts at the Lexington Casino, Philadelphia, 1941. Owner Harry Weinberg stands front and center. Back, left to right: unidentified bassist, Richard Bach, Bernard Flood, Garvin Bushell, Herbie Cowens, Johnny Russell, unidentified pianist.

Garvin Bushell's Italian-American Restaurant, Harlem, mid-1940s

Peekaboo Jimmy's "gig band," Carver Auditorium, Harlem. Left to right: *"Peekaboo" Jimmy Davis, Claude Blakemore, unidentified, Garvin Bushell, Jock Martin, unidentified.*

In his New York studio, 1950s

Marching in a parade honoring Sidney Bechet, Juan-les-pins, France, 1960. Left to right: *Wilbert Kirk, Sidney De Paris, Garvin Bushell, Doc Cheatham, Wilbur De Paris.*

Wilbur De Paris's New New Orleans Jazz Band. Left to right: *Sonny White, Wilbert Kirk, Hayes Alvis, John Smith, Garvin Bushell, Doc Cheatham (hidden), Wilbur De Paris, Sidney De Paris.*

Bushell (at left) in
Rhodesia, 1964

The Bushells in Las
Vegas. Left to right:
Philip, Louise, Garvin,
Garvin Jr.

*With George Popo's
Concert Jazz Band, Las
Vegas*

*In his Las Vegas studio,
1983. (Photograph by
Patricia Mortati.)*

me see the man's application." In the meantime, he had pencilled in flute to the job description, and he'd also taken the bassoon and tenor book and slipped a flute part in it.

The agent said, "Well, all right. But if I find out that you've done anything you shouldn't do, you're going to pay this man. You're going to hire him and pay him for every week for fifteen weeks."

I called up Nat Reines and told him about the job, saying they needed a bassoon player. Nat went down there and got the job; it didn't call for flute at all. I told the agent what had happened, and he said, "You want to sue him? You can sue him and get every penny for the fifteen weeks you're supposed to get, the $350 a week." So I began to think. I wanted to get into radio on a staff position. If I made it uncomfortable for them now, then I wouldn't get the opportunity. So I just let it slide. Whiteman had never had a black musician in his orchestra, and he wasn't about to start then.

WILD BILL AND BUNK

Meanwhile, people were beginning to recreate so-called Dixieland jazz, and I was getting a lot of calls on clarinet. In 1946 and 1947 I had the opportunity to play with two well-known trumpet players, Wild Bill Davison and Bunk Johnson.

Rudi Blesh hired me for one date with Wild Bill Davison, way up in Vermont or New Hampshire. After that I played on all Wild Bill's things around New York for a while. Bill had a lot of drive in his playing. You felt like playing when he kicked off a tempo. There was nothing laid back about it.

We mainly played for white audiences around town. I don't think the people of Harlem would have accepted what we were doing. For black audiences, music has to have a certain feeling, a certain groove. It also has to tell a story. They don't absorb it just because it's music. It may be a dangerous story, or a wild one, but it must be expressed.

In 1946 I got called to do a date with Bunk Johnson at the Stuyvesant Casino. Bunk had moved to New York the previous year, and this was the first time he'd heard me. From then on he wanted me to play with him, and I recorded an album with him. When we got out of the record date it was snowing outside and the traffic was all tied up in knots.

Bunk said, "My God, look at all this snow. You *know* I'm going back to New Orleans." He did go back, and died not long after.[3]

Bunk was one of the few New Orleans musicians who could read. But he didn't play the New Orleans style I expected to hear. He played the way they used to all up and down the East Coast, in New York, or even in Springfield—he sounded more like Jack Hatton or Seymour Irick. It was a ragtime style of trumpet. When we played "The Entertainer" we sounded just like an old-time pit orchestra playing those orchestrations. I didn't hear any traces of Freddie Keppard, Fats Williams, Joe Sutler, Mutt Carey, or Louis Armstrong in Bunk's playing.

I have to say that Bunk never impressed me as a trumpet player. I certainly wouldn't rank him with the great trumpeters from New Orleans. His reputation is such because history and the media made it so. You don't get anything from these guys coming out who haven't played in twenty years, but it's a commodity for marketing. Maybe Bunk didn't sound better because he was having problems with his teeth or was past his prime. But where is the evidence of his playing when he was in his prime? We don't have it.

PEEKABOO

I was also with a gig group in Harlem in the late forties led by Peekaboo Jimmy. His name was Jimmy Davis, but everybody called him Peekaboo. He was an ex-fighter and used to be one of the bouncers at the Savoy. But he was so vicious and knocked out so many people that they had to put him out of the job. He was built like Rocky Marciano, and wobbled when he walked.

Peekaboo was a mediocre drummer but a good performer. He used to play with the Clef Club groups and had been trained in the Clef Club tradition of being very polite and gracious. You'd never know he was a tough guy. He was in his late fifties when I played with him.

Our group had Jock Martin on trumpet, Claude Blakemore on tenor, Carl Diton on piano, Peekaboo on drums, and I was on alto. We had gigs all around Harlem playing for Negro society balls and club dances. These jobs never paid more than ten dollars a man, but I enjoyed doing them. Peekaboo also played alto, so we could have four-part harmony with the trumpet taking the lead and Peekaboo beating the bass drum. If we were performing in a little hall and using a microphone we sounded like a big band. All these creative things were done to compensate for what you didn't have. The music was interesting because every time you played you were challenged to create something new.

Carl Diton was a concert pianist and composer who had studied in Germany and at Juilliard. He was a very cultured man. I wasn't in his league, but I became good friends with him. People would be amazed to see him with this gig band: "Professor Diton!" they'd exclaim in disbelief.

Peekaboo and I finally had a falling out. We were playing a job, I made some comment, and he replied, "What are you doing, trying to run my band?" That hit me hard, because I didn't need his work. I had my own teaching business by then.

So I said, "Anything I've ever done or said in this band, I did it for you. I need this job like I need a hole in the head."

A left hook wouldn't have hurt him more than that. The next time he called me for a gig, I said no thank you.

NOTES

1. Rust lists the bassist as Slam Stewart on four sides made in August 1940, then Nick Fenton on four sides recorded in September. But Bushell has identified one of the singers on the September date as Slam Stewart (see app. A).
2. Bushell became a Mason—together with Milt Hinton and Ben Webster—in St. Paul, Minnesota, while on tour with Cab Calloway.
3. The record was Bunk Johnson's *Last Testament,* recorded 23, 24, and 26 December 1947 (see app. A). Johnson died 7 July 1949 in New Iberia, Louisiana.

13

Settling Down

In 1950 I was in Chicago with *Angel in the Pawnshop*, which eventually became a Broadway show; we went there to break it in. Eddie Dowling and Joan McCracken starred in it, and Willie Lewis played in the band. Willie had a walk-on part with spoken lines. One night I took his place when he didn't make it. In the first scene I ran into a pawnshop to hawk my clarinet. Eddie Dowling asked me, "What's the matter with you, boy? Who you running from?"

"Landlord and stomach." I had had stage experience and knew what to do and how to move. There was no fooling around.

We were with the show in Chicago several months. I stayed with Edith Wilson, out on the South Side, and Willie lived next door with Edith's uncle.

During this time I heard of a bassoon chair vacancy in the Chicago Civic Symphony. Since I wanted to keep up my bassoon playing, I went to the rehearsal.

At the rehearsal they put me in the first bassoon chair. We were running through Dvořák's *New World* Symphony, and when it came time to play a brief passage in the first movement, my horn wouldn't make a sound. The conductor pointed to me again. Still nothing came out. So he pointed to the woman sitting next to me in the second bassoon chair, and she played it in a certain fashion, though it wasn't what he wanted. Meanwhile I had taken the wing joint off my bassoon and discovered that during intermission someone had dropped a nail down into the boot joint of my bassoon. I got right up in the middle of the movement and said, "Look what's happened to my bassoon! This is why I couldn't play, there was a nail in it."

The conductor stopped the orchestra and said, "That's one of the most despicable tricks I have seen perpetrated in an orchestra where there are professionals and artists." Then he explained to them that racial attitudes were out of place in the orchestra, and gave me back my first chair.

Some of the orchestra members stayed belligerent the whole time I was there. But I was a fighter. I knew I had to fight to get what I wanted, since in these cases I was often the first black that had done this kind of thing. I'd conditioned my mind to accept it and be ready to fight back. That was my creed then. I surely wasn't the bassoonist then that I later became. But I was as good as any of the rest of them.

Those were critical times for a black person. Any time you left home you had problems—even in your home you had problems with basic maintenance. It was a problem trying to get a job with a decent salary, because they conspired to get you out. They figured you weren't supposed to achieve something unusual, so you always had to be on your toes. It was the same situation with musicians: if you had a job, you had to be careful to protect it, because they'd always foment some bit of chicanery, some scheme by which they could get you fired.

There was another problem, too. Classical players tended to look down their noses at jazz musicians, assuming you were less accomplished (and envying the fact that you were making money). If a jazz musician came along who could do what a classical player did, you were the enemy, especially if you were a doubler. Today that's changed; to play jazz is considered much more of an accomplishment.

TEACHING IN THE STUDIO

When I came back from Chicago in 1951, one of the players with the show knew that John Costello wanted a woodwind teacher for his studio on 49th Street, just off Seventh Avenue. I went down to see John and he said, "Sure, like to have you." He gave me the inside studio that looked out both on 49th Street and Seventh Avenue. It was a very good location, right off Broadway in the heart of Times Square. So I started teaching there and wound up staying for fifteen years. Costello had his trumpet students, and I brought in woodwind students, which enhanced his business. I never had to advertise. I had a big sign on the window that read, "Garvin Bushell Woodwind Studio." And I brought students downtown who had been coming to my place in Harlem.

In those days I was getting five dollars an hour for teaching. I worked my butt off and would come home with fifty dollars if I'd had ten pupils that day. Steve Lawrence, the singer, was struggling along then, too; his agent was right down the hall from our studio, and I used to see him waiting outside the door for ten-dollar gigs. That was when his name was still Sidney Finkelstein.

In time, though, the studio business became quite successful. I taught clarinet, saxophone, bassoon, oboe, and flute. The Whiteman incident had opened up my eyes to the fact that I needed to know flute—all successful saxophone players on Broadway played it—so I took some lessons with Victor Just, and picked up the rest on my own. I also taught some trumpet. Eddie Smith, who'd been a waiter in my restaurant, was a trumpet student of mine. I could play a little, knew the fingering and the embouchure, and could read the music. Someone in the Springfield YMCA band had taught me the basics. I even had bass students. I'd teach anything. At least for the instruments I didn't play I could get students started, then they had to go find somebody else.

I taught my students how to play their instruments, not jazz. My theory was, and still is, that you have to know your instrument thoroughly—have the facility and the imagination to produce whatever sound comes into your mind—before you can play jazz. I found out myself that the more I learned about my instrument, the better I could play jazz. The records I made in the fifties and sixties prove it, as opposed to the ones from the twenties, when I wasn't practicing at all.

One day the phone rang in my studio. The voice said, "My name is Curtis Ousley. I live in Forth Worth, Texas, and I'm coming to New York and want to study with you."

"Fine, be glad to have you."

"Where's your studio, on 49th and Broadway?"

"Yeah."

"I'll be in to see you Monday morning about eleven o'clock." This was tenor saxophonist King Curtis. Sure enough, he showed up and began studying with me five days a week for about a year. I felt proud of him, since he was one of the students I turned out early on in my teaching.

King Curtis was a big, strong kid, and had a temper he couldn't control. He knew his size, and he didn't let anybody tell him anything. That was the cause of his death, in 1971. He got in an argument on 86th Street with a guy he'd told to move off his property. King started whaling on him, and the guy pulled a knife and jugged him. I was shocked to hear that he had died.

One student who wanted to study jazz with me was Dick Hadlock. He came in with his clarinet, and after the first lesson I walked to the elevator with him and he said, "I'm going to study with you, but I'm going to resent it."

"What do you mean?"

"I'm going to fight back," he said.

"You keep on fighting," I replied. "It's all right. As long as you come in and pay for your lessons, you can fight all you want." I never did get an explanation for what he meant. But evidently I helped him some—so did Sidney Bechet. Dick turned out to be one of my best friends, and for a long time he's been very much in the corner of black jazz artists and performers.

In 1955 I played bassoon and tenor saxophone in an off-Broadway show called *Phoenix '55*, that starred Nancy Walker. There were four blacks in the orchestra, including Lawrence Brown and Ernie Royal, brother of Marshall Royal of the Basie band.

Another show I played in was Langston Hughes's *Simply Heavenly*, in 1957. Claudia McNeil was the star, and I performed in a small group backstage. That lasted about three or four months. It was a hit, in a way, but something happened and it didn't hold up.

Besides teaching in the studio and playing shows, I did a lot of recording work in the fifties. People just sent for me when something would come up. I worked with Ralph Sutton, Charlie Shavers, even with the Everly Brothers for one of their albums! One time I got a chance to play several instruments on a date with singer Barbara Lea in 1957. Dick Cary was the arranger, and he wrote parts for me on bassoon and oboe. It was an enjoyable session.

Since playing with Peekaboo Jimmy I'd gotten out of the Harlem gig scene. Anyhow, by this time jazz wasn't featured in as many clubs and cabarets; rhythm and blues had replaced it, also rock and roll—which is really an old form of blues from back in the twenties, done with a different tempo and rhythm.

Occasionally I'd go down and do jazz concerts at the Stuyvesant Casino, on Second Avenue near Ninth Street. Jack Crystal—comedian Billy Crystal's father—used to produce shows there on the weekends.

During this time I was also playing oboe with the Prince Hall Masonic Band. We had something like sixty men, and I conducted them. We rehearsed every Sunday, and did concerts and parades around Harlem, sponsored by the union. When we had parades, Eddie Barefield would do the marching in front of the band.

One time I got a call from the union to play second oboe in a revival of the Creatore band. Creatore was one of the great band conductors, like Goldman, and they had gathered a lot of old-timers who had played under him. I think I was probably the only one in the band who didn't speak Italian. The rehearsal worked out all right, then I went to play the concert out at Coney Island.

Before we started, the first oboe player started playing a solo from Dvořák's *New World* Symphony; it's actually a duet for flute and oboe, in the key of C-sharp minor.[1] I looked over at him fingering it in C minor and said, "Now why don't you try playing it in the right key?"

"Who the hell are you to challenge me what key?"

"E-natural is what you start on, not E-flat."

He started on E-natural and fumbled around, and muffed it up. Then I went ahead and played it for him. The guy was shocked. Being a Negro, I was supposed to tell him that he was a great oboe player who had played with Creatore in Italy. And he couldn't play the passage.

This oboist had on a long, black cape and a slouch hat like Verdi used to wear. He took off his coat, folded it, and put it on the back of his chair, took off his hat and put it on his case, then we started playing. Since we were on the beach, the wind started blowing. Presently the wind caught his toupee, which made it stick up in the back just like a fan. It's a good thing I was playing second oboe, because I couldn't play at all, I was screaming. In fact, a whole lot of parts were missed, since all the guys were turning around and laughing. It was a bad day for this guy. I guess if he thought he could whip me he'd have jumped on me.

These were productive and prosperous years. I turned in my Pontiac and got a 300c Chrysler. I practiced oboe, clarinet, and bassoon very religiously, taught during the days, and played shows and did record dates on the side. When I wasn't working at night, I'd stay home with Hilda. Nightlife didn't appeal to me much any more; there was nothing out there I wanted to do. Things were flourishing on 52nd Street, but I wasn't in the jazz scene too much. I had stopped drinking in '46, so that held no appeal for me. I was getting opportunities to perform on all of my instruments, and that was the challenge.

NOTE

1. Beginning m. 46 in the second movement ("Un poco più mosso").

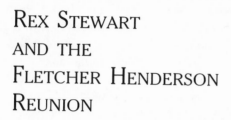

14

REX STEWART
AND THE
FLETCHER HENDERSON
REUNION

I used to carry a six-piece band Friday and Saturday nights over to a place in Jersey City. Sammy Price would play piano for me, and I'd use Herman Autrey, Louis Metcalf, Benny Morton, and Sonny Greer. For a month or two Rex Stewart was my permanent trumpet player. Rex had played with the greats—with Fletcher Henderson and Duke Ellington—but in 1956 he was struggling in New York. He had a room up on St. Nicholas Avenue with his wife. Later he told me I'd saved his life with that Jersey gig. And for a while he'd take me on any job he could get.

Rex was a dynamic trumpet player. But he was self-taught, and he fingered his horn wrong. That's how he got those very peculiar sounds. Coleman Hawkins always criticized Rex severely for playing out of tune. But he was sensational in the things he played.

In a way, Rex represented one of the great faults of black musicians. In creativity they were tops, but since many of them didn't have basic training to begin with, they did a lot of things wrong, and it showed up in bands—like weaknesses in overall range and intonation problems. They became such great creators because jazz was their main object, not whether they could play in tune or not. Many a black musician in the 1920s couldn't blow his nose. Like Tommy Morris. He had some great ideas, but no lip—it just splattered all over the place.

Today that's different. In this era, if a player has jazz talent and wants to go in that direction, he's got fundamentals to go on. The musicians of today are so well trained technically, and able to read, that they don't depend on creativity, they depend on what you put on paper for them. The educational process is making fantastic imitators out of young players.

Anyway, Rex had a great ear, and could almost play whatever he heard. He could move fast and had the range. He just lipped and fingered his horn wrong.

I don't know how Rex got fired from Duke's band. That was a funny band, the way they fired you, or made you quit. Louis Metcalf told me a story about how they'd gotten him out. He hadn't been in the band too long, but they wanted to get rid of him—so he later found out. (I think the whole thing was probably arranged by Duke.) One night down in the dressing room some band members started complaining, "Duke shouldn't do that." "That's a damn shame how Duke treats us. What do you think about it, Metcalf?"

"Y'all right." He didn't know better.

"Well Metcalf, you know, you see what's going on. Why don't you say something to Duke about it?"

"I don't know. What about you?"

"No, man, he won't listen to us. He'll listen to you, cause you're new in the band, you know, you're a sensation."

And Metcalf, like a jackass, went to Duke and told him he didn't think he was doing right.

Duke said, very quietly, "Oh no? Well, all right." The next day Metcalf got his notice.

I do know why they let Ben Webster out, though. He was a troublemaker, a house-wrecker. He'd break down doors in hotels when you were on the road. Ben was a great artist but a very bad boy.

Back to Rex. He had made a lot of good white friends who were interested in jazz, and in the late fifties his name was still big so he started getting jobs up in Connecticut and on Long Island. In 1957 someone wanted to put together a Fletcher Henderson reunion band at a festival in East Islip, Long Island [Great South Bay Jazz Festival]. So they got Rex to lead it and hired a lot of guys who had been with Fletcher: Emmett Berry, Bobby Williams, Joe Thomas, Paul Webster, J. C. Higginbotham, Alton Moore, Fernando Arbello, Benny Morton, Hilton Jefferson, Jimmy Wright, Edgar Sampson, Haywood Henry, and myself, Red Richards, Bernard Addison, Hayes Alvis, and Jimmy Crawford. We had a big audience, I remember, and I think it may have been a financial success. Then we did the same thing in the studio using some different guys, including Hawk and Ben Webster. There was a lot of jealousy between them—more so on the part of Ben, who was fearful of Hawk. They played back to back and wouldn't look at each other. Hawk didn't bother about anybody, because he knew he could blow. He also knew how limited Ben was—how little harmony and theory he knew. Still, when Ben matured, he became one of the greatest ballad players there ever was.

For the reunion we used Fletcher's original arrangements, but they'd been doctored and modified some. In addition, a white arranger had taken some arrangements off records, but we had to change around a lot of things because we didn't like the way they sounded.[1]

The next year, in '58, I did a record with Rex called *Rendezvous with Rex*. Stanley Dance produced it, and Dick Cary did the arrangements. The songs were originals, in most cases. It turned out to be a cute record— not sensational, but cute. It was incidental music for a nice, quiet evening, with the lights turned low. Very peaceful. I played bassoon on it, also clarinet. Hilton Jefferson was on the date, too. He was a great saxophone player. He was born in Connecticut, but he didn't sound like a northern boy. He had a weird way of thinking, but he could hit all the notes.

Dick Cary's arrangements always reminded me of Willard Robison, who wrote for the Deep River Quartet. It's that peaceful style—you're down on the river, the steamboats are going by, the weeping willows are hanging over the water, and you've got a straw in your mouth. It's a picture. Nobody arranged like that except Willard Robison—and Dick Cary, who sounds like him.

NOTE

1. For an account of the Henderson reunion, see Allen, *Hendersonia,* 476–80. Francis Thorne organized the event, which took place 19–21 July 1957. Leora Henderson, Fletcher's widow, contributed some of the bandleader's original charts for the occasion. There were also arrangements by John Nesbitt and Teo Macero. It is not clear, however, which arrangements Bushell believes were taken off records by a white arranger.

   In late July and early August 1958 the Henderson reunion band assembled again at Great South Bay, and parts of the August concert were recorded (see app. A).

15

From Dixieland
to Dolphy

Jimmy Ryan's is where I first joined Wilbur De Paris, in 1959. I replaced Omer Simeon, who had throat cancer and died soon after I went with Wilbur.[1]

I already knew the De Paris brothers. In those days you knew everybody: even if you didn't play with them you knew them from the Rhythm Club. That's the first place a black musician went when he came to town. If he was smart he'd introduce himself; if he was stupid he'd hang in the corner and wait 'til somebody asked him to play. He either made a good impression or a bad one.

At Ryan's we did six hours a night, from 9:00 P.M. to 3:00 A.M., six nights a week. I was clearing ninety dollars a week, plus what I got from teaching. Wilbur was withholding all the money from Social Security and the union. But later I found out he didn't pay it; when I applied for Social Security, I found out he hadn't put any in for five years. Wilbur was a shrewd businessman. He died owing me about a thousand dollars.

I enjoyed Wilbur's band because I got a chance to play clarinet. I had to bend my style a little bit and bring it closer to the old New Orleans way of playing. I was pleased with Sonny White's piano, but I didn't care for Wilbert Kirk's drumming—Wilbur had him playing that boom-chank, boom-chank, two-to-the-bar, Leroy Smith style; Kirk was a better drummer than that. But it was a challenge memorizing all the arrangements. Nothing in that band was ever written down. It was the faking-est band for harmony I'd ever seen in my life!

The band was billed as playing "new" New Orleans jazz. It was an extension of the same concepts we had in the 1920s, but by now everyone was playing better technically. And our arrangements may have been more flexible than in the twenties. Wilbur was responsible for coming up with most of them. He was the boss from start to finish. He was a disciplinarian, but you could get along with him. His brother Sidney was his biggest problem; he was bullheaded, came in late, and always played sharp, on top of the pitch. But Wilbur couldn't do much to change Sidney's habits, because Sidney could take him in the back and whip him any day of the week. The band always sounded better when Doc Cheatham was with us. Doc didn't play with us at Ryan's, but he joined us on the road and for recording dates. Doc was always on time, never any trouble. The world was a bowl of cherries, as far as Doc was concerned.

Around this time some changes were taking place in my personal life. Hilda and I started having problems and separated. Meanwhile I'd met a young woman, Louise Olivari, who had brought her daughter to the studio for clarinet lessons. Louise and I hit it off and began seeing one another quite a bit. Soon we were married.

In 1960 I went with Wilbur's band to Juan-les-Pins, France, for a jazz festival. Except for Doc Cheatham we had our regular Ryan's lineup: Wilbur on trombone, his brother Sidney on trumpet, Sonny White on piano, John Smith on banjo and guitar, Hayes Alvis on bass, Wilbert Kirk on drums, and myself on clarinet. We stayed for two weeks and were received wonderfully. Charlie Mingus was on the same bill with us. On opening night, the audience booed Mingus because he was playing these long, repetitious numbers. The French weren't used to his version of modern jazz. After he finished, Mingus went up to the microphone and said, "I'm sorry y'all don't like what I play, but that's the way I play and I don't give a damn whether you like it or not!" There were 20,000 people in the audience booing him.

Eric Dolphy was with Mingus at the time. He was very intelligent, a high-class musician. He and I became good friends in Nice. Later, when we got back to New York, he played flute in my woodwind quintet. He could play good, legitimate flute. He was also a hell of a clarinet player, especially on bass clarinet.

I loved Eric Dolphy. When I met him I said to myself, "This is the guy I want to hang out with, the guy I want for a buddy." We had a lot of things in common, but he had some more things I didn't have. There was so much I could gain from him—his idea of finesse, for example—and he used to show me things on his horns. I don't know of a musician I respected or admired more.

In Juan-les-Pins they were unveiling a monument to Sidney Bechet, and our band played and marched in the parade. We went through several small towns, and eventually had a huge crowd by the time we got to Sidney's statue. I remember a woman asking me, "Are you a ce-leb-ri-ty?"

"You better believe it," I said.

We played "Muskrat Ramble," "Tiger Rag," and various other jazz things. The French thought so much of Sidney. He was no doubt the biggest musician that had ever come from America.

COLTRANE

It was through Eric Dolphy, I believe, that I met John Coltrane. One day Coltrane sought me out in my studio. He was always having mouthpiece troubles. He'd grab Hawk and go uptown with him and try to talk about mouthpieces. When he came to me he was trying to find out why he never got the sound he wanted. He had the finger ideas and technique, but not the sound. I tried to change his embouchure, but he was too far gone. He stayed with me three or four weeks. But he was never satisfied with his playing. To my mind, Eric was a much better performer.

In 1961 I played with Coltrane at the Village Vanguard and on a record date. There was a big band at this one session. The guy who made the arrangements came in and was high as a kite. He scored for saxophones, two bassoons, and five French horns. He must have been a genius to distribute all those horns the way he did. I remember being impressed by Elvin Jones. That son-of-a-gun beat so much drums, he was sensational. He sounded almost African playing so many different rhythms. One of the numbers was called "Africa"; another was "The Damned Don't Cry." Sometimes the titles could be more spectacular than the music. When we played at the Vanguard, Louise was there. Louise is quite affected by music; she has a good sense of rhythm and melodic line. After we finished she said, "I never heard anything that bad in my life." She had a headache from the experience.

There were no written parts when I played with Coltrane's group at the Vanguard. They just talked about the atmosphere of a piece, and set up a vamp. The minute I heard the vamp, I knew how it should be interpreted.

All my experience, from Leroy's to orchestras to quintets, prepared me how to react in that situation.

With Coltrane's band there wasn't too much variety. They didn't play powerful ballads or strong melodic lines—they were playing these weird new things, originals. They were trying to establish a new approach to American music. I found it difficult to absorb what they were doing melodically, although I could follow it harmonically. I will say that Coltrane had a phenomenal sense of harmony. I just wasn't impressed when he got into a lot of monotonous scales going up and down. In a way, it was a technical exercise, like gymnastics: he was reviewing the things he practiced every day. But it's like a guy standing on one finger, and you say, "That's fantastic." Then you find out he has a steel pin down in his hand. That's not so fantastic.

VISIT TO PUERTO RICO

For a time in 1963 Wilbur started laying off, so I did a lot of free-lancing: Marine band concerts, gigs with Henry Goodwin, Sundays with Sonny Greer out on Long Island, and many other things. Sonny used to take Joe Thomas, Sammy Price, J. C. Higginbotham, and myself out to this Long Island date. Once Sonny got drunk and fell off the elevated bandstand. Another time Higginbotham came out with his case but no horn in it. A strange bunch of guys—but they could all play. Meanwhile, I was doing well, making lots of money.

In September of that year, Garvin Jr. was born. Since most of Louise's family had moved from New York back to Puerto Rico, she went down there when she was pregnant, and I joined her after Garvin Jr.'s birth. I wanted to get away from the Dixieland thing, change my program around, and see what I could do otherwise.

In San Juan I found work in a Latin band led by Noro Morales at the La Concha Hotel. I had a hell of a time trying to play my parts with that band. I never did my job as I was supposed to, because I hadn't learned how to play Latin music. Their charts were hard to read, and I had trouble interpreting the rhythms. Maybe I didn't stick with it long enough. But I know they weren't too happy with what I played.

Then in November, when Kennedy was assasinated, all of Puerto Rico closed down. The Puerto Ricans loved JFK, since he had been responsible for so much aid through Project Bootstrap. I decided to return to

New York and told Louise I'd send for her when I found some steady work.

I moved back to my apartment on St. Nicholas Avenue. Wilbur De Paris had started working again, so I went back with him, and a bit later sent for Lu and Garvin Jr. to come up to New York.

GIL AND MILES

In the spring of 1964, while I was playing with Wilbur De Paris at Ryan's, Gil Evans called me to do a record date. I was one of the only black musicians around who played all the winds—English horn, bassoon, oboe, clarinet, and all that. So I went to one rehearsal at Gil's apartment, and we recorded soon after. Some of the same people were there who had been on the Coltrane big band session a few years earlier—like Paul Chambers, Elvin Jones, Eric Dolphy, Bill Barber, Bob Tricarico (a student of mine), and some others. On this date I got to play English horn and bassoon.

Gil had weird ideas. On his charts, nothing seemed to blend; but that was his style. When he put it together, it made sense. We did a tune called "Las Vegas Tango," but it was misnamed—it sounded more like Malaysia or Morocco than Vegas. It would have been good in a movie clip.

I also had a session with Miles Davis around the same time; I don't remember what tunes we did. I think Gil Evans was involved, but it was Miles's date. When Miles found out I was a sportscar bug, he challenged me: "Hey Bushell, let's get out of here and drag tonight. We'll see what you got."

"Miles, I don't want to discourage you, but my Jaguar will do 155 miles an hour." Miles's Ferrari was pretty fast. So when we got out of the studio that night, we dragged up the street. I had a 411 gear in my Jaguar for dragging. That gave me a good takeoff, and I could do 150–152 miles an hour. I ate him up for a while, but overall Miles could outrun me with his Ferrari.

The next day they had to stop Miles from talking so we could start rehearsal. He said, "That motherfucker ran out past me like I was standing still. He threw shit in my face all the way up Fifth Avenue. That motherfucker, he could fly! But I'll whip his ass yet, you wait." Miles never got over that. We became good friends. Never argued music; always automobiles.

To be perfectly truthful about it, Miles never impressed me as a trumpet player. He missed more notes than anybody I'd ever seen. Dizzy was head and shoulders above him; when Dizzy put down his fingers, the right notes came out. Miles could never compete with guys like Clifford Brown or Fats Navarro. He did have good ideas, I'd never question that. What I'd question is his ability to execute those ideas.

NOTE

1. Simeon died 17 September 1959.

16

A Trip to Africa

In August of 1964 Phil Shapiro called me from the union office and asked if I'd like to go on a three-month tour of Africa, traveling with a State Department band. Sure I would, I told him. So I put in my notice with Wilbur. He said, "O.K." At the end of two weeks, Wilbur came up to me and said, "Well, I've decided to change clarinet players, so I'm giving you notice."

"But I gave my notice two weeks ago, have you forgotten?"

"Oh yeah, is that the way it was?"

"Sure, what else could it be? I'm leaving, going to Africa."

I went to the first rehearsal, an all-day affair, and after about four hours it began to sound like a band. Paul Taubman was our conductor. He was a Canadian who had a weekly radio show years ago. We had a group of thirty men, and I played in the saxophone section, occasionally doubling on oboe. There were a few other black musicians in the band, among them the trombonist Benny Morton.

The second day we had inspection and were given shots. You never know how peculiar mankind appears until you see thirty bare asses at one time. We also heard lectures by State Department officials, who explained how we were supposed to make a good impression over there.[1]

On the flight over, I had a long session with the baritone horn player and snare drummer. It was an interesting trio—a Negro, a Russian, and a Jew. When you get thrown into a thing like that, people start expressing their views. It was surprising how different they were. We got into a discussion of the race situation, and started probing into each other's minds. They knew they were going to Africa and that their attitudes would have to change. As a matter of fact, they were scared to death. It was strange for me, because I'd never lived with so many white people before. But I was excited. At last I'd have the opportunity to see my homeland, to see the people as they really are.

The plane stopped in Lisbon and we picked up an Ethiopian crew. I'd never seen an all-black crew on a plane before. We flew so close over Gibraltar it looked like you could touch it. Very soon we were over Africa, flying over the desert.

When we got to Dakar, Senegal, I started rooming with Benny Morton, who stayed my roommate for most of the whole trip. Benny was pretty articulate and had good business sense. But he also had something wrong with his mind. He never went outside the whole time we were in Africa, just stayed in the hotel room and slept. He never had anything to say, never talked.

This was a concert band, not a jazz group. We did Sousa marches, Victor Herbert's *Babes in Toyland,* some modern pieces, and arrangements of jazz things like "St. Louis Blues."[2]

In some areas our audiences enjoyed the music; in others they were cold as a mackerel. The Africans aspiring for European culture were aware of the music we played and responded favorably, especially in Nigeria. Paul Taubman came out there and gave a big speech in French about how we'd come thousands of miles to give the audience impressions of American music and musicians. Someone called out in English, "Stop all that malarkey and let's get on with the concert!"

Taubman was a great showman, but as a conductor he didn't know too much about what he was doing. He also overplayed his part in exacting discipline. The guys sometimes reacted against it. Once the drummer, a guy who'd been raised on the streets of Brooklyn, must have frowned at Taubman, who said, "Don't you dare look at me like that!"

The drummer replied, "With a face like yours, what other expression could I make?"

Benny and I went to meet a French jazz record collector while we were in Abidjan, Ivory Coast. This guy had copies of everything both of us had ever made, and he started pulling the records off his shelf. He even had the first Mamie Smith recordings, and the ones I'd made in Europe with Wooding. Then he proceeded to pull out things Benny had done with Fletcher Henderson, and went through Coleman Hawkins's entire career. We listened for three hours and discussed every record.

In Dabou, Ivory Coast, the people had assembled for us five small musical groups. They all joined under one conductor to play their national anthem, then the "Star-Spangled Banner." Each unit was made up of all brass, except in one there was a single saxophone. They played without music, but badly out of tune.

For our concert in Dabou, Taubman deviated from his regular program, looking for a groove that would satisfy everybody. He clowned and ran all around the audience. They did not get the message, but stayed orderly and quiet, and applauded politely. American jazz was not to their taste, nor were the classics.

I heard little evidence that jazz originated on the west coast of Africa. The musicians had tremendous stamina but no imagination. In Togo, though, at a native cabaret, I did hear musicians who played things that sounded very much like some of the Latin styles heard in the States and Puerto Rico—the mambo, cha-cha, and pachango. People told us these dances came from the Congo and had been around as long as anyone could remember. After a while this four-piece band (two guitars, bass, drums) started really swinging, so I went up to the mike and sang four choruses of the blues. Maybe I missed my calling!

Dahomey [Benin] provided one of my most memorable experiences. A group of us took a bus out into the bush, then arrived at a narrow, brown lagoon. There we boarded a motor boat and started out, as everybody started singing "Sleepy Lagoon." The lagoon opened up to a large lake, and far over the horizon we saw a line of buildings, like a village in the sky. It was the weirdest sight. Apparently, long ago this tribe had been driven from their home and decided to settle in the middle of this lake, where they'd lived ever since, perhaps ten miles off shore. There were about 20,000 inhabitants living in huts on stilts ten feet above the water. It took us nearly an hour to get out there. The huts were gray with age. Most of the children were naked, and they crowded around our party, begging for money. We went up and down the streets—all water, no place to walk—and suddenly came upon a hut with a sign that said, "Swing Club." It was a cabaret where you could get soft drinks, including Coca Cola. I never thought a place like that could exist.

Another place where you really saw a different side of Africa was Chad. At Fort-Lamy [now Ndjamena] literally thousands of people met us at the airport. There were black sheikhs on Arabian horses, with gold and silver saddles, and all their wives and servants walking behind them. The women did wild chanting, dressed in colorful costumes. We played our concert, which they seemed to enjoy, and then they put on a dance spectacle for us in front of the big outdoor coliseum.

In Rhodesia every hotel had a sign up: "We reserve the right to exclude whom we wish." One night in Salisbury a guy took me up to the top of the city's highest building. Salisbury is a beautiful, modern, well-planned city. To see it from above is like a dream. We looked down on the lights, and he said, "You know, it's pathetic"—this was 1964—"but we're going to have to give all this up one of these days. It's inevitable." This man was one of the intellegentsia of the town, and he knew that one day their dominance of the majority would come to an end. Since then it's happened.

But things were different when I was there. In Salisbury I was staying at a hotel and went down to the grill. This grill had some African help, but blacks weren't allowed to come in the restaurant. Since I was with the State Department, they didn't dare segregate me. The people saw me walk in with my sports jacket, which had the emblem of the Sports Car Club of America.

"Hey chappie! You wish to join us?"

"Well, O.K."

"We see you're a member of the Sports Car Club of America? Is that right?"

"Yes."

"You're an American, a member of that club?" They were aghast that a colored person—which is what I was to them—could belong to the most prestigious auto club in America. To them I was God. So I sat down and had some drinks with them. They turned out to be race drivers.

On Sunday there was an event out at the track to which they invited me. They said, "We'll see that you get in the gate." They were worried, since they didn't allow coloreds in. But when I got there they admitted me and let me drive a car around the track. They wouldn't even allow a black to be a porter at that racetrack. But they tolerated one, since I was a member of that club.

With all prejudice and segregation, I've found this out: as narrow-minded as people are who perpetrate this bigotry, they always tolerate *one*. Even in the States, when I joined this club, I went to a function at the Tavern on the Green and sat across from a couple. The lady said, "Are you a doctor?"

"No."

"A lawyer?"

"No, no, just a normal person." You see, for me to be accepted into the Sports Car Club of America, I had to be different, way above them. That's how asinine people can be in their opinions.

Prejudice can also result from misinformation. Some of the black Africans I met had been very much influenced by propaganda about life for blacks in America. I'd sit down with them and find out that they believed that the American black man was a slave, a third-class citizen—that he was segregated, lynched, and didn't get jobs. In many respects this was true. But the people I talked with didn't believe that there were blacks who lived on the level of whites in America. And their opinion of the black American's intelligence was often not high. I did my best to convince them that their opinions were exaggerated. But I didn't expect these attitudes, and it hurt me.

I remember in Somalia, a very poor and communist country, I met residents who said they hated white Americans. They would ask me, "How can you like whites after the way they treat you in America?"

My only answer was, "Things aren't quite as bad as you've been led to believe." Then they would bring out pictures of police beating women with clubs and shooting men in the streets, police dogs attacking Negroes, and the Harlem riots. I said these were extreme cases. Then they would bring up Rochester, Birmingham, Jersey City, Chicago, Mississippi, New York. How much more did I want to be convinced of a general picture of what was going on?

What could I say? They were so right.

Somalia was also the one place in Africa where we had problems. First, people didn't want me to take photographs because they thought I'd be showing how bad things were. They threatened to take away my camera if I kept on shooting. Then, on the day we were to leave, we suddenly got orders to get out of Mogadishu on the double. We scrambled on the bus and raced to the airport, which they feared was going to be shut down. We had to wait around, but finally got off and flew to Nairobi. Later we found out there had been violent anti-American demonstrations and burning of cars in front of the American embassy.

By this time I was very anxious to get home. We had several days off in Nairobi, then went to Morocco before flying to Paris en route to New York. When we arrived back at U.S. customs I looked up and saw Lu there with Garvin Jr. and Lu's son Paul. I was relieved and happy. Although I'd had this family only a short while, it doesn't take long to love something you've always wished for.

NOTES

1. The entire trip lasted from 12 September to 10 December 1964. Throughout the period Bushell recorded his impressions in a detailed, 240-page journal which he called "B-flat Safari."
2. A printed program from a 2 November 1964 concert in Tananarive, Madagascar, lists the following repertory:

> First part: "Seventy-Six Trombones," Wilson: *William Tell* Overture, Rossini; "American Salute," Gould; "Funiculi, Funicula," Denya; "African Blues," Taubman; Concerto for Piccolo, Bergeim; "St. Louis Blues," Handy; Finale, Symphony No. 4, Tchaikovsky. Second Part: "American Patrol," Meacham; "Old Timers' Waltz," Lake; "Tribute to Col. John Glenn," Taubman; "Bugler's Holiday," Anderson; "Victory at Sea," Rodgers; "My Fair Lady," Lerner and Loewe; "Stars and Stripes Forever."

> At the top is the notice, "Sous reserve de Modification."

17

Puerto Rico

Things were rough when I got back from Africa. I was happy to be home, but I had to reorganize. My son Philip was born in 1965, so there were expenses for the kids, I had a big garage bill from storing my Jaguar for three months, and I had to pay rent on my studio. I didn't save much money from the African trip, even though I'd been sending home $200 a week to Louise. I did a little gigging with Henry Goodwin, went back with Cab Calloway for a brief time, and had some union things, but otherwise it was thin.

One day I got a telegram from Fernando Arbello in Puerto Rico, the trombonist who had played with Fletcher Henderson, Jimmy Lunceford, and other big bands. He told me they were looking for a bassoonist in the state concert band, and asked if I was interested in coming down. I was.

At the time I didn't even have a bassoon, because I'd sold my Heckel to Charlie Ponte. But I went to the union to get a loan, bought a brand-new bassoon from Ponte, and moved my family to Puerto Rico.

In 1966, when I went to the first rehearsal in San Juan, people flipped, because they'd never had a bassoon in that band. I told them I wanted to stay in Puerto Rico the rest of my life, and they thought that was great. I was only in Puerto Rico to do what I could do, playing my different instruments.

I stayed in the national band less than a year, and pretty soon I started getting jazz gigs. Bill Williams, an American publisher down there, and a frustrated pianist, wanted me to get a group together to play at a cabaret in San Juan. I put together a jazz band made up of both Americans and Puerto Ricans, but we never made much money. We were playing Dixieland, and most of the audience who came in there wanted to hear Latin music. The few Puerto Ricans who subscribed to American jazz weren't enough to keep the place open.

For a short time I was with an English vaudeville group called the Nitwits. They'd been in Vegas for about ten years before coming to Puerto Rico. It was a real comedy act. To introduce me, one of them said, "And now ladies and gentlemen, for the pièce de résistance, we present to you Silas McDougal, from Dublin, Ireland." The audience would be expecting an Irishman, and out I came, a Negro with a clarinet. I wore full dress but with short pants and tennis shoes, and a red sash. Then we'd do our special material and parade around the audience. We'd stop the show every night. Recently some of the remaining Nitwits asked me to join them again in Vegas, but there was too much jumping and running around on stage, I just couldn't do it.

When I worked with jazz groups down in Puerto Rico, I often had problems with local drummers. They wanted to play jazz their own way, and didn't want me to show them the right way (chances are that I knew what the right way was). I was just as bullheaded as they were. One night a drummer told me he wasn't going to take orders from me. I got so mad I was going to kill him. I went down to my locker to get my gun but the guys stopped me. I fired the guy, but eventually hired him back after he apologized.

In the meantime I'd started studying oboe and bassoon at the conservatory, also theory. I was in a solfège class, singing a passage, when one of the students criticized me. Then the teacher explained that I was using the movable "do" system, while she was teaching a fixed "do" approach. I remember her saying, "His system is an old system, but let me tell you, I wish I could teach it to you, because it's a better one." From that time on I was tops in the class. I had no problem with that.

Studying at the conservatory got me into the symphony. Victor Teva, the conductor, came down and heard me play a long English horn solo by Sibelius, and he seemed to like it.

For two seasons I played in the Puerto Rican symphony. We appeared in all the big cities in the Caribbean, and from one end of Puerto Rico to the other. It was a full-time job, with two rehearsals a week, and a regular paycheck. Teva was the regular conductor, but two or three times they brought in Pablo Casals to conduct, and Zubin Mehta would occasionally do a guest spot, too. I'm proud of my classical experience. I've worked under Dmitri Mitropolous, Zubin Mehta, Victor Teva, Everett Lee. I've had a hell of a lot more training in classical than in jazz.

I also found work playing oboe, clarinet, and bassoon at the Americana Hotel with Ralph Font's band. Then eventually the manager of the Cerromar Beach, one of the Rockefeller-owned hotels, heard about my jazz group and said he'd keep me in mind if he ever had an opening. The call finally came, and I went there in '72 for two weeks, ended up staying four and a half years.

At the Cerromar Beach we had to play shows as well as on our own. We backed visiting performers who'd come there with their acts. It was great for me and my family. We lived in a big house on the hotel grounds, and I was averaging $800–$900 weekly.

I heard some fantastic singers in Puerto Rico. The folk singers—especially the males—were among the greatest singers I've ever heard. And they played small guitars with a lot of technique. I also got to hear Spanish acts at the hotel—flamenco guitarists and dancers. The Puerto Ricans also played flamenco style, sometimes with a little more soul than the Spaniards!

I composed a piece, "Lament Africaine," when my boys were small. Garvin Jr. was fooling around on an mbira I'd brought back from Nigeria. Kenty, one of his cousins, was playing two chords on a guitar. I was just noodling around on flute. I had in mind an experience in Uganda when I looked out and saw a camel train going over the hill; I was also thinking of Willard Robison, and the sound of his Deep River Orchestra. I turned on the tape recorder and started playing these fantastic things on flute that I've never been able to do since. Later an arranger, Bob Hammer, took it off the tape and scored it for large orchestra.

On Friday and Saturday nights people would be out on the highway dragging. Puerto Rican drivers have steel nerves. I'd take my Jaguar and Porsche and go out there and race, too. They had Volkswagens with Porsche motors in them. Someone got killed nearly every week.

After I'd been there a few years, I had a bad accident on the road. I ran into the rear of a truck with no lights. It knocked me out. Eventually I got $11,000 for the case. Around then I started thinking about coming back to the States.

When you go to a foreign country—I found this out in Europe, South America, and Africa—you eventually reach a point where you want to get back to your own background. I was trying to function in Spanish all the time, and when I heard English I couldn't interpret it fast enough. My kids were going to American schools, but they were having a hell of a time trying to speak English. Finally I'd had enough of Puerto Rico. I wanted my two sons to learn more about American customs, and to speak better English. I also got tired of the mosquitos there; Puerto Rican mosquitos just eat you alive.

My pianist, Gene Gilboa, said to me, "Fess, you can make $1,200 a week out in Las Vegas. Doublers get big money there."

"That's all I want, a chance to play on my horns and be in a band." I'd been playing too much Dixieland and wanted to buckle down. Since leaving the symphony, I'd lost the precision I once had. I wanted to try a new field.

18

LAS VEGAS

When I left Puerto Rico in 1976 I wanted to get back into the swim of things. I'd been out of exposure for a good many years, but I didn't want to return to New York. It didn't have what I wanted when I left there, and I saw no evidence of its having changed. I thought Las Vegas would be the spot. I figured that jazz was at its height here, and I found it was just the opposite. Also, I had no ideas that the barriers would still exist here.

While Lu stayed with the kids in Puerto Rico, I made a trip to Las Vegas with my nephew to look for a house. I went to a real estate operator and spent two days looking. Finally I found one I wanted to buy. It was $52,000, had a pool and a two-car garage. They agreed to sell it to me. I was getting ready to finalize it and go back to Puerto Rico when she called me at the hotel.

"Well, Garvin, the deal is off."

"What happened?"

"Well . . ." she said.

"What, they don't want to sell it to me?"

"That's it."

Because I was black, I couldn't buy the place. So the next day I started looking again, and finally wound up leasing a townhouse for six months. I went back to Puerto Rico and played for a little while longer, then gave my band notice and told them I had to go to the States for eye surgery.

So we flew to Miami, then on to Jacksonville, where we picked up our car. We hit Route 10 about four o'clock in the morning. At the time I had cataracts and couldn't see when it got cloudy. I was wearing black glasses to keep out the light. So when it got dark, I didn't have a chance and had to pull over.

It took us about four days to get to Vegas. We arrived a day late, so they put the furniture in storage and I had to pay $400 to get it back. This was Labor Day, 1976.

At first I had to concentrate all my efforts on getting my eyes straightened out. I had a couple of operations and started wearing glasses.

Then one day I met Bardu Ali in the lobby of one of the clubs. He remembered me from the days with Chick Webb. Now he was Redd Foxx's manager. He told me about Monk Montgomery.

Monk was Wes Montgomery's brother. He's credited for pioneering the electric bass, and he was a very smart businessman. He founded the Las Vegas Jazz Society and promoted much of the jazz activity in this town when I first arrived.

Monk said he'd try to get me a job in the relief band at the Dunes. But when they found out I was black, they canceled it.

Later I met a friend here who told me, "Garvin, they're not going to hire you. First place, you're black. Second, you're old. Third, you don't have hair." So the only thing I could do was take whatever subs and jazz concerts Monk could get for me.

Black musicians have a hard time of it in Las Vegas. Many can't find work so they go back to L.A. or wherever they came from. But I came prepared to stay. I bought a house and my kids were here, so I had to resort to teaching.

When I first came through Las Vegas, on the Pantages Circuit with "Modern Cocktail" in 1922, they wouldn't even let me get off the train. Las Vegas was a stop where the train took on cattle and water. When I went to go outside, the conductor stopped me and said, "Boy, you'd better not get off here." There were cowboys sitting around on horses. "Those boys out there are a little rough. Better stay on the train." Las Vegas used to be a very prejudiced and segregated place. Even in the 1950s, black entertainers like Sammy Davis, Jr., still had to go on the west side to live. Today it's better, but the town does very little to promote black entertainment. The segregation is never obvious—you don't see it on the surface.

The only contacts I made were through Monk. He had me work with Carmen McRae, and featured me during Jazz History Week. But since Monk's death in 1982, there's been much less jazz activity.

Jazz has never been a great sensation in Las Vegas. Several people have tried to promote it, but it's been coolly received. For most of the people who come to settle here, jazz is not a big part of their lives. Las Vegas musicians are among the best in the country for technique and training. But they're not creative: they all play alike. If you want to bring down the curtain on your creative abilities, just sit in a show band for three or four months and play the same thing every night. Very soon your creativity goes out the window.

Some of my students want to play jazz, but most are more interested in being classical players. For five years I taught summers at a school up in the mountains near here. I taught woodwinds and coached sections. The sixth season they wrote saying they wouldn't need me any more, since they were starting a jazz program and were going to hire some jazz teachers. Those people knew nothing about me at all—who I was, or who I'd played with, or what I'd done. I wrote back and said, "Read your history of American music, and find out whether I would fit into your jazz program or not." But after that I wasn't interested.

The teaching business started booming; I had about fifty students a week after the first year. I got in touch with different bandleaders at the junior and senior high schools, that's how it developed. The fact that I could teach flute, bassoon, and oboe, in addition to saxophone and clarinet, enhanced my reputation.

I still experiment with my horns. That's why I'm able to give good lessons. If somebody plays badly, I'll go miles to hear them to see what makes them play that way. I can also demonstrate what sounds good and what sounds bad. Most teachers don't do that. They just put the horns in their mouth and tell them to blow.

For the last three years I've been practicing every day, three to four hours. When I first came to Vegas, I wasn't as sharp as I am now, because I'd been playing a lot of jazz. These days I'm most interested in concentrating on bassoon. The bassoon is a lifetime study. Just last year I arrived at a different type of reed. I keep working at it, and I enjoy playing with the Las Vegas Civic Symphony.

When I start out practicing, it's always with long tones, to strengthen the muscles in the embouchure so you can maintain pitch. I do long tones and octaves all over the horn, then finger exercises, scales (both legato and staccato), and arpeggios. Then I read music—etudes or excerpts, usually. Sometimes I practice with a metronome. Invariably you have a tendency to pick up tempo, especially if you're a jazz musician.

In Puerto Rico I used to do a lot of racing, but I haven't done much since coming here. When I'd go up to the mountains to teach, I used to have the opportunity to put my foot through the floor, so to speak. But my reflexes at this age aren't as fast as they used to be, so I don't take too many chances. I have the hardest time when these kids pull up alongside my Camaro Z-28 and want to drag. Every once in a while I challenge one of them and throw dust in his face.

Garvin Jr. lives here in Las Vegas since getting out of the Air Force. Right now he's in sales and marketing, and his younger brother Philip is a communications major at the University of Utah. I know Louise would move back to New York in a second, but it looks like we'll stay out in Nevada for the time being.

In August of 1984 I received a Lifetime Achievement Award from the National Association of Negro Musicians. Black deans, professors, and music teachers from all around the country came here for a symposium. I gave quite a long address about my relationship with Eubie Blake, then after the final dinner they presented me with a plaque and I had to give a brief talk about my career. I didn't have anything prepared. I got up there and thought, "What the hell am I gonna say?"

Then it came to me. I started telling them how I'd played for European nobility and African tribesmen around the world, but that nothing compared to having received this award from my own people. That's what I've wanted all my life, and now it's finally come.

I said to them, "I've waited a lifetime for this, which goes to show, just have faith, baby, and all good things will come to you."

Looking back, I realize I could have made some better decisions about finances and focused more on the commercial aspect of the music business. But all I wanted was to be a great jazz clarinet player, a fine first alto player, and a first-chair bassoonist. That was my motivation, not money. That's why I don't have any now! But I can play my instruments better.

I don't think anybody should go through life not having done what you want to do. Maybe it's the reason I've gone this far.

NEW YORK SOCIETY LIBRARY
53 EAST 79 STREET
NEW YORK, NEW YORK 10021

APPENDIXES

Appendix A

A Garvin Bushell Discography
with Selected Comments and Identification of Soloists

The following is a chronological list of all known commercially released recordings upon which Garvin Bushell appears. In compiling it I have drawn upon two major discographies: Brian Rust, *Jazz Records: 1897–1942*, 4th ed. 2 vols. (New Rochelle, N.Y.: Arlington House, 1978); and Walter Bruyninckx, *50 Years of Recorded Jazz: 1917–1967* (Mechelen: private printing, 1968).

Unless otherwise noted, all recordings were made in New York City. Listings for pre-1943 recordings take their information from Rust, listings for those made 1943 and after rely upon Bruyninckx. For the most part, issues before 1944 are 78 r.p.m. recordings and those after 1944 are microgroove (LP). Exceptions are marked with the abbreviation LP, 78, and 45 next to the record number.

I have included only original issue numbers next to each title. A dash indicates the same issue number as that for the preceding title. For matrix numbers and fuller information on each recording, consult Rust and Bruyninckx.

If individual players are not known, only instruments are listed.

Bushell's comments and identification of soloists were made during the course of my interviews with him in the summer of 1986. In some cases, his memories of personnel contradict those given by Rust or Bruyninckx. For ease of comparison, I have left intact the personnel as it appears in the discographies and cited Bushell's observations below in italics (often following the titles of pieces under consideration).

The following abbreviations are used for instruments.

ah	alto horn	con	conductor
arr	arranger	dir	director
as	alto saxophone	d	drums
bar	baritone saxophone	f	flute
bb	brass bass (tuba/sousaphone)	frh	French horn
bcl	bass clarinet	g	guitar
bsn	bassoon	h	harmonica
bsx	bass saxophone	o	oboe
c	cornet	or	organ
ca	cor anglais (English horn)	p	piano
cel	celeste	pic	piccolo
cl	clarinet	sb	string bass
cbsn	contrabassoon	ss	soprano saxophone

t	trumpet	v	vocalist
tb	trombone	vn	violin
ts	tenor saxophone	vtb	valve trombone
tu	tuba	x	xylophone

The following abbreviations are used for record labels.

Atl	Atlantic	OK	Okeh
BB	Bluebird	PA	Pathe Actuelle
Br	Brunswick	Pm	Paramount
CC	Collectors' Corner	Pol	Polydor
Col	Columbia	Prest	Prestige
Dec	Decca	UA	United Artists
DG	Deutsche Grammophon	Vic	Victor
Em	Emerson	Voc	Vocalion
Gnt	Gennett	Vri	Variety
HMV	His Master's Voice	VT	Velvet Tone
Imp	Impulse		

Mamie Smith and Her Jazz Hounds

Mamie Smith, v; Johnny Dunn, c; ? Dope Andrews, tb; Garvin Bushell, cl; Leroy Parker, vn; Porter Grainger, p; ? George Howell, d
5 November 1920
Mem'ries of You, Mammy   OK/Phonola 4228
If You Don't Want Me Blues   ⸺

If You Don't Want Me Blues:
   I think this was 1921, not 1920. [Perry Bradford supplied dates for these Okeh sessions.] It could be Cutie Perkins on drums. Dope Andrews on trombone.

Mamie Smith's Jazz Hounds

Johnny Dunn, c; Dope Andrews, tb; Garvin Bushell, cl; ? Leroy Parker, vn or a second reed?; p; ? Mert Perry, x
January 1921
Royal Garden Blues   OK 4254
Shim-Me-King's Blues   ⸺

Shim-Me-King's Blues:
   The trombonist might be Dope Andrews, but Dope had a little more vibrato in his sound. The xylophone might be Raymond Green; I can't recall any other xylophone player around at that time. The Paul Biese trio, a white group on Columbia, used a combination of xylophone, saxophone, and banjo, but using xylophone was new for our group.
   This tune could have been by Porter Grainger, H. Qualli Clark. Freddie

Bryant, or Shep Edmonds. The composer was usually the producer of the record date.

The title comes from the "shimmy" dance; a shimmy was just shaking your rear end. But this tune is too slow for blacks to shimmy to—it was just a title. I think Perry came up with the "Jazz Hounds" name.

Royal Garden Blues:

You see, nobody could blow their notes since no one practiced in those days! You just picked up your horn, went out, and made the record. In the last five years I've practiced more than I did during the whole 1920s.

Battle Axe might be playing xylophone. He was a drummer who also played bells and xylophone. He's the only drummer I know who did that.

"Royal Garden Blues" was one of our opening numbers with Mamie Smith. It might have been Johnny Dunn's choice to record that.

Lavinia Turner Accompanied by Her Jazz Band
Lavinia Turner, v; [possible personnel] Gus Aiken, c; Jake Frazier, tb; Garvin Bushell, cl, as; Willie Gant, p; ——— Spivey, bj; Joe Banks, d [For this session, the two entries following, and the 17 May 1921 Lavinia Turner date, Martin Rust lists Bushell on alto saxophone. Bushell, however, claims he did not play the instrument until 1923.]
March 1921
How Many Times?   PA 020544
Can't Get Lovin' Blues   ———

Lillyn Brown Accompanied by Her Jazzbo Syncopators
Lillyn Brown, v; Ed Cox, c; Bud Aiken or Herb Flemming, tb; Garvin Bushell, cl, as; Johnny Mullins, vn; p; Lutice Perkins, d
ca. 29 March 1921
If That's What You Want, Here It Is   Em 10366
Ever-Lovin' Blues   ———

Daisy Martin Accompanied by the Five Jazz Bell-Hops
Daisy Martin, v; [probable personnel] Gus Aiken, c; Jake Frazier, tb; Garvin Bushell, cl, as; Dude Finlay, p; bj; d
March–April 1921
Royal Garden Blues   Gnt 4712
Spread Yo' Stuff   ———

Daisy Martin Accompanied by Her Five Jazz Bell-Hops
Personnel probably as above, with bb instead of d
ca. 15 April 1921

Play 'Em for Mama Sing 'Em for Me   OK 8001
I Won't Be Back 'Til You Change Your Ways   ———

Lulu Whidby Accompanied by Henderson's Novelty Orchestra
Lulu Whidby, v; t; Chink Johnson or George Brashear, tb; Garvin Bushell or
Edgar Campbell, cl; probably Cordy Williams, vn; Fletcher Henderson, p;
? John Mitchell, bj; bb
ca. April 1921
Home Again Blues   BS 2005
Strut, Miss Lizzie   ———

Strut, Miss Lizzie:
  I don't think I'm on this one. It sounds more like Ed Campbell. It might be
Speedy [Sam Speed] on banjo.

Lavinia Turner
Lavinia Turner, v; [possible personnel] Gus Aiken, c; Jake Frazier, tb; Garvin
Bushell, cl, as; Willie Gant, p; ——— Spivey, bj; Joe Banks, d
17 May 1921
A-Wearin' Away the Blues   PA 020572
Sweet Man O' Mine   ———

Katie Crippen Accompanied by Henderson's Novelty Orchestra
Katie Crippen, v; t; tb; Buster Bailey, cl, as; Garvin Bushell, cl; Fletcher
Henderson, p
ca. June 1921
That's My Cup Blues   BS 2018
When It's Too Late (You're Gonna Miss Me, Daddy)   ———

Daisy Martin Accompanied by Her Jazz Masters
Daisy Martin, v; [probable personnel] Gus Aiken, c; Jake Frazier, tb; Garvin
Bushell, cl; Dude Finlay, p; bj; d
ca. early July 1921
Won't Someone Help Me Find My Lovin' Man   OK 8008
Everybody's Man Is My Man   ———

Mamie Smith Accompanied by Her Jazz Band
Mamie Smith, v; t; tb; cl; vn; p; d
ca. 18 August 1921
Sax-O-Phoney Blues   OK 4416
Sweet Man O' Mine   OK 4511

Sweet Man O' Mine:

This might be George Bell, the violin player we picked up in Detroit. The trumpet might be Ed Cox; Dope Andrews on trombone; Cordy Williams on violin; Charlie Summers on piano. If we had drums on there it was Cutie Perkins.

Things that sound like this are all arrangements. Tim Brymn may have been responsible for this one—or possibly H. Qualli Clark or Bill [William Grant] Still. Still didn't just arrange for Black Swan; if you paid him his price he'd arrange for anyone.

Ethel Waters Accompanied by Her Jazz Masters

Ethel Waters, v; t; tb; Garvin Bushell, cl; ? Charlie Jackson, vn; Fletcher Henderson, p
ca. August 1921
One Man Nan   BS 2021
There'll Be Some Changes Made   _____

One Man Nan:

Most of this number was down on paper; we were reading. It might have been a stock arrangement supplied by the publisher. Will Vodery did a lot of these arrangements for recordings, too.

I don't recall Fletcher arranging any of the numbers. At the time we made these Black Swan recordings we didn't recognize Fletcher as an arranger.

Often we'd never play these tunes again after we recorded them, unless they became a hit.

There'll Be Some Changes Made:

There's a tuba in there—could be Bill Benford. The trumpet could be Luke Smith or Elmer Chambers. It's not Gus Aiken's style. That's Cordy Williams or Lorenzo Caldwell on violin.

This was our big hit on the road when we played theaters.

Ethel Waters Accompanied by Her Jazz Masters

Ethel Waters, v; t; ? Chick Johnson, tb; Garvin Bushell, cl; 2d cl; ? Charlie Jackson, vn; Fletcher Henderson, p; ? Ralph Escudero, bb
ca. August 1921
Dying with the Blues   BS 2038
Kiss Your Pretty Baby Nice   _____

Dying with the Blues:

This might be Ed Cox or Elmer Chambers on trumpet. Or perhaps Luke Smith, brother of Joe and Russell Smith.

The violin is cross-firing with everybody else, playing the lead right against the singer. He was reading that line.

This was a very modern arrangement for the day. In those days tuba players didn't seem to know how loud to play. That's why some smart guy found out they could get better results with a bass player. Old Braud [Wellman Braud] was one of the people responsible for that.

There's no ad lib here, it's all arrangement. It sounds like something [William Grant] Still might have done.

Kiss Your Pretty Baby Nice:
   I hear four horns—trumpet, trombone, clarinet, and alto saxophone. It might be Herschel Brassfield on saxophone.

Ethel Waters' Jazz Masters
Gus Aiken, c; Bud Aiken, tb; Garvin Bushell, cl; ? Joe Elder, cl, as; bsx;
Fletcher Henderson, p
ca. September 1921

'Frisco Jazz Band Blues	BS 2037
Royal Garden Blues	BS 2035
Bugle Blues (Intro. Old Miss Blues)	BS 2037

Edith Wilson Accompanied by Johnny Dunn's Original Jazz Hounds
Edith Wilson, v; Johnny Dunn, c; tb; ? Garvin Bushell, cl; vn; p
12 September 1921

Nervous Blues	Col rejected

15 September 1921

Nervous Blues	Col A-3479
Vampin' Liza Jane	————

Nervous Blues:
   Bud Aiken might be on trombone, since the playing is clean and not boisterous—Buddy was never boisterous. It might be Herb Flemming, too, who played down at Leroy's several times.

Vampin' Liza Jane:
   Hear Johnny Dunn do that old Geechie call?

Johnny Dunn, cornet break (after patter section)

The Geechies brought that up from South Carolina. Someone would whistle it, and if a Geechie heard it he'd know there was another Charlestonian around. Pretty soon every jazz player on the East Coast picked it up.

   Another one was:

Later they made it into a song, "Organ Grinder's Swing." But that was a Geechie whistle, too.

Edith Wilson Accompanied by Johnny Dunn's Original Jazz Hounds

Edith Wilson, v; Johnny Dunn, c; tb; ? Garvin Bushell, cl; p

24 September 1921	
Old Time Blues	Col rejected
30 September 1921	
Frankie	Col rejected
6 October 1921	
Old Time Blues	Col A-3506
Frankie	———

Old Time Blues:

That thing Johnny Dunn plays came out of the West, from Chicago or New Orleans:

Johnny Dunn, cornet, Introduction, mm. 5-6

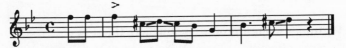

They used to sing:

Some-bo-dy done   snagged their brit-ches

Later they changed it to, "Somebody done snagged the blue note." That's probably from Joe Oliver or Freddie Keppard. Johnny may have heard them play it in Chicago.

This sounds like Buddy [Aiken] on trombone; I never heard Herb Flemming play with a mute.

Frankie:

Overall, Edith's records are much better instrumentally than Mamie Smith's were. One of those clarinet breaks sounds like something I used to do.

Mamie Smith and Her Jazz Hounds
Mamie Smith, v; ? Bubber Miley, c; tb; ? Garvin Bushell, cl; ? Leroy Parker, vn; p
ca. 12 October 1921
Let's Agree to Disagree   OK 4511
Rambling Blues   OK 8024
Cubanita   _____

Let's Agree to Disagree:
   *I hated dates like this because you had to read so much. You had no chance
to put in anything of your own. I didn't want to read, because I figured I could
play it better than they could write.*
   *I don't remember this tune, but it sounds like me playing the second part. It
could have been somebody else. . . . [middle section, instrumental break] We're
ad libbing now! Ha!*
   *This is either me or Buster Bailey on clarinet. No, it's not me—I never had
that fast vibrato. And that high G—it couldn't be Ernest Elliott, because I never
heard him go up to a high G in my life! Actually, it could be Mayland Hall; he's
the only one I know who had that fast vibrato. There was also an old West
Indian from Philadelphia who had that vibrato. . . . It might be Nelson Kincaid,
too.*
   *The cornet has a mute in so it's hard to identify the player, but I'd say Ed
Cox. I don't think they'd hire Bubber Miley for a date like this where reading
was involved; Bubber didn't have much chops then. Besides, that cornet is too
stiff to be Bubber.*

Essie Whitman Accompanied by the Jazz Masters
Essie Whitman, v; [probable personnel] Gus Aiken, c; Bud Aiken, tb; Garvin
Bushell, cl; Joe Elder, cl, ts; Charlie Jackson, vn; Fletcher Henderson, p
ca. October 1921
Sweet Daddy It's You I Love   BS 2036
If You Don't Believe I Love You   _____

Eliza Christmas Lee Accompanied by Her Jazz Band
Eliza Christmas Lee, v; Gus Aiken, c; Jake Frazier, tb; Garvin Bushell, cl; vn;
Willie Gant, p; ——— Spivey, bj; Joe Banks, d
October 1921
I Ain't Givin' Nothin' Away   Gnt 4801
Arkansas Blues   _____

Edith Wilson Accompanied by Her Jazz Hounds
Edith Wilson, v; Johnny Dunn, c; Herb Flemming, tb; Garvin Bushell, cl; Will

Tyler, vn; Dan Wilson or Leroy Tibbs, p; John Mitchell, bj
20 May 1922
Mammy, I'm Thinking of You   Col A-3634
Take It 'Cause It's All Yours   ———

Edith Wilson Accompanied by Her Jazz Hounds
Edith Wilson, v; Johnny Dunn, c; Herb Flemming, tb; Garvin Bushell, cl; Dan
Wilson or Leroy Tibbs, p; John Mitchell, bj
9 June 1922
He May Be Your Man (But He Comes to See Me
  Sometimes)   Col A-3653
Rules and Regulations "Signed Razor Jim"   ———

13 July 1922
Lonesome Mama Blues   Col A-3674
What Do You Care (What I Do)?   ———

Lucille Hegamin Accompanied by Wooding's Society Entertainers
Lucille Hegamin, v; Sam Wooding, p, dir; Elmer Chambers, t; Herb Flemming,
tb; Garvin Bushell, cl, as; Rollin Smith, ts; Charlie Dixon, bj; bb; Joe Young, d
16 July 1922
I've Got to Cool My Puppies Now (I've Got to Cool
  My Doggies Now)   Pm 20151
Send Back My Honey Man   ———

Mamie Smith's Jazz Hounds
Johnny Dunn, ? Bubber Miley, c; ? Herb Flemming, tb; ? Garvin Bushell, cl;
? Herschel Brassfield, as; Coleman Hawkins, ts; ? Everett Robbins, p; Sam
Speed, bj; d
ca. 15 August 1922
Stuttering   OK 8036
Those Longing for You Blues   OK 8072

Mamie Smith's Jazz Hounds
Mamie Smith, v; Johnny Dunn, c; ? Herb Flemming, tb; ? Garvin Bushell, cl;
? Herschel Brassfield, as; Coleman Hawkins, ts; ? Everett Robbins, p; Sam
Speed, bj; d
ca. 22 August 1922
Got to Cool My Doggies Now   OK 4670
You Can Have Him, I Don't Want Him, Didn't
  Love Him Anyhow Blues   ———

Got to Cool My Doggies Now:

That's a tenor sax in the lower register. It could be Hawk. He used to do a lot of slap tongue in those days.

After Mamie takes the first chorus, the band "tears out" in the middle. "Tear out" was a term meaning every man for himself. But as a clarinet player I had to follow a certain format. It was the custom to play a third above the trumpet player, and I'd try to emulate or answer his patterns—like a fugue, more or less.

You Can Have Him, I Don't Want Him, Didn't Love Him Anyhow Blues:

That could be Ernest Elliott on clarinet, but it sounds like me. We played a lot alike then. Perry [Bradford] was always insisting on the clarinets hitting the high notes; he loved that. It may be George Bell on violin.

That middle part, on a vocal number, was called the "patter section." On an instrumental number it was called the "trio."

Josie Miles

Josie Miles, v; Joe Smith, c; Jake Frazier, tb; Garvin Bushell, cl; ? Fletcher Henderson, p [Bruyninckx gives the foregoing personnel; Rust lists Joe Smith, c; ? George Brashear, tb; ? Clarence Robinson, cl; Fletcher Henderson, p; ? Ralph Escudero, bb.]
ca. September 1922

If You Want to Keep Your Daddy Home	BS 14130
You're Foolin' with the Wrong Gal Now	————

Eva Taylor

Eva Taylor, v; ? Johnny Dunn, c; ? Garvin Bushell, cl; as; ? Clarence Williams, p
ca. September 1922

New Moon	BS 2103

Edith Wilson Accompanied by Her Jazz Hounds

Edith Wilson, v; Johnny Dunn, c; Herb Flemming, tb; Garvin Bushell, cl; Will Tyler, vn; Dan Wilson or Leroy Tibbs, p; John Mitchell, bj
18 September 1922

Evil Blues	Col rejected

19 September 1922

Pensacola Blues (Home Again Croon)	Col rejected

2 October 1922

Evil Blues	Col A-3746
Pensacola Blues (Home Again Croon)	————

Evil Blues:

That sounds like Johnny Mitchell or Sam Speed on banjo. It may be Danny

Wilson, Edith's husband, on piano; he made a lot of Edith's things. Will Tyler was the greatest Negro violinist in the country at that time.

Pensacola Blues:
   This doesn't really sound like Edith to me. That's pretty high for her. It sounds more like Lena Wilson. I'm not too sure that's Johnny Dunn, either. That's not his sound, and besides, by that time everybody was double-timing.

Edith Wilson Accompanied by Her Jazz Hounds

Edith Wilson, v; Johnny Dunn, c; Herb Flemming, tb; Garvin Bushell, cl; Will Tyler, vn; Dan Wilson or Leroy Tibbs, p; John Mitchell, bj
22 November 1922
Dixie Blues   Col rejected
He Used to Be Your Man but He's My Man Now   ———

Lena Wilson Accompanied by Johnny Dunn's Jazz Hounds

Lena Wilson, v; Johnny Dunn, c; Earl Granstaff, Herb Flemming, or Calvin Jones, tb; Garvin Bushell, Ernest Elliott, and/or Herschel Brassfield, cl, as; Leroy Tibbs, George Rickson, or Dan Wilson, p; John Mitchell or Sam Speed, bj; others?
26 February 1923
I Don't Let No One Man Worry Me   Col rejected
Humming Man   ———

Lena Wilson Accompanied by Perry Bradford's Jazz Phools

Personnel as above?
April 1923
Deceitful Blues   Pm 12029
I Don't Let No One Man Worry Me   ———
Here's Your Opportunity   Pm 12042
Memphis, Tennessee   ———

Lena Wilson Accompanied by Her Jazz Hounds

? Gus Aiken, c; Herb Flemming, tb; Garvin Bushell, cl; ? George Rickson, p; John Mitchell, bj
12 May 1923
Deceitful Blues   Col A-3915
Memphis, Tennessee   ———

The Gulf Coast Seven

Gus Aiken, c; Bud Aiken, tb; Garvin Bushell, cl; Ernest Elliott, cl, ts; Leroy Tibbs, p; John Mitchell, bj

17 May 1923
Fade Away Blues   Col A-3916
Daybreak Blues   ———

Fade Away Blues:
   That's an alto saxophone in the middle duet. But I never heard Ernest Elliott
play saxophone. Maybe it was Herschel Brassfield.
   We weren't using music for this number.

Daybreak Blues:
   That cornet has to be Johnny Dunn!

Perry Bradford's Jazz Phools
Gus Aiken, c; Bud Aiken, tb; Garvin Bushell, cl, as; Charles Smith, p; Samuel
Speed, bj
May–June 1923
Fade Away Blues   Pm 12041
Day Break Blues (Original Bugle Blues)   ———

Fade Away Blues:
   If that's Gus Aiken, he's playing Johnny Dunn's patterns note for note.

Day Break Blues:
   That's not Johnny [Dunn], but he sure plays like Johnny. This date puzzles
me, because I don't recall Gus playing so much like Johnny. There's a
saxophone in there, so there had to be two reeds.

Ethel Ridley Accompanied by Perry Bradford's Jazz Phools
Ethel Ridley, v; Gus Aiken, c; Buddy Aiken, tb; Garvin Bushell, cl, as; Ernest
Elliott, ts; Leroy Tibbs, p; Samuel Speed, bj
26 June 1923
Memphis, Tennessee   Vic 19111
If Anybody Here Wants a Real Kind Mama (Here's
   Your Opportunity)   ———

The Gulf Coast Seven
Gus Aiken, c; 2d c; Bud Aiken, tb; Garvin Bushell, cl; Ernest Elliott, cl, ts;
Leroy Tibbs, p; ? Sam Speed, bj
7 August 1923
Papa, Better Watch Your Step   Col A-3978
Memphis, Tennessee   ———

Papa, Better Watch Your Step:
   There are a lot of bad notes in there, because we were reading. This is a
pretty bad recording. Again, it sounds like Johnny Dunn to me on cornet.

Memphis, Tennessee:
The clarinet doesn't sound like me; I never had that vibrato. This could be George Brashear on trombone, it's not Buddy's sound at all. The arrangement could be by Qualli Clark.

Mary Jackson Accompanied by Perry Bradford's Jazz Phools
Mary Jackson, v; [probable personnel] Gus Aiken or Bubber Miley, c; Bud Aiken or Herb Flemming, tb; Herschel Brassfield or Garvin Bushell, cl, as; Leroy Tibbs, p; Sam Speed, bj
October 1923

All the Time	PA 032013
Who'll Get the Man When I'm Gone?	———

Perry Bradford's Jazz Phools
Herb Flemming, tb, dir; Johnny Dunn, Bubber Miley, c; ? Garvin Bushell, Herschel Brassfield, cl, as; ? Leroy Tibbs, p; Samuel Speed, bj; ? Harry Hull, bb
February 1924

Charlestown, South Carolina	Pm 20309
Hoola Boola Dance	———

I doubt if I was playing clarinet on this session, because at the time I was playing saxophone with Wooding and wouldn't have taken a clarinet date.

Hoola Boola Dance:
That sounds like Brassfield on saxophone. I don't think Bubber Miley would have been on a date with Johnny Dunn, since by this time he'd established himself down at the Kentucky Club with Ellington. [Miley joined the Washingtonians at the Hollywood Cafe (later Kentucky Club) in the fall of 1923.]

Sam Wooding and His Orchestra
Sam Wooding, p, dir; Bobby Martin, Maceo Edwards, Tommy Ladnier, t; Herb Flemming, tb; Garvin Bushell, cl, as, o; Willie Lewis, as, bar, v; Gene Sedric, cl, ts; John Mitchell, bj; John Warren, bb; George Howe, d
Berlin, July 1925

O Katharina	Vox 01882
Shanghai Shuffle	Vox 01890
Alabamy Bound	———
By the Waters of Minnetonka	Vox 01882
O Katharina	Vox 1883
Shanghai Shuffle	———
Alabamy Bound	Vox 1891
By the Waters of Minnetonka	———

O Katharina:

Solos: Gene Sedric, ts (after first full chorus); Herb Flemming, tb (against trumpet figures)

This is Sam's arrangement. We had a weak spot: Bobby Martin could play anything, but he had a bad sound. Hear that banjo player? Johnny Mitchell. Oh, he was a genius.

Shanghai Shuffle:

Solos: Sedric, bsx; Martin, c; Tommy Ladnier, c; Flemming, tb; Willie Lewis, cl; Martin, c; Bushell, cl (leading glissando); Flemming, tb

[On the middle section, before clarinet solo:] Everything was so expressive then. If we had just played on pitch instead of scooping into notes! That's what spoils the records. If they could take some of those same arrangements today, played by musicians of today, you wouldn't hear all those slurs.

Alabamy Bound:

Solos: George Howe, slide and train whistles; Ladnier, c; Sedric, ts; Mitchell, bj; Flemming, tb

I'm playing lead saxophone here. At first Sam voiced the reeds with tenor in the middle, and second alto taking the bottom. That was too hard, so he switched it around so tenor was on the bottom.

By the Waters of Minnetonka:

Solos: Lewis, as; Bushell, o; Martin (or Maceo Edwards), t; Sedric, bsx; Flemming, tb; Bushell, o; Lewis, f (backed by two clarinets); Flemming, tb

Arthur Lange made this arrangement, and we bought it.

I had a military system oboe, which has very few keys. It had a plastic reed on it. That's why I got such a gosh-awful sound. I wasn't a good oboe player then. I wasn't a good musician at all in those days. They thought I was good, but I just stunk all over the place. Now I hear so much wrong with the things that I did it's amazing.

A lot of papers wrote up about [Flemming]; they thought he was singing through his horn.

This band could play, no question about it. They made good music.

Sam Wooding and His Orchestra

Sam Wooding, p, dir; Bobby Martin, Maceo Edwards, t; Herb Flemming, tb; Garvin Bushell, cl, as, o; Willie Lewis, as, bar, v; Gene Sedric, cl, ts; John Mitchell, bj; Sumner Leslie "King" Edwards, bb; Percy Johnson, d
Berlin, September 1926

Black Bottom	DG/Pol 20689
Behind the Clouds	————
By the Waters of Minnetonka	DG/Pol 20690
Dreaming of a Castle in the Air	————
Just a Cottage Small	DG/Pol 20693

Milenberg Joys	DG/Pol 20691
Lonesome and Sorry	DG/Pol 20693
Tampeekoe	DG/Pol 20691
Am I Wasting My Time on You?	DG/Pol 20692
Dreaming of Tomorrow	———

Johnny Dunn and His Band

Johnny Dunn, c; ? Herb Flemming, tb; ? Garvin Bushell, cl, as; Jelly Roll
Morton, p; John Mitchell, bj; Harry Hull, bb; ? Mert Perry, d
13 March 1928

Sergeant Dunn's Bugle Call Blues	Col 14306-D
Ham and Eggs	Col 14358-D
Buffalo Blues	Col 14306-D
You Need Some Loving	Col 14358-D

Sergeant Dunn's Bugle Call Blues:

I remember this date for Columbia, with Jelly Roll and Mert Perry.

*The trombone doesn't sound like Herb Flemming; it's too rough for Herb. It
sounds more like Jimmy Harrison. Also, I don't remember being able to tongue
that fast on saxophone. The sound is like mine, though. As for the tuba, I
don't think Harry Hull could have played that fast double-tonguing; it may be
Chink Johnson.*

*This is what a big band used to sound like without music: a conglomera-
tion of nothing. Now you can see why Fletcher Henderson's band became
such a sensation, because they had it down on paper and played in tune.*

Buffalo Blues:

*These are head arrangements. It sounds like Chink Johnson to me, not
Harry Hull.*

*This is a pretty number. If an arrangement could have been made for it, it
would have been a fantastic record.*

Some parts of the clarinet solo sound like me, others like Percy Glascoe.

Dunn's Original Jazz Hounds

Johnny Dunn, c; ? Herb Flemming, tb; ? Garvin Bushell, cl, as; as; James P.
Johnson, Fats Waller, p; ? John Mitchell, bj
26 March 1928

| What's the Use of Being Alone? | Voc 1176 |
| Original Bugle Blues | ——— |

Louisiana Sugar Babes

Jabbo Smith, c; Garvin Bushell, cl, as, bsn; James P. Johnson, p; Fats Waller, or
Camden, N.J., 27 March 1928

Willow Tree	Vic 21348
Willow Tree	HMV 7EG-8215
'Sippi	Vic 21348
'Sippi	BB B-10260
Thou Swell	———
Thou Swell	Vic 21346
Persian Rug	———

Willow Tree:

This was in the show [Keep Shufflin']; it might have been a soft-shoe number.

'Sippi:

We were reading here at the beginning.

This [bassoon solo] was probably some of the first jazz bassoon on record—for Victor, at least. It was the first time I really soloed on bassoon for records; with Sam I'd been reading parts. You can hear the Adrian Rollini influence!

I don't remember using bassoon in Keep Shufflin'. *I think James P. just wanted me to carry it along for the record date.*

Thou Swell:

As loose as this sounds, it took us a long time to get it that much together, since we had no drums and bass, and the organ pipes were in the other room.

[Alto saxophone solo:] I wasn't a jazzman there; I wanted to play lead saxophone.

Persian Rug:

James P. and Fats chose this one, they both knew it. I may have played it with Sam as a big orchestral thing with an oriental introduction.

Roy Evans

Roy Evans, v; J. C. Johnson, p; Garvin Bushell, cl, as
20 June 1928

| How Long Is That Train Been Gone? | Col 2257-D |
| Georgia's Always on My Mind | Col 1449-D |

I remember this date. Roy Evans was a tall, brown-skinned fellow. Like Harry White, he was a baritone with a range into the tenor area. We did shows together at Small's Paradise.

Bessie Smith

Bessie Smith, v; Ed Allen, c; Garvin Bushell, as; Greely Walton, ts; Clarence Williams, p; Cyrus St. Clair, bb

15 May 1929
I've Got What It Takes (But It Breaks My Heart
    to Give It Away)   Col 14435-D
Nobody Knows You When You're Down and Out   Col 14451-D

I've Got What It Takes:

   *It would have been better if we'd had a banjo, guitar, or drums to keep
tempo. Still, nobody could sing the blues like Bessie, bless her heart.*

Margaret Webster

Margaret Webster, v; Ed Anderson, c; ? Alberto Socarras, cl; ? Garvin Bushell,
as; Clarence Williams, p
13 February 1930
Wipe 'Em Off   VT 7076-V
How Can I Get It (When You Keep On Snatchin' It Back)?   VT 7066-V

Catherine Henderson [Eva Taylor]

Eva Taylor, v; Ed Anderson, c; ? Alberto Socarras, cl; ? Garvin Bushell, as;
Clarence Williams, p
13 February 1930
What If We Do?   Diva 6050-G
Keep It to Yourself   Diva 6040-G

   *I did some things with Socarras, I remember. He was Cuban, and a terrific
flutist. He usually played flute, because his clarinet wasn't jazz.*

Bessie Smith

Bessie Smith, v; Louis Bacon, t; Charlie Green, tb; Garvin Bushell, cl, as;
Clarence Williams, p
27 March 1930
Keep It to Yourself   Col 14516-D
New Orleans Hop Scop Blues   ——————

Keep It to Yourself:

   *Clarence Williams knew more what he was doing in the studio than Perry
Bradford did. But couldn't he or the producers hear that things weren't
together with no drums and bass? Couldn't they see there was no foundation?
It's incomplete; there's too much missing.*

   *Before recording something like this we'd run it through a couple of times
and Clarence would give some idea of what he wanted you to play. Then you
were off by yourself.*

New Orleans Hop Scop Blues:

   *That's a famous New Orleans walking bass—they called it a "hopscotch
bass."*

Sam Wooding and His Orchestra

Sam Wooding, p, dir; [probable personnel] Frank Newton, John Swan, t; Nat
Story, tb; ? Garvin Bushell, cl, as; another cl, as; Gene Sedric, cl, ts; g; sb; d
29 January 1934
My Gal Sal   Col test
Weary Blues   ———

Cab Calloway and His Orchestra

Cab Calloway, v, dir; Shad Collins, Irving Randolph, Lammar Wright, t; Claude
Jones, Keg Johnson, De Priest Wheeler, tb; Garvin Bushell, Andrew Brown, as,
cl; Ben Webster, Walter Thomas, ts; Bennie Payne, p; Morris White, g; Milt
Hinton, sb; Leroy Maxey, d
21 May 1936
Love Is the Reason   Br 7677
When You're Smiling   Br 7685
Jes Natch'ully Lazy   Br 7677
Are You in Love with Me Again   Br 7685

15 September 1936
Copper-Colored Gal   Br 7748
Frisco Flo   Br 7756
The Wedding of Mr. and Mrs. Swing   Br 7748
The Hi-De-Ho Miracle Man   Br 7756

Copper-Colored Gal:
   Solos: Randolph, t; Bushell, cl; Webster, ts
   *This was a big piece in the Cotton Club show; Bill Robinson did a tap
number to it.*
   *Cab didn't want to pay enough money for his arrangements. Bennie Payne
used to arrange for him and would only get ten dollars.*

The Wedding of Mr. and Mrs. Swing:
   Solos: Webster, ts; Bushell, cl
   *We had no business recording this. In the show it was great, but as a
record sitting at home . . . .*
   *The rhythm's heavy, it doesn't move. The horns want to go, but the rhythm
section's holding them back.*

Cab Calloway and His Orchestra

Cab Calloway, v, dir; Shad Collins, Irving Randolph, Lammar Wright, t; Claude
Jones, Keg Johnson, De Priest Wheeler, tb; Garvin Bushell, Andrew Brown, as,
cl; Ben Webster, Walter Thomas, ts; Bennie Payne, p; Morris White, g; Milt
Hinton, sb; Leroy Maxey, d
3 March 1937

Don't Know If I'm Comin' or Goin'	Vri 535
My Gal Mezzanine	Vri 593
That Man Is Here Again	Vri 501
Peckin'	Vri 612
Congo	Vri 593
Swing, Swing, Swing	Vri 501

Peckin':
   I remember playing this arrangement. Fruit [Morris White] never had much life in him as a guitar player, he didn't have any drive. The tempo's dying. That clarinet doesn't sound like me, more like Jerry Blake.

Victoria Spivey
Victoria Spivey, v; Sidney De Paris, t; Garvin Bushell, cl; as; ts; Porter Grainger, p; sb; Wilbert Kirk, d
12 March 1937

One Hour Mama	Voc 03505
Harlem Susie-Kue	unissued
Give It To Him	Spivey 2001 (LP)
Got the Blues So Bad	Voc 03505

Cab Calloway and His Orchestra
Cab Calloway, v, dir; Doc Cheatham, Irving Randolph, Lammar Wright, t; Claude Jones, Keg Johnson, De Priest Wheeler, tb; Garvin Bushell, Andrew Brown, as, cl; Chu Berry, Walter Thomas, ts; Bennie Payne, p; Morris White, g; Milt Hinton, sb; Leroy Maxey, d
17 March 1937

Wake Up and Live	Vri 535
Goodnight, Baby	rejected
Manhattan Jam	Vri 612

Manhattan Jam:
   Again, that sounds like Jerry Blake on clarinet.

Cab Calloway and His Orchestra
Cab Calloway, v, dir; Doc Cheatham, Irving Randolph, Lammar Wright, t; Claude Jones, Keg Johnson, De Priest Wheeler, tb; Garvin Bushell, Andrew Brown, as, cl; Chu Berry, Walter Thomas, ts; Bennie Payne, p; Morris White, g; Milt Hilton, sb; Leroy Maxey, d
24 August 1937

Moon at Sea	Vri 651
I'm Always in the Mood for You	Vri 643
She's Tall, She's Tan, She's Terrific	———

31 August 1937

Go South, Young Man	Vri 644
Mama, I Wanna Make Rhythm	———
Hi-De-Ho Romeo	Vri 651
Queen Isabelle	Vri 662
Savage Rhythm	———

Chick Webb and His Orchestra

Chick Webb, d, dir; Mario Bauza, Bobby Stark, Taft Jordan, t; Sandy Williams, Nat Story, tb; Garvin Bushell, cl, as; Louis Jordan, as; Ted McRae, ts; Wayman Carver, ts, f; Tommy Fulford, p; Bobby Johnson, g; Beverly Peer, sb; Ella Fitzgerald, v

Savoy Ballroom broadcast, 10 December 1937

Bronzeville Stomp	Jazz Archives JA33
She's Tall, She's Tan, She's Terrific	———
Honeysuckle Rose	———

Bronzeville Stomp:

Solos: Bushell, cl; Williams, tb; McRae, ts

Our rhythm sounds smoother in person than in the recording studio. We never played our best in the studio.

She's Tall, She's Tan, She's Terrific:

Solos: Jordan, t; McRae, ts

This doesn't have good balance in the [microphone] pickup. The harmonic parts are closer than the melodic line, it's way out of balance.

Honeysuckle Rose:

Solos: Jordan, t; Bushell, cl; McRae, ts; Bushell, cl; ? Bushell, as

This arrangement may have been by Charlie Dixon or Dick Vance.

17 December 1937

I Want to Be Happy	Dec 15039
I Want to Be Happy	Dec Z-778
The Dipsy Doodle	Dec 1587
If Dreams Come True	Dec 1716
Hallelujah!	Dec 15039
Midnite in a Madhouse (Midnite in Harlem)	Dec 1587
Midnite in a Madhouse	Dec Y-5208

If Dreams Come True:

Solos: McRae, ts; ? George Matthews, tb

As a rule, Chick wanted Taft to play lead on the final ensembles. Otherwise, Mario played lead. When Vance came into the band, Chick didn't have to switch them like that.

Chick Webb and His Orchestra

Chick Webb, d, dir; Mario Bauza, Bobby Stark, Taft Jordan, t; Sandy Williams,
Nat Story, George Matthews, tb; Garvin Bushell, cl, as; Louis Jordan, as; Ted
McRae, ts; Wayman Carver, ts, f; Tommy Fulford, p; Bobby Johnson, g; Beverly
Peer, sb; Ella Fitzgerald, v
2 May 1938

A-Tisket, A-Tasket	Dec 1840
Heart of Mine	Dec 2721
I'm Just a Jitterbug	Dec 1899
Azure	————

I'm Just a Jitterbug:
  Solos: Jordan, t, Webb, dr
  *This is typical of a white band playing. That was the problem with Chick's
band, although Chick thought it was great.*

3 May 1938

Spinnin' the Wheel	Dec 2021
Liza (All the Clouds'll Roll Away)	Dec 1840

Hilton Jefferson, as, replaces Louis Jordan
9 June 1938

Pack Up Your Sins and Go to the Devil	Dec 1894
MacPherson Is Rehearsin'	Dec 2080
Everybody Step	Dec 1894
Ella	Dec 2148

Everybody Step:
  Solos: Jordan, t
  *You can hear Webb holding back the tempo. My claim is that no jazz band
in the world that holds exactly strict tempo has drive. Benny Goodman proved
that. He held reasonable tempos, but then let them go. If you hold or pull
back the tempo, the bottom drops out of the feeling.*

Chick Webb and His Orchestra

Chick Webb, d, dir; Mario Bauza, Bobby Stark, Taft Jordan, t; Sandy Williams,
Nat Story, George Matthews, tb; Garvin Bushell, cl, as; Louis Jordan, as; Ted
McRae, ts; Wayman Carver, ts, f; Tommy Fulford, p; Bobby Johnson, g; Beverly
Peer, sb; Ella Fitzgerald, v
17 August 1938

Wacky Dust	Dec 2021
Gotta Pebble in My Shoe	Dec 2231
I Can't Stop Loving You	Dec 2310

18 August 1938

Who Ya Hunchin'?	Dec 2231

| I Let a Tear Fall in the River | Dec 2080 |

Dick Vance, t, replaces Bauza
6 October 1938

F. D. R. Jones	Dec 2105
I Love Each Move You Make	———
It's Foxy	Dec 2309
I Found My Yellow Basket	Dec 2148

Recorded by RCA Victor for NBC, 9 January 1939

Tea For Two	Pol 423248 (LP)
How Am I to Know?	———
One O'Clock Jump	———
The Blue Room	———
Crazy Rhythm	———
Sugar Foot Stomp	———
Grand Terrace Rhythm	———
By Heck	Pol 236524 (LP)
Blue Skies	Pol 423248 (LP)
Dinah	———
Who Yuh Hunchin'?	Pol 236524 (LP)
Liza (All the Clouds'll Roll Away)	Pol 423248 (LP)

Blue Room broadcast, 10 February 1939

Let's Get Together	Cicala (Italy) BJL8010 (LP)
Blue Room	———
Deep in a Dream	———
One O'Clock Jump	———
That Was My Heart	———

Chick Webb and His Orchestra

Chick Webb, d, dir; Mario Bauza, Bobby Stark, Taft Jordan, t; Sandy Williams, Nat Story, George Matthews, tb; Garvin Bushell, cl, as; Louis Jordan, as; Ted McRae, ts; Wayman Carver, ts, f; Tommy Fulford, p; Bobby Johnson, g; Beverly Peer, sb; Ella Fitzgerald, v
17 February 1939

Undecided	Dec 2323
'Tain't What You Do (It's the Way That Cha Do It)	Dec 2310
In the Groove at the Grove	Dec 2323
One Side of Me	Dec 2556
My Heart Belongs to Daddy	Dec 2309

John Trueheart, g, replaces Johnson
2 March 1939

| Sugar Pie | Dec 2665 |

It's Slumbertime Along the Swanee	Dec 2389
I'm Up a Tree	Dec 2468
Chew-Chew-Chew	Dec 2389

21 April 1939

Have Mercy	Dec 2468
Little White Lies	Dec 2556
Coochi-Coochi-Coo	Dec 2803
That Was My Heart	Dec 2665

Southland Cafe broadcast, Boston, 4 May 1939

Let's Get Together	CC 11 (LP)
Poor Little Rich Girl	_____
Break 'Em Down	_____
If I Didn't Care	_____
The Stars and Stripes Forever	_____
My Wild Irish Rose	_____
Chew-Chew-Chew (Your Bubble Gum)	_____

Ella Fitzgerald and Her Famous Orchestra

Ella Fitzgerald, v; Dick Vance, Bobby Stark, Taft Jordan, t; George Matthews, Sandy Williams, Nat Story, tb; Garvin Bushell, cl, as; Hilton Jefferson, as; Ted McRae, ts, bar; Wayman Carver, as, ts, f; Tommy Fulford, p; John Trueheart, g; Beverly Peer, sb; Bill Beason, d

29 June 1939

Betcha Nickel	Dec 2904
Stairway to the Stars	Dec 2598
I Want the Waiter (with the Water)	Dec 2628
That's All, Brother	_____
Out of Nowhere	Dec 2598

I Want the Waiter (with the Water):
Solos: Jordan, t; McRae, ts; Jordan, t; Fulford, p
This sounds like an Al Feldman arrangement.

That's All, Brother:
Solos: Matthews or Williams, tb
Another Feldman arrangement.

Stairway to the Stars:
The band has good quality, but the only originality comes from Ella.

Out of Nowhere:
Solos: McRae, ts
[Middle instrumental section:] That's the best I've heard this band sound!
The rhythm section with Bill Beason is better by all means. Beason wasn't the soloist Chick was, but he was a better all-around drummer.

Ella Fitzgerald and Her Famous Orchestra

Ella Fitzgerald, v; Dick Vance, Bobby Stark, Taft Jordan, t; George Matthews, Sandy Williams, Nat Story, tb; Garvin Bushell, cl, as; Hilton Jefferson, as; Ted McRae, ts, bar; Wayman Carver, as, ts, f; Tommy Fulford, p; John Trueheart, g; Beverly Peer, sb; Bill Beason, d

18 August 1939

My Last Goodbye	Dec 2721
Billy (I Always Dream of Bill)	Dec 2769
Pleast Tell Me the Truth	———
I'm Not Complainin'	Dec 3005
Betcha Nickel	rejected

Ethel Waters

Ethel Waters, v; Eddie Mallory, t; Benny Carter, cl; Garvin Bushell, as; Reg Beane, p; Charlie Turner, sb

22 September 1939

Baby, What Else Can I Do?	BB B-10517
I Just Got a Letter	———

Ethel always had great diction; you could hear every word. You see where Lena Horne got her style from?

I think Eddie Mallory or Benny Carter did the arrangements, probably Eddie. It's similar to the kind of writing Charlie Shavers did for the John Kirby band.

Ella Fitzgerald and Her Famous Orchestra

Ella Fitzgerald, v; Dick Vance, Bobby Stark, Taft Jordan, t; George Matthews, Sandy Williams, Nat Story, tb; Garvin Bushell, cl, as; Hilton Jefferson, as; Ted McRae, ts, bar; Wayman Carver, as, ts, f; Tommy Fulford, p; John Trueheart, g; Beverly Peer, sb; Bill Beason, d

Chicago, 12 October 1939

You're Gonna Lose Your Gal	Dec 2816
After I Say I'm Sorry	Dec 2826
Baby, What Else Can I Do?	———
My Wubba Dolly	Dec 2816
Lindy Hoppers' Delight	Dec 3186
Moon Ray	Dec 2904

26 January 1940

Is There Somebody Else?	Dec 2988
Sugar Blues	Dec 3078
The Starlit Hour	Dec 2988
What's the Matter with Me?	Dec 3005

Slim Gaillard and His Flat Foot Floogie Boys

Slim Gaillard, g, v; Henry Goodwin, t; Garvin Bushell, cl; Loumell Morgan, p;
Slam Stewart, sb, v; Hubert Pettaway, d
2 August 1940

Don't Let Us Say Goodbye	OK 5792
Rhythm Mad	OK 6015
Bongo	————
Broadway Jump	OK 5792

Rhythm Mad:

Slim was truly an artist. Talk about talent! I loved this group.

Bongo:

*[Trumpet solo:] Henry Goodwin was an erratic sort of guy. He wasn't much
of a trumpet player, but he had a lot of good ideas.*

Nick Fenton, sb, replaces Stewart
24 September 1940

Put Your Arms Around Me, Baby	OK 6088
Lookin' for a Place to Park	OK 6260
Hit That Mess	————
Hey! Chief (Hey! Chef)	OK 6088

Hey! Chief:

*This must have been written, probably by Loumell Morgan. You can hear
how I'd been influenced by some of Goodman's things. There's a tenor sax in
here, too; I don't remember who it might have been. He must have been
brought in for the date.*

That's Slam Stewart singing, not Slim.

Garvin Bushell

? Pat Rossi, v; unidentified group
13 October 1944

White Sands	No Record no.
	A-1
Don't Ever Leave Me	————
Hold Back the Dawn	————
The Stars Look Down	————

Bunk Johnson and His Band

Johnson, t; Ed Cuffee, tb; Garvin Bushell, cl; Don Kirkpatrick, p; Danny Barker,
g; Wellman Braud, sb; Alphonse Steele, d
Stuyvesant Casino, 8 November 1947

Please Don't Talk about Me When I'm Gone	Nola LP3
Peg O' My Heart	————

You're Some Pretty Doll	Nola LP3
Please	———
Pagan Love Song	———
Margie	———
Royal Garden Blues	———
Sweet Lorraine	———
Darktown Strutter's Ball	———
Tishomingo Blues (1)	———
Tishomingo Blues (2)	———

Johnson, t; Ed Cuffee, tb; Garvin Bushell, cl; Don Kirkpatrick, p; Danny Barker, g; Wellman Braud, sb; Alphonse Steele, d

23 December 1947	
The Entertainer	Col GL520
The Minstrel Man	———
Chloe	———
Someday	———

24 December 1947	
Hilarity Rag	Col GL520
Kinklets	———
You're Driving Me Crazy	———
Out of Nowhere	———

26 December 1947	
That Teasin' Rag	Col GL520
Some of These Days	———
Till We Meet Again	———
Maria Elena	———

I was experimenting with a crystal mouthpiece on this date, and you can hear the difference. It had a "ping" to it, but it was too small a sound for the band.

Wild Bill Davison

Davison, c, v; Jimmy Archey, tb; Garvin Bushell, cl, bsn; Ralph Sutton, p, cel; Sid Weiss, sb; Morey Feld, d

27 December 1947	
Just a Gigolo	Circle J1032 (78)
She's Funny That Way	Circle J1034
Ghost of a Chance with You	Circle J1033
Yesterdays	———
Why Was I Born?	Circle J1032
When Your Lover Has Gone	Circle J1034

She's Funny That Way:
A Harlem audience wouldn't have accepted this; there'd have to be more of a blues idiom and construction to it.

When Your Lover Has Gone:
Now, a black audience would accept this. That's what they call getting down with it. Bill would have wrecked the Apollo with a thing like that. He sounds like Freddie Keppard in the good old days.

Louis Metcalf

Louis Metcalf, Dick Vance, t; Alva McCain, ts; Ernie Mauro, as; Garvin Bushell, bar; Ken Kersey, p; Lord Westbrook, g; Lemont Moten, sb; Cozy Cole, d; Nick Mayo, v; Eddie Barefield, arr
1955

Frenchman Boogie	Franwill F5026
	(45?)
Underneath the Harlem Moon	————
Sugar Coated Love	Franwill F5027

Barbara Lea

Barbara Lea, v; Dick Cary, ah; Garvin Bushell, o, bsn; Ernie Caceres, bar, cl; Jimmy Lyon, p, cel; Jimmy Raney, g; Beverly Peer, sb; Osie Johnson, d
24 April 1957

Sleep Peaceful Mr. Used-to-Be	Prest LP7100
I'm Old Fashioned	————
The Very Thought of You	————
I've Got My Eyes on You	————

26 April 1957

Mountain Greenery	Prest LP7100
Am I in Love?	————
We Could Make Such Beautiful Things	————
More Than You Know	————

Rex Stewart and the Henderson All Stars

Rex Stewart, c; Emmett Berry, Taft Jordan, Joe Thomas, t; J. C. Higginbotham, Benny Morton, Dickie Wells, tb; Buster Bailey, cl; Garvin Bushell, Hilton Jefferson, as, cl; Coleman Hawkins, Ben Webster, ts; Haywood Henry, bar; Red Richards, p; Al Casey, g; Bill Pemberton, sb; Jimmy Crawford, d
late November 1957

Sugar Foot Stomp	Jazztone J1285
King Porter Stomp	————

King Porter Stomp:

[Dickie Wells solo:] You never knew what Dickie was playing! Always like he was hiding behind something—the mystery man. We had three of the wackiest trombone players; they all played something different.

The single thing I find wrong with this album is intonation. No one tuned up well. Black musicians are notorious for playing sharp.

Dick Vance, t, and Norman Thornton, bar, replace Berry and Henry
29 November 1957
Honeysuckle Rose   Jazztone J1285
Wrappin' It Up   ⸺
The Way She Walks (Rex's Tune)   ⸺

I enjoyed this date; these guys could all play. The most uncomfortable thing was between Hawk and Ben. Hawk blew Ben out of the studio that day.

Rex Stewart and His Orchestra

Rex Stewart, c, v; Hilton Jefferson, cl, as; Garvin Bushell, cl, bsn; Dick Cary, p, t; Everett Barksdale, g; Joe Benjamin, sb; Mickey Sheen, d [Bushell does not play on "My Kind of Gal."]
31 January 1958
Pretty Ditty   Felsted FAJ7001
My Kind of Gal   ⸺
Trade Winds (Danzon d'amour)   ⸺
Blue Echo   ⸺
Mauve   unissued

Rex Stewart and the Fletcher Henderson Alumni

Rex Stewart, c; Allan Smith, Joe Thomas, Taft Jordan, Paul Webster, t; (James) Leon Comegys, Benny Morton, Dickie Wells, tb; Garvin Bushell, Hilton Jefferson, as, cl; Buddy Tate, Bob Wilber, ts, cl; Haywood Henry, bar; Dick Cary, ah; Red Richards, p; Chauncey Westbrook, g; Bill Pemberton, sb; Mousie Alexander, d; Clarence H. "Big" Miller, v
East Islip, N.Y., 1–2 August 1958
Wrappin' It Up   UA UAL 4009
D Natural Blues   ⸺
These Foolish Things (Medley)   ⸺
  Willow Weep for Me
  Over the Rainbow
  Hello Little Girl
Georgia Sketches   ⸺
  1st mvt. Motion
  2d mvt. Tiempo Espagnole
  3d mvt. The Earth is Good

Luckey Roberts

Luckey Roberts, p, dir; Garvin Bushell, as, cl; Joe Benjamin, sb; Herbert
Cowens, d
1958

By the Beautiful Sea	Period RL1929
St. Louis Blues	———
If You Knew Susie	———
After You've Gone	———
Darktown Strutter's Ball	———
Bill Bailey	———
Ballin' the Jack	———
Honeysuckle Rose	———
Runnin' Wild	———
Sweet Georgia Brown	———
I'm Just Wild about Harry	———

*On this session the engineer told me I was too good for the date!
Apparently they wanted more ricky-ticky. They didn't even use a grand piano,
but had Luckey play an upright.*

*I think some of my best playing is on this record. I was as sharp on this
date as I ever was. I was using a Selmer Albert system clarinet; I loved the
sound of that horn.*

*In this period I had a good, happy feeling about jazz. I didn't have any
responsibilities, so I felt better.*

Luckey was great. Whatever he did he excelled in.

Wilbur De Paris

Wilbur De Paris, tb, vtb; Sidney De Paris, c; Doc Cheatham, t; Garvin Bushell,
cl, pic, bsn; Sonny White, p, or; John Smith, bj, g; Hayes Alvis, sb; Wilbert
Kirk, d, h; Louis Bacon, v
9–10 May 1960

Minorca	Atl LP1363
Creole Love Call	———
Tell 'Em About Me	———
Baby Won't You Please Come Home	———
That Thing Called Love	———
Railroad Man	———
Twelfth Street Rag	———
Shim-me-sha-wabble	———
When My Sugar Walks Down the Street	———
Runnin' Wild	———
The Charleston	———
Blues Ingee	———

Wilbur De Paris

Wilbur De Paris, tb, vtb; Sidney De Paris, c; Doc Cheatham, t; Garvin Bushell,
cl, pic, bsn; Sonny White, p, or; John Smith, bj, g; Hayes Alvis, sb; Wilbert
Kirk, d, h; Louis Bacon, v
"Jazz Festival," Antibes, France, 9 July 1960

Fidgety Feet	Atl LP1363
Tres Moutarde	————
St. Louis Blues	————
South Rampart Street Parade	————
Sensation Rag	————
Clarinet Marmalade	————
Muskrat Ramble	————
Battle Hymn of the Republic	————

18 November 1960

How You Gonna Keep Them Down on the Farm	Atl SD1552
Wabash Blues	————
Jada	————
Royal Garden Blues	————

19 November 1960

Over and Over Again (first version)	Atl SD1558
Careless Love	————
Just a Closer Walk with Thee	————
Goodnight Irene	————

Just a Closer Walk with Thee:

*[Clarinet solo:] This, I think, was a very good job. I was thinking of one of
the mourners coming back after they'd buried their loved one.*

John Coltrane Orchestra

Coltrane, ts; Booker Little, Freddie Hubbard, t; Julian Priester, Charles
Greenlee, euphonium; Julius Watkins, Donald Corrado, Bob Northern, Jimmy
Buffington, Robert Swisshelm, frh; Bill Barber, tu; Eric Dolphy, as, f, bcl;
Garvin Bushell, reeds, woodwinds; Laurdine "Pat" Patrick, bar; McCoy Tyner,
p; Paul Chambers, Reggie Workman, sb; Elvin Jones, d
Englewood, N.J., 23 May 1961

Greensleeves	Imp A-6, AS9223-2
Song of the Underground Railroad	Imp 9273
Greensleeves	————
The Damned Don't Cry	Imp IZ9361-2
Africa	————

I mostly played bassoon on the orchestra things with Coltrane.

Africa:

In the first two minutes, Coltrane plays some good, legitimate African chants. When he buckles down and plays themes, it's fantastic. But after that it just gets ridiculous. Also, his harmonics don't come out—I know that, since I'm a teacher.

The Damned Don't Cry:

I think this piece is trying to depict a group of people that has been downtrodden and subjected to all sorts of iniquities. Despite that, they don't cry. With all the slavery, segregation, and browbeating, they come through just the same, with flying colors.

I go along with trying to put a political message across through music. It's been done for hundreds of years, and it's worked.

Wilbur De Paris

Wilbur De Paris, tb, vtb; Sidney De Paris, c; Garvin Bushell, cl, pic, bsn; Sonny White, p, or; John Smith, bj, g; Hayes Alvis, sb; Wilbert Kirk, d, h; Mae Barnes, Hoagy Carmichael, v ["Maple Leaf Rag" (1) adds Eubie Blake, Dick Wellstood, Ralph Sutton, Hoagy Carmichael, p.]
summer 1961

Bill Bailey	RCA LO8P-4126
Do That Ragtime Dance	_____
Maple Leaf Rag (1)	_____

From soundtrack of NBC TV series, "Those Ragtime Years."

Elmer Snowden Mysterical Six

Elmer Snowden, bj; Garvin Bushell, ts, bsn, cl; Gene Sedric, cl, ts; Ray Bryant, p; Jimmy Rowser, sb; Mickey Roker, d
11 October 1961

Keepin' Out of Mischief Now	unissued
Black Bottom	_____

John Coltrane Group

John Coltrane, ts, ss; Eric Dolphy, as, bcl; Garvin Bushell, ca, cbn; McCoy Tyner, p; Ahmed Abdul-Malik, oud; Jimmy Garrison, Reggie Workman, sb; Elvin Jones, d
Village Vanguard, 2 November 1961

India	Imp rejected
Spiritual	Imp rejected

John Coltrane Group

John Coltrane, ts, ss; Eric Dolphy, as, bcl; Garvin Bushell, ca, cbn; McCoy Tyner, p; Ahmed Abdul-Malik, oud; Jimmy Garrison, Reggie Workman, sb;

Elvin Jones, d [Bushell plays English horn on "India," contrabassoon on
"Spiritual."]
Village Vanguard, 5 November 1961
India   Imp AS9325
Spiritual   _____

Wilbur De Paris' New New Orleans Jazzband
Wilbur De Paris, tb; Sidney De Paris, t; Garvin Bushell, cl; Sonny White, p;
John Smith, bj; Hayes Alvis, sb; Wilbert Kirk, d
late 1961
Wrought Iron Rag   RCA (F)430362S
From soundtrack of the film *Nuits d'Amérique*

Gil Evans Orchestra
John Coles, Bernie Glow, t; Jimmy Cleveland, Tony Studd, tb; Ray Alonge, frh;
Bill Barber, tu; Eric Dolphy, Garvin Bushell, Bob Tricarico, reeds; Steve Lacy,
ss; Gil Evans, p, arr, con; Kenny Burrell, g; Paul Chambers, Ron Carter, sb;
Elvin Jones, d [Bushell can be heard on bassoon on "Hotel Me," oboe on
"Las Vegas Tango."]
6 April 1964
Hotel Me   Verve MGV8555
Las Vegas Tango   _____

APPENDIX B

A GLOSSARY OF MUSICIANS AND PERFORMERS

The following roster is devoted to lesser known figures mentioned in the course of Garvin Bushell's narrative. The principal sources of biographical information for these entries are: Walter C. Allen, *Hendersonia* (Highland Park, N.J.: privately published, 1973); John Chilton, *Who's Who of Jazz*, 4th ed. (New York: Da Capo, 1985); Leonard Feather, *The Encyclopedia of Jazz* (New York: Horizon Press, 1960); Roger Kinkle, *The Complete Encyclopedia of Popular Music and Jazz, 1900–1950*, 4 vols. (New Rochelle: Arlington House, 1974); Eileen Southern, *Biographical Dictionary of Afro-American and African Musicians* (Westport: Greenwood Press, 1982).

Aiken, Augustine "Gus" (1902–73). Trumpeter from Charleston, South Carolina. Like his older brother, trombonist Gene "Buddy" Aiken (d. 1927), Gus received his musical training in the Jenkins' Orphanage Band. He performed with vaudeville acts (Gonzelle White, Drake and Walker) in the 1920s and many big bands in the 1930s, including those of Charlie Johnson, Luis Russell, and Alberto Socarras.

Ali, Bardu (1910–81). Conductor, singer, and dancer from New Orleans who moved to New York in the late 1920s. Best known for fronting Chick Webb's band in the 1930s. Later he worked as Redd Foxx's manager.

Arbello, Fernando (1907–70). Trombonist and arranger from Puerto Rico who was active in New York from the mid-1920s through the late 1960s. He performed with the big bands of Claude Hopkins (1931–34), Fletcher Henderson (1936–37, 1941), and Jimmy Lunceford (1942–46), and spent the last years of his life in Puerto Rico.

Barefield, Edward "Eddie" (b. 1909). Saxophonist, clarinetist, and arranger whose early experience was in territory bands of the Midwest and Southwest, most notably Bennie Moten's orchestra (1932–33). Later he played with Cab Calloway, Fletcher Henderson, Don Redman, and served as musical director for various ensembles and theatrical productions.

Barksdale, Everett (1910–86). Guitarist, married to pianist Victoria Barksdale. He performed in Eddie South's band from 1932 through 1939. Based in New York from late 1939 through the 1970s, he was best known as a session guitarist.

Briggs, Arthur (b. 1899). Trumpeter raised in Charleston, South Carolina, and tutored by Eugene Mikell. He performed with Will Marion Cook's Southern Syncopated Orchestra in 1921 and Noble Sissle's orchestra in the late 1920s. For many years he has been based in Europe as a performer and teacher.

Brown, Lawrence (b. 1907). Trombonist in Duke Ellington's orchestra, 1932–51, then again 1960–70. He moved to Los Angeles in the mid-1970s and has retired from music.

Caldwell, Lorenzo. New York–based violinist who may have taken part in Black Swan recording sessions in the early 1920s.

Calloway, Blanche (1902–78). Singer and sister of bandleader Cab Calloway. She toured frequently with revues in the 1920s and led her own band from 1931 through 1938.

Carver, Wayman (1905–67). Flutist and reed player who appeared with bands led by Elmer Snowden (1931–32), Benny Carter (1933), Chick Webb (1934–39), and Ella Fitzgerald (early 1940s). Later he became associate professor of music at Clark College, in Atlanta, Georgia.

Cary, Richard "Dick" (b. 1916). Arranger and multi-instrumentalist (piano, trumpet, alto horn). In the 1940s and 1950s he arranged for the bands of Benny Goodman and Bobby Hackett. Based on the West Coast since 1959, he has been active as an arranger, composer, and touring performer.

Cheatham, Adolphus "Doc" (b. 1905). Trumpeter from Nashville, Tennessee. He went to Europe with Sam Wooding in the late 1920s, and subsequently worked in McKinney's Cotton Pickers and bands led by Cab Calloway, Teddy Wilson, and Benny Carter. His experience includes regular stints with Latin bands and society orchestras, and innumerable appearances with small groups in clubs and at festivals, both as trumpeter and occasional vocalist.

Clark, H. Qualli (1883–1932). Cornetist, arranger. From Missouri, he was cornet soloist with W. C. Handy's Mahara Minstrels and also organized the Tennessee Ten, touring with the group. In 1914 he began working as an arranger for Will Vodery in New York, then joined Pace and Handy's music publishing company in 1918. He arranged for many recording bands in the 1920s.

Creath, Charles "Charlie" (1890–1951). Trumpeter from Ironton, Missouri, also a saxophonist and accordionist. He toured with circus bands and vaudeville troupes ca. 1906–18, then led bands in St. Louis during the 1920s and 1930s. Later he ran his own nightclub in Chicago and worked as an inspector in a factory.

Crippen, Katie (ca. 1895–1929). Singer in Harlem cabarets, wife of trombonist Lew Henry. From 1925 through 1929 she performed in New York theaters and on the vaudeville circuit.

Curtis, King [Curtis Ousley] (1935–71). Saxophonist, guitarist, and singer from Fort Worth, Texas. He played in bands behind singers in the 1950s, among them the Coasters and Buddy Holly. Soon he began recording under his own name, both in R&B and jazz formats. In the late 1960s he recorded for Atlantic and backed Aretha Franklin.

De Paris, Wilbur (1900–73). Trombonist and bandleader. Early on he played in circus bands, with tent shows, and on the TOBA Circuit. In the 1920s he led groups in Philadelphia, then worked as a sideman in various big bands (Leroy Smith, Edgar Hayes, Teddy Hill, Duke Ellington). Beginning in the late 1940s he fronted combos that often featured his brother Sidney (1905–67) on trumpet and tuba.

Diton, Carl (1886–1962). Concert pianist, singer. A 1909 graduate of the University of Pennsylvania, he studied piano in Munich (1910–11) and opened a studio in Philadelphia after settling there in 1918. In the late 1920s he was president of the National Association of Negro Musicians. Based in New York after 1929, he received a diploma from Juilliard (1930) and accompanied such singers as Jules Bledsoe, Marian Anderson, and Ezio Pinza.

Dowell, Edgar. Pianist and composer from Baltimore (according to Bushell). He played with Bushell at the Libya Cafe in Harlem (West 139th Street), behind the Garden of Joy. He recorded with singers Viola McCoy, Julia Moody, Rosa Henderson, and possibly Kitty Brown.

Dunn, Johnny (1897–1937). Trumpeter from Memphis, Tennessee. He worked under W. C. Handy in the late 1910s, then was featured in bands backing Mamie Smith and Edith Wilson. He went to Europe with Will Vodery's Plantation Orchestra in 1923, led bands and toured as a soloist in the States, then returned to Europe in 1928, where he spent the rest of his life performing mainly in Holland, Denmark, and France.

Edwards, "Junk," Sr. Drummer with the Clef Club bands. Around 1920 he and his son Junk Jr. lived close to Bushell, on 133rd Street near Seventh Avenue.

Edwards, "Junk," Jr. Drummer. Junk Edwards, Jr., went with a band to Thailand and died there.

Edwards, Maceo "Eddie." Trumpeter with Sam Wooding's orchestra in the mid-1920s, and brother of bassist Leslie "King" Edwards.

Elgar, Charles "Charlie" (1885–1973). Violinist, reed player, and bandleader from New Orleans who moved to Chicago ca. 1913, where he led orchestras in the 1920s at the Sunset Cafe, Dreamland, Savoy Ballroom, and other dance halls. Later he was active as a teacher and officer in the musicians' union.

Elliott, Ernest (b. 1893). Clarinetist and saxophonist from Missouri who moved to New York ca. 1919–20, and made many recordings in the 1920s, including sides with Mamie Smith, Eva Taylor, Thomas Morris, Johnny Dunn, and Bessie Smith. In the 1940s he worked in small groups with Willie "The Lion" Smith and Cliff Jackson.

Feldman, Al [Van Alexander] (b. 1915). Pianist, arranger, composer, and bandleader. He began arranging for Chick Webb in 1936, and was responsible for "A-Tisket A-Tasket" and other Webb novelty numbers. He began leading his own bands in the late 1930s, arranged for Tommy Tucker and Abe Lyman, and eventually directed his writing efforts toward film and television projects in Hollywood.

Flemming, Herb [Niccolaiih El-Michelle] (1898–1976). Trombonist who played with Jim Europe's 369th U.S. Infantry Band during World War I. He toured with Sam Wooding in Europe (1925–27, 1930), then traveled widely as a trombonist in orchestras and as a solo singer. He worked with Fats Waller in the early 1940s, retired briefly from music, then came back on the scene in New York in the 1950s. In the 1960s he had residencies in Spain and Germany.

Frye, Donald "Don" (1903–81). Pianist from Springfield, Ohio. He worked with Cecil and Lloyd Scott in New York in the 1920s, and later played in bands led by John Kirby, Lucky Millinder, and Zutty Singleton, among others. From the mid-1940s through the 1960s he was active in New York as a soloist, including a long stint as house pianist at Jimmy Ryan's.

Glascoe, Percy. Clarinetist, saxophonist, and bandleader from Baltimore. In the 1920s he recorded with Julia Moody, Mamie Smith, and pianist Lemuel Fowler.

Gorman, Ross (ca. 1890–1953). Multi-reed player, bandleader. He was featured with Paul Whiteman's orchestra (1921–25) and led his own band, Ross Gorman and His Novelty Stompers. During the 1920s he recorded extensively. Later he became a staff musician for NBC radio.

Green, Raymond. Drummer, xylophonist. He toured with Fletcher Henderson and Ethel Waters (1921–22), then went on the road with other vaudeville troupes. He may have played with Fess Williams in 1919 and 1924.

Gross, Leon (1900–1943). Originally a truck driver, he became a saxophonist and led gig bands mainly in Harlem. His obituary in the October 1943 *Music Dial* (a magazine for Harlem musicians) stated that he was a popular performer, and had lived for nineteen years at the home of Fletcher Henderson.

Harper, Leonard. Dancer, show producer, and choreographer. With his wife, Osceola Blanks, he performed as a dance team at Connie's Inn, the Lafayette Theater, and other New York night spots. He produced many revues during the 1920s, both in Harlem and midtown Manhattan.

Harper, William Emerson "Geechie" (b. ca. 1896–98). Alto saxophonist and oboist. From 1912 through 1914 he was an instructor at the Jenkins' Orphanage in his hometown of Charleston, South Carolina. He played in Leroy Smith's orchestra (1918–33), then joined Fletcher Henderson (1944–46).

Haughton, Chauncey (b. 1909). Clarinetist and saxophonist from Maryland. His early experience was in the Baltimore area before coming to New York in the early 1930s. He worked under many bandleaders (Blanche Calloway, Claude Hopkins, Noble Sissle, Fletcher Henderson, Chick Webb, Cab Calloway, Duke Ellington) before leaving music in the late 1940s.

Hayes, Edgar (1904–75). Pianist, arranger, and bandleader from Lexington, Kentucky. He received a music degree from Wilberforce before going on the road with Fess Williams and Lois Deppe. In the 1930s he was associated with the Mills Blue Rhythm Band and Lucky Millinder, then led his own group 1937–41. After 1942 he was based in California, working as a solo pianist and leader of combos.

Henry, Lew [or Lou]. Trombonist and bandleader. He toured with "A Modern Cocktail" (1921–22) and Liza and Her Shuffling Sextet (1922–23) and led his own band, the Creole Syncopators, in New York in 1925. According to Bushell, he was from Maryland, and returned there in the late 1920s or 1930s to become an undertaker in Annapolis.

Hill, Theodore "Teddy" (1909–78). Saxophonist, clarinetist, and bandleader from Birmingham, Alabama. He worked under Luis Russell in the late 1920s and led a big band 1932–40. Later he managed Minton's Playhouse in Harlem.

Hudgins, Johnny. A popular black comedian in New York and on the vaudeville circuit. He appeared in the Club Alabam revue during Sam Wooding's tenure there (1924–25) and shared billing with Wooding at the Lafayette Theater in January of 1925. He often worked with a cornetist, and his specialty was miming speech while a muted horn "spoke" for him.

Irick, Seymour. Trumpeter. In the 1920s he recorded with Lucille Hegamin, Martha Copeland, and Lemuel Fowler.

Jackson, Charles E. "Charlie." Violinist who toured with Ethel Waters 1921–22 and recorded for Black Swan during the same period. He performed with the Aiken brothers and Bushell at Leroy's and was a member of Sam Wooding's orchestra in 1922.

Jefferson, Hilton (1903–68). Alto saxophonist from Danbury, Connecticut. He worked with Julian Arthur's band in the mid-1920s, then played in many New York bands. His longest associations were with Fletcher Henderson (1932–34, 1936–38) and Cab Calloway (1940–49). He appeared sporadically with Chick Webb's band and briefly with Duke Ellington's (1952–53). In later years he remained active as a free-lancer while holding a day job in a bank.

Johnson, Herb. Saxophonist and double-reed player with Sam Wooding's orchestra at the Nest Club, 1923–24. According to Bushell, he had received training at the Boston Conservatory.

Johnson, Percy. Drummer with Sam Wooding's orchestra in Europe, 1926–27. Later he recorded with Cliff Jackson and Blanche Calloway.

Jones, Claude (1901–62). Trombonist and singer. Originally from Oklahoma, he attended Wilberforce College in Ohio and joined the Synco Jazz Band in Springfield in 1922. He stayed with the ensemble after it became McKinney's Cotton Pickers, leaving in 1929 to go with Fletcher Henderson. In the 1930s he worked with Don Redman and Cab Calloway (1934–40), then played valve trombone with Duke Ellington (1944–48, 1951) before retiring from music.

Jones, Palmer. Black pianist active in Paris in the mid-1920s (married to cabaret singer Florence Jones) who played in the house band at Chez Florence. Apparently he had a hand in bringing Ada "Bricktop" Smith to Paris.

Kewley, Fred. Clarinetist. In 1921, while on tour in Detroit with Mamie Smith, Bushell heard Kewley play at the Copeland Theater on Gratiot Avenue.

Ladnier, Thomas "Tommy" (1900–1939). Trumpeter from Mandeville, Louisiana. He was based in Chicago in the early 1920s, then joined Sam Wooding on tour in Europe (1925–26, 1928–29). He appeared with Sidney Bechet in the early 1930s, also at the 1938 "Spirituals to Swing" concert.

Lewis, William T. "Willie" (1905–71). Clarinetist and saxophonist from Texas. After formal training at the New England Conservatory he toured with the Musical Spillers, and with Sam Wooding in Europe in the late 1920s. He led his own groups in Europe throughout the 1930s before returning to the States in 1941 and leaving a full-time musical career.

McKinney, William "Bill" (1895–1969). Drummer from Kentucky who settled in Springfield, Ohio, after World War I. In the mid-1920s he took over the Synco Septet, which eventually became McKinney's Cotton Pickers. He remained with the Cotton Pickers, in its various incarnations, through 1937, then managed bands before retiring from music in the 1940s.

Madison, Bingie S. (1902–78). Reed player, pianist, and arranger from Des Moines, Iowa. In the late 1920s he worked in groups led by Cliff Jackson and Lew Henry, then joined Elmer Snowden's band ca. 1930. Through much of the 1930s he was a member of Luis Russell's orchestra, and later appeared with Edgar Hayes and Alberto Socarras.

Major, Addington. Trumpeter who toured on the vaudeville circuit with "A Modern Cocktail" (1921–22) and (possibly) recorded a few sides with Mamie Smith and Clarence Williams.

Mallory, Eddie (ca. 1905–61). Trumpeter, saxophonist and arranger. Active in Chicago in the late 1920s and early 1930s, he worked in New York with the Mills Blue Rhythm Band and Charlie Turner's orchestra. He was married to Ethel Waters in the late 1930s and served as her musical director. After leading his own bands in the 1940s he left the music business.

Martin, Daisy. Singer who recorded sixteen sides for Okeh, Gennett, and Banner between 1921 and 1923, accompanied by five-piece bands.

Martin, Robert "Bobby" (b. 1903). Trumpeter from Long Branch, New Jersey. He worked in Europe and the States with Sam Wooding (1925–31), and went abroad again with Willie Lewis's orchestra (1932–36) and his own band (1937–39). In the early 1940s he appeared with small groups in New York before retiring from music.

Metcalf, Louis (1905–81). Trumpeter from St. Louis, he played with Charlie Creath before moving to New York in 1923. He was a sideman in many

bands (Andy Preer, Tim Brymn, Elmer Snowden, Duke Ellington, Luis
Russell), and led his own groups from the 1930s through the late 1960s.

Mikell, Francis Eugene (1885–1932). Trumpeter, composer, and influential
teacher at the Jenkins' Orphanage in Charleston, South Carolina. During
World War I he assisted James Reese Europe in leading the 369th Infantry
Band, and later taught in New Jersey and New York.

Mitchell, Abbie (1884–1960). Singer and actress. In the early 1900s she starred
in theatrical productions of Williams and Walker, Cole and Johnson, and
Will Marion Cook (her husband from 1899 to 1906). One of the Original
Lafayette Players in 1914, she later toured widely as a concert singer, taught
at Tuskeegee Institute, and acted in straight drama.

Morton, Henry Sterling "Benny" (1907–85). Trombonist from New York, he
performed in the big bands of Fletcher Henderson (1926–28, 1931), Chick
Webb (1931), and Count Basie (1937–40). In the 1940s he free-lanced in
small groups, theater orchestras, and the studios, remaining active through
the late 1970s.

O'Bryant, Jimmy (ca. 1896–1928). Clarinetist and saxophonist based in Chicago who recorded frequently in the 1920s with his own groups, also with
Ma Rainey, Lovie Austin, Alberta Hunter, and other singers.

Pensacola Kid [J. Paul Wyer or Wyre]. Clarinetist, bandleader. Born in
Pensacola, he played with W. C. Handy around 1916, then served in the
army 1918–19. In the 1920s he spent time in Chicago and New Orleans
before moving to Argentina, where he continued to perform and lead his
orchestra, the Dixy Pals, into the 1950s.

Perry, Mert. Drummer who played in vaudeville, and recorded with Mamie
Smith in 1921, possibly with Johnny Dunn in 1928. (Rust gives the first name
as "Mort," but Bushell recalls it as "Mert.")

Phillips, William King. Clarinetist, saxophonist. In 1909 he was playing tenor
saxophone in a quartet with Allen's Minstrels. Subsequently he worked with
theater orchestras in Jacksonville and Savannah, also on the road. He was
composer of "Florida Blues," recorded by W. C. Handy, and appeared with
John Wickliffe's band in 1917.

Robinson, Clarence. Choreographer, dancer, and show producer active in New
York in the 1920s and 1930s. He was known for revues he staged at the Club
Alabam, Cotton Club, Lafayette Theater, Apollo Theater, and other well-
known New York night spots and theaters.

Rollini, Adrian (1904–56). Bass saxophonist and vibraphonist. His bass saxophone was featured in the California Ramblers during the 1920s, in
England with the orchestra of Fred Elizalde, and on many recordings with
pickup bands. From the mid-1930s on he was known primarily as a
vibraphonist.

Royal, Ernest "Ernie" (1921–83). Trumpeter from California, he appeared in bands led by Lionel Hampton (1940–42), Count Basie (1946), and Woody Herman (1947). From the 1950s on he was active in New York as a free-lancer, specializing in television, radio, and recording work.

Scott, Cecil Xavier (1905–64). Clarinetist and saxophonist from Springfield, Ohio, brother of drummer Lloyd Scott (b. 1902). In the 1920s the Scott brothers played in bands with pianist Don Frye around Ohio, and eventually in New York, Pennsylvania, and Canada. Later Cecil Scott worked with Teddy Hill, Alberto Socarras, and Art Hodes, remaining active in small groups through the 1960s.

Sears, Albert "Al" (b. 1910). Tenor saxophonist best known for his work with Duke Ellington (1943–49) and Johnny Hodges (1951–52). Since 1952 he has been based in New York.

Senior, Milton "Milt" (ca. 1900–ca. 1948). Saxophonist and clarinetist from Springfield, Ohio. He worked with the Willis and Wormack band in Dayton, and helped found the Synco Septet (later McKinney's Cotton Pickers). In the early 1930s he led his own groups in the Toledo area before leaving music.

Smith, Cladys "Jabbo" (b. 1908). Trumpeter and trombonist raised in the Jenkins' Orphanage of Charleston, South Carolina. Based in New York from 1925 through 1928, he then worked in Chicago with the bands of Carroll Dickerson, Charlie Elgar, Erskine Tate, and others. He played with various groups in Milwaukee and lived there for many years. More recently he has appeared in the musical revue *One Mo' Time* and with trumpeter Don Cherry at jazz festivals.

Smith, Joseph "Joe" (1902–37). Trumpeter from Ohio who worked with Fletcher Henderson in the 1920s and backed many singers on recordings. For a time he accompanied Johnny Hudgins in his act. He was a member of McKinney's Cotton Pickers (between 1929 and 1934) before his health failed.

Smith, Luke M., Jr. (ca. 1890–1936). Trumpeter from Ohio, brother of Joe and Russell. He played in New York pit orchestras in the early 1920s, possibly on some Black Swan recordings, and briefly with Fletcher Henderson (1925–26).

Smith, Rollin [or Rollen, Roland]. Saxophonist. In the early 1920s he recorded with Johnny Dunn and Lucille Hegamin, and may have been a member of the Black Swan "house orchestra." He performed with the *Dover to Dixie* revue in 1923, and later that year joined Elmer Snowden's Washingtonians at the Hollywood Cafe on saxophone and bassoon.

Smith, Russell T. (ca. 1890–1966). Trumpeter, older brother of Joe and Luke Smith. Primarily a lead trumpeter rather than soloist, he played in various theater orchestras in the 1920s, also with Fletcher Henderson (between 1925 and 1934, and 1936–39), Claude Hopkins (1935–36), and Cab Calloway (1941–46).

Snowden, Elmer Chester (1900–1973). A native of Baltimore, he played banjo there with Eubie Blake in the late 1910s and in Washington in the early

1920s (often with the young Duke Ellington on piano). He led bands at the Nest, the Hot Feet Club, and Small's Paradise in New York, performing on guitar and saxophone. Through the late 1960s he remained active in small groups in New York, San Francisco, and Philadelphia.

South, Eddie (1904–62). Violinist from Chicago who studied with Charlie Elgar and worked in local bands before traveling to Europe in the late 1920s. In the 1930s he performed both in the States and abroad, and later became known through his work on radio and television.

Speed, [also Speede], Sam. Banjo player who recorded in the 1920s with Ethel Ridley, Leroy Smith, Mamie Smith, Edith Wilson, Lena Wilson, and others.

Sweatman, Wilbur C. (1882–1961). Clarinetist, bandleader, and vaudevillian from Brunswick, Missouri. He began playing in circus bands, later with W. C. Handy (1902) and his own groups. His first cylinder recording was made in 1903; in the late 1910s he was featured on many Columbia recordings. A prominent touring performer in the early 1920s, he became less active in the 1930s but in the following decade returned with his own trio.

Thomas, Walter "Foots" (1907–81). Reed player, flutist, and arranger who started out in Southwest territory bands, then worked with Jelly Roll Morton, Luis Russell, and the Missourians in New York. He remained with the latter band, under Cab Calloway's direction, until 1943.

Turner, Charles "Charlie" ("Fat Man") (d. 1964). Bassist and bandleader, a frequent performer at the Arcadia Ballroom in the mid-1930s. His band was used by Fats Waller and Fletcher Henderson in the 1930s, and he appeared with Eddie Mallory's orchestra backing Ethel Waters (1938–39).

Wethington, Arthur Crawford (b. 1908). Saxophonist, singer. From Chicago, he studied at the Chicago School of Music, then worked with Lottie Hightower's Night Hawks and Carroll Dickerson. He played with the Mills Blue Rhythm Band and Edgar Hayes in the 1930s, subsequently retiring as a performer but continuing to teach music.

Whaley, Thomas L. "Tom" (ca. 1900–1986). Pianist, arranger from Boston. He studied at the New England Conservatory, worked with Wilbur Sweatman, then was active in New York as a rehearsal pianist and musical director for shows and revues. In 1941 he became associated with Duke Ellington, for whom he served as copyist, arranger, and assistant conductor for many years.

Wilborn, David "Dave" (1904–82). From Springfield, Ohio, he played banjo with Cecil and Lloyd Scott, the Synco Septet, and McKinney's Cotton Pickers. From the late 1930s through 1950 he led his own groups, playing guitar. Beginning in 1972 he was featured as vocalist with the New McKinney's Cotton Pickers.

Williams, Te Roy. Trombonist. He recorded in 1921 with Leroy Smith, and in 1927 with both Leroy Tibbs and a group under his own name.

NEW YORK SOCIETY LIBRARY
53 EAST 79 STREET
NEW YORK, NEW YORK 10021

INDEX